GREEK AMERICAN FAMILIES
Traditions and Transformations

GREEK AMERICAN FAMILIES:

TRADITIONS AND

TRANSFORMATIONS

Edited by

Sam J. Tsemberis

Harry J. Psomiades

Anna Karpathakis

PELLA
PELLA PUBLISHING COMPANY, INC.
New York, NY 10018-6401
1999

This book was published for The Center for Byzantine and Modern Greek Studies, Queens College of the City University of New York, which bears full editorial responsibility for its contents.

MODERN GREEK RESEARCH SERIES, VIII, SEPTEMBER 1999

GREEK AMERICAN FAMILIES
Traditions and Transformations

Library of Congress Catalog Card Number 99-76195

ISBN 0-918618-76-2

PRINTED IN THE UNITED STATES OF AMERICA
BY
ATHENS PRINTING COMPANY
337 West 36th Street
New York, NY 10018-6401

To

the new generation

Alexander, Christine,

Elena, Kathy, & Themis

Table of Contents

MODERN GREEK RESEARCH SERIES

The purpose of this monograph series is to promote and disseminate scholarly works on the history, institutions, and the culture of the Greek people. It is sponsored and edited by the Center for Byzantine and Modern Greek Studies, Queens College of the City University of New York (formerly jointly with the Greek Seminar of the Center for Mediterranean Studies of the American University). This is the eighth publication within the framework of the Modern Greek Research Project—Harry J. Psomiades, Professor of Political Science, Queens College of the City University of New York, Director

MODERN GREEK RESEARCH SERIES

Preface

THE BULK OF THE PAPERS contained in this volume were presented at a conference sponsored by the Center for Byzantine and Modern Greek Studies of Queens College, the City University of New York. The conference, entitled "The Greek American Family in Transition: Assimilation and Acculturation," was held at Queens College and at the Hellenic Cultural Center in Astoria, New York, on December 5–6, 1996.

The conference was made possible by grants primarily from the New York City Council, Peter F. Vallone, president; the General Secretariat of Greeks Abroad, Greek Ministry of Foreign Affairs, Athens; AHEPA Educational Foundation; the Alexander S. Onassis Public Benefit Foundation; the Atlantic Bank of New York; the Hellenic Society of Constantinople; and Polytimi Karolidou-Divack, John Hancock Financial Services of Astoria (New York). Other grants came from Interbank of New York, Marathon National Bank of Astoria, and Citibank—Hellenic Banking Centers of Astoria and Whitestone. Material support was also provided by the Ikaros Greek Club of Queens College, Dr. Florentia Christodoulidou, and Andrew A. Athens.

We are also grateful for the hospitality provided to the conference by Uncle George's Restaurant and the Athens Café, both of Astoria, New York. We wish to express our deep appreciation to all those who participated in the conference and to Effie Lekas and Sonya Allin and their staffs for their excellent administrative support. We also thank those authors and publishers who so kindly granted permission to reproduce materials. We regret that, for a variety of reasons, not all of the papers presented at the conference appear in this volume.

Finally, we wish to acknowledge our very special debt to the New York City Council and its president, Peter F. Vallone; the Alexander S. Onassis Public Benefit Foundation; and the General Secretariat for Greeks Abroad, Greek Ministry of Foreign Affairs, Athens, for grants which largely made possible the publication of this volume. We are also indebted to Yiota Papadopoulos, who served with distinction as managing editor; to Beatrice Gregory, whose intelligence, erudition, and skill as copy editor greatly enhanced the quality of this work; and to Betsy Warren, who graciously contributed her talent to designing the beautiful book cover (she appears on the cover, second from left). Finally, on behalf of all the contributors to this volume, we wish to emphasize that the views expressed in this publication are those of the individual authors and do not necessarily reflect the views of the individuals and organizations that helped to make the conference and this publication possible.

H.J.P.
S.J.T.
A.K.
Flushing, New York

Editors' Note on Transliteration

It proved impossible, despite the best efforts of the editors, to maintain a consistent system of transliterating Greek words, terms, and names throughout the text of this collaborative work. Not merely were different forms of the language involved (classical, koine, Byzantine, and the various local and stylistic variants of modern Greek), but the various authors often had strong—and conflicting—views on the correct way to transcribe various letters and letter combinations, some favoring a phonetic and some an etymological system. We have, however, made every effort (assisted by the search-and-replace features of modern computerized word processing) to ensure that words are spelled consistently within each article.

Introduction

GREEK AMERICANS ARE ENTERING into a vitally important stage of their acculturation to the United States, a stage that will challenge the identity of Greek Americans and the continuation of the Greek American community. Will Greek Americans continue to reference their Greek ancestry or will they assimilate fully and identify wholly as Americans? This question is addressed both directly and indirectly by the authors in this volume. Dan Georgakas's penetrating analysis of census tract data over three decades leads him to conclude that there is a predictable pattern in the history of European immigration to the United States. Most northern European white ethnic groups were completely assimilated into the vast homogeneity of American culture by the fifth generation. The Greek Americans in the United States and Canada are rapidly approaching that critical period. The transmission of Greek language and culture diminished with each successive generation: the children, grandchildren, and great-grandchildren of these immigrants speak little or no Greek and observe few if any Greek customs. Will Greek Americans follow in the footsteps of the European immigrants who preceded them?

The two chapters concerned with the issue of intermarriage confirm Georgakas's findings that Greek Americans are rapidly blending into the heterogeneity of the American melange. Chimbos and Constantelos report very high rates of intermarriage between Greeks and non-Greeks in Canada and the United States. Chimbos regards interethnic marriages as inevitable, and in an effort to maintain the cohesion of the Greek American community, discusses strategies that may reduce its impact. Constantelos discusses intermarriage from the perspective of preserving Greek Orthodoxy in America.

The destiny of the fifth generation of Greek Americans is yet to be determined. Sutton's and Karpathakis's papers observe that immigrants make accommodations to sustain Greek customs after arriving in the United States. Sutton's astute observations of Greeks and Greek Americans leads her to conclude that Greek American family structures reflect the conditions of American life as much as they do the maintenance of unbroken tradition. Karpathakis's social and economic analysis of Greek American families argues that for Greek women, assimilation into American culture requires a trade-off: they achieve a better economic position, but give up some real power, being no longer *noikokyres*, but just "ladies."

Two excellent historical papers report on the longevity and durability of Greek family life and customs. The paper by the late Alexander Kazhdan of the Center for Byzantine Studies at Dumbarton Oaks in Washington, D.C., illuminates the long-standing traditions of Greek family organization, customs, and roles through his analysis of the family in the Byzantine Empire. Alice-Mary Talbot, also of Dumbarton Oaks, graciously completed the revisions to Dr. Kazhdan's paper after his death on May 29, 1997. The central theme in Paul Sant Cassia's lively and entertaining paper on the evolution of marriage and family life in modern Greece is that during the 19th century the shape of marriage and family life was redefined by the primacy of the new capital, the emerging trend of mobility of dowry, and the urbanization of country folk.

Three papers by experienced clinicians present issues often observed in Greek American families who seek therapy. Hibbs discusses the dilemmas of Greek mothers and Greek American daughters struggling with issues of separation-individuation. Halkitis presents a moving and informative perspective on being gay and Greek American. He observes that the Greek American struggle to maintain and perpetuate Greek culture within a dominant American culture has led to views that are often conservative and rejecting of differences and has thus created complicated realities for gay and lesbian Greek Americans. In my paper on Greek American families who seek therapy, a family systems approach is used to describe the etiology and manifestation of problems presented by the children and marital partners in immigrant families. Strategies and interventions for therapists working with such families are also provided.

This volume is timely and informative. It documents Greek American family life at a critical juncture in the acculturation process. It describes Greek families past and present and offers provocative speculation concerning the uncertain future of Greek American families.

Sam J. Tsemberis
October 28, 1999

The current state of Greek America

1. The America beyond Ellis Island

DAN GEORGAKAS

This essay argues that the history of the Greeks in America is best understood in the context of European immigration to America rather than in the context of the global Greek diaspora. The essay further argues that the story of the Greeks in America is not synonymous with the evolution of a Greek American identity. The essay concludes that the small number of third- and fourth-generation Greek Americans with pre-World War II immigrant parents or grandparents indicates that Greek American families are no more successful in reproducing or retaining their European culture in the United States than other European immigrants.

SOME 12 MILLION INDIVIDUALS, mostly European, voluntarily immigrated to the United States between 1880 and 1924. Studies focusing on any particular ethnic group participating in that unprecedented historical phenomenon have tended to downplay the American side of the immigration dynamic and largely to ignore the experience of other immigrant groups of the same period. Greek American studies have not been an exception to this general rule.

The inevitable result of minimizing the American component of immigration is that the uniqueness of each group under study is inflated and the broad historical forces in play devalued. Most of the myths and misconceptions about Greek Americans that abound stem from this unbalanced analysis. Not the least of these errors is to consider the story of the Greeks in America synonymous with the evolution of a Greek American community with a distinct Greek American consciousness. Without a full understanding of the politics, culture, and economy of the United States, it is impossible to understand the evolution of Greek American identity or the fate of those immigrants who did not enter the American mainstream.[1]

Coming or going to America?

Most studies of the Greeks in America begin in the homeland. We learn why Stella or Costa (and it is usually Costa) opted to go to America. A major agricultural crop has failed, a regional war is brewing, a military dictatorship has taken power, or poverty has simply become unbearable. But these and related factors were in place in the 1860s and the 1930s as well as from 1900 to 1924, the peak years of Greek immigration. The determining factors in setting off and terminating immigration were on the other side of the Atlantic.

The difference between "going" and "coming" to America involves more than semantics. If we speak of "going" to America, the cultural center of the tale is Greece. Ultimately, if that orientation persists, the Greeks in America must be regarded as Greeks living abroad, and their major concern will be how to retain their Greek core in an American environment. If we speak of "coming" to America, the cultural center is the United States. Ultimately, that leads to regarding the Greeks in America as Americans of Greek ancestry, and their major concern will be assimilation to the American mainstream. Although retention of Greekness will still be a major issue, it will be placed in the context of other European ethnic groups' assimilating to America rather than the context of a worldwide Greek diaspora. Common sense dictates that these orientations should not be considered rigid categories, but by and large, they determine the tone of any given narrative of the Greeks in America.

The pattern for massive immigration was established in the very first large settlement of Greeks in America, the New Smyrna experiment of 1768. In that instance, a Scotsman in London, married to a Greek woman from Smyrna, had decided to invest in a colony in the New World, not unlike other English colonies. His wife and others persuaded him that immigrants from the Mediterranean would be good but inexpensive workers. In due course, approximately 500 Greeks, mainly males from Mani, joined an equal number of Italians and Minorcans as indentured workers of the ill-fated venture. The courage of these immigrants, like that of their many successors, is in no way diminished by the fact that they were fetched instead of having made a decision to immigrate based on their own resources and needs.[2]

The Great Migration of 1880–1924 follows a similar pattern. With the failure of Reconstruction after the Civil War, American capitalists needed hundreds of thousands and then millions of workers for the industrialization that would elevate the United States to a world power by the time of World War I. With the option of moving black labor north rejected for a complex of reasons, the industrialists turned to Europe for most of their labor. Beginning in the 1880s they would recruit systematically, first beginning in central Europe and then proceeding eastward and southward in search of ever cheaper labor.

The establishment of Ellis Island was part of this vast project. Arrangements involving steamship companies and the use of labor agents in Europe were central to the enterprise. Once a country was targeted, ads in the local press and other outreach efforts were put into motion. By the turn of the century, active recruitment had reached Greece and other nation-states with large Greek populations.

Industry not only fetched immigrants, it earmarked places of settlement and determined the kind of work to be offered. Greek immigration hit full stride when the textile industry was flourishing in New England. Not coincidentally, the first large waves of Greeks would settle in the area stretching from New York City to lower Maine and New Hampshire to work in the shoe, fur, and textile industries. In 1910, Lowell, Massachusetts, would be the third largest Greek center in America, with a population of 10,000 Greeks. Smaller but significant numbers of Greeks were found in the surrounding mill towns.[3]

With the advent of mass production in the automobile industry and the related boom in the steel, tire, glass, iron, and coal industries, Greeks would swarm to industrial centers in a broad belt reaching from Chicago in the west to Baltimore in the east, with the heaviest concentration in the area between Detroit and Pittsburgh. Greeks also found work in the Mesabi Iron Range in Minnesota and the cigarette factories of Philadelphia (Georgakas 1987).

An additional 40,000 to 50,000 Greeks took on work available in the West. A great many of them got jobs on railroad gangs, where for a considerable period they made up 20 percent of the total workforce. Large numbers were also lured to southwestern coal and copper mines. Yet another group worked in and around various Pacific ports. A smaller percentage became lumber workers.[4]

Where Greeks did *not* settle was also determined by American needs and politics. Only a small fraction ventured into the Deep South, where a coalition of xenophobic nativist forces, exemplified by but not limited to the Ku Klux Klan, were hostile to immigrants. Nor were Greeks drawn to the Great Plains region, which was already settled. Only small numbers joined the huge migratory harvest force which worked seasonally for marginal wages.

The major exception to these patterns was the immigration of mostly Dodecanesian sponge divers to Tarpon Springs, Florida, in the first years of the 20th century. This is one of the few instances where Greek technology was in advance of that in the United States. The Greeks ousted local economic rivals with ease and established a prosperous family-based Greek enclave. That community has proven to have the strongest and longest transmission of Greek language and culture in the United States.

The geographic and employment factors just outlined have left an enormous long-term imprint on the formation of Greek American culture. A majority of Greek immigrant males lived under geographic, social, or economic circumstances where they could not form Greek families. That was most obviously the case with the shoeshine boys of the East who worked for subsistence wages and workers in the West where there were few Greek women. Having more positive long-term consequences was the fact that Greeks had been drawn to the very urban areas that would be the center of American reform and economic prosperity, offering the material conditions for ethnic advancement in education, industry, politics, and business.

Just how formative the geographic patterns proved to be can be seen in the 1980 census, which reveals that a hundred years after major Greek immigration began, over 600,000 of the million self-identified Greeks lived in New York, Illinois, Massachusetts, New Jersey, Pennsylvania, Ohio, Michigan, and Maryland. Most of these Greeks lived within 50 miles of New York City, Chicago, Boston, Detroit, Philadelphia, Baltimore, Cleveland, Pittsburgh, or Akron. Another 100,000 were located in the port cities of the Pacific coast. The only major Southern settlement was in the St. Petersburg-Tarpon Springs region, with some 30,000 inhabitants (Saloutos 1964, 250).

The Jazz Age, the Great Depression, and the New Deal

No ethnic history of Greeks in America fails to mention the formation of the American Hellenic Progressive Association (AHEPA) in 1922 and the Greek American Progressive Association (GAPA) in 1923. No cultural history fails to outline the historic newspaper battle waged by the democratic *Ethnikos Kyrix* (national herald) and the monarchist *Atlantis*. No local history is without mention of the founders of the first Greek Orthodox church. What is not noted is that the 1944 membership of AHEPA was only 20,000, and GAPA's was 10,000. Similarly, the combined circulation of all the Greek-language press in 1944, a time when interest in foreign affairs was intense, was only 80,000.[5] These figures come to only 5 percent and 11 percent respectively of the total of Greek immigrants and much less if we assume that numerous children had been born. On the other hand, a fraternal event or a member of a fraternal order might influence many in the community who were not formal members, and there were a considerable number of pass-along readers of newspapers. The point here is not to denigrate the impact of those institutions but to give context to the following questions: What were the majority of Greeks reading? What organizations did they belong to? In which domestic political movements did they participate? Only by considering such questions can we understand the entire dynamic within the Greek community. And one must hasten to add, a Greek immigrant who belonged to AHEPA might also belong to the Rotary Club, the United Steel Workers, or the YMCA. The reader of *Kyrix* or *Atlantis* might also be a reader of the American press or a listener to English-language radio.[6]

However deeply immersed in Greek culture individuals or families might be, they were not immune to the powerful cultural forces of mainstream America. The 1920s and 1930s were distinctive American eras marked by an accelerating movement from farms to cities. The impact of the popularly priced automobile and the chaos brought on by Prohibition transformed domestic society. No less transformative was the impact of the women's rights movement, which had scored a major triumph with the passage of the women's suffrage amendment in 1920. Women living and working outside the parental home became a mass phenomenon. Women began to go to college in greater numbers and women were even smoking in public! Any Greek woman going to a public school or having access to mass media would be influenced by these cultural changes even if she was not immediately able to embrace them in her everyday life.

The interaction of Greek and American culture is a subject particularly well suited to exposition in fiction. That theme has characterized the work of Harry Mark Petrakis, the most prolific chronicler in fiction of the Greeks in America. His novel *The Odyssey of Kostas Volakis* is especially sensitive to cultural interactions within a Greek family headed by an immigrant male. His *Collected Stories* are also valuable in this respect. Particularly pertinent are the short introductions he offers to each tale, in which he describes the cultural context out of which it emerged. In the short story collection *The apple falls from the apple tree*, Helen Papanikolas emphasizes the cultural problematics of Greek women. "County hospital, 1939" is a novella-length exposition of a young woman living in one culture at home and another at work. The volume's title story, "The apple falls from the apple tree," uses an interdenominational marriage, in which a Greek woman marries a Mormon, to probe profound cultural dichotomies. Similar themes in various literary genres can be found in *Hellenes & hellions*, a guide to the modern Greek characters in American literature by Alexander Karanikas.

The impact of the Great Depression on the foreign-born was even more severe than on the rest of the American population. Among the most rueful effects was that marginal small businesses of the kind run by newly arrived immigrants were often wiped out. Nor were immigrants likely to have cash reserves to meet mortgages on newly acquired homes. No less an authority than John Constant noted that the Great Depression had wiped out much of the economic progress Greeks had made to that time.[7] Relief for most workers did not come until the passage of the Wagner Act in 1935. In the next ten years, nearly 50 percent of American workers would be unionized, often after bloody mass struggles in exactly those cities where Greeks were most densely congregated.

A related phenomenon that greatly affected Greeks in America was that ever since the mid-1880s, the American educational system, American industry, and American social organizations had devised programs to Americanize immigrants. The first to be treated to this kind of planned assimilation were immigrants from Germany and central Europe. By the time the children of Greek immigrants arrived in the public schools, the system had become highly refined. Social agencies also worked closely with some Greeks, the most famous being the work of Hull House with the Greeks of Chicago.[8]

When Franklin D. Roosevelt began to shape New Deal programs devised to end the Great Depression he initiated policies designed to end conflict between the needs of the immigrants who had become citizens and those of the native-born. With the onset of World War II, his administration worked even more zealously to stress the value and loyalty of the foreign-born, a theme carried out in motion pictures, political rallies, federally sponsored theater, commercial radio programs, and the public schools.

Any study which tries to determine how Greek families and institutions translated language skills, religious traditions, gender relationships, sibling obligations, and the like during the 1920–1945 period without serious consideration of the American cultural and political forces surrounding each and every Greek is skating on very thin ice. *Philotimo* (honor) and *dropi* (shame) were certainly operative forces, but so too was the enormous power of American mass culture. That anything Greek managed to survive the process is more remarkable than that much did not.

Greek, but not Greek American

Further complicating any cultural evaluation of Greeks in America is the fact that only a minority of Greek immigrants evolved into Greek Americans or produced Greek American offspring. This blunt reality is evident from comparing the total number of Greek immigrants and the number of persons, as of 1990, who considered themselves to be Greek Americans.[9]

Before 1880 there had been only 1,000 Greek immigrants to America, and the only communities were small merchant enclaves found in port cities. From 1880 to 1890, there would be an increase of 20,000. From 1900 to 1924, 520,000 Greeks immigrated. They would be joined by an additional 30,000 from 1924 to 1946. We can assume a probable 100,000 more arrived illegally or on passports not indicating Greek nationality. This gives from 600,000 to 700,000 Greek immigrants through 1946.

From 1947 to 1965, there were 75,000 legal immigrants, mostly displaced persons, and 75,000 sailors who jumped ship. From 1966 through 1979, the Hart-Celler Act helped produce 160,000 immigrants, in what is known as the Second Wave of Greek immigration. That wave ebbed to approximately 25,000 immigrants from 1980 to 1990.[10] These figures indicate a total of some 335,000 postwar immigrants. When they are added to the earlier immigration numbers, we have approximately one million Greek immigrants from 1890 to 1990.[11]

In the census of 1990, only 900,000 Americans identified themselves as having some Greek ancestry, a lesser number than those who responded to the 1980 census. The 1990 census also shows that 200,000 of the respondents were Greek-born. We can assume that a large portion of this number were postwar immigrants and that a considerable portion of the 350,000 second-generation were their children. Only 250,000 identified themselves as third-generation, and only 100,000 were fourth-generation. These figures are not set in concrete, to be sure. Many Greeks might not have responded to the census. Such persons, however, are likely to be recent immigrants rather than American-born. Moreover, many of those responding that they were Greek may have minimal Greek identity. What is inescapable is the pattern of reduced ethnic identification. The 600,000–700,000 Greeks who arrived before World War II did not reproduce themselves. The vast majority of Americans who identify themselves as having Greek ethnicity are postwar immigrants or their children.

Taking these figures and the underlying patterns into account, the much heralded tightly knit Greek family and closely bonded Greek community proves to be a myth. The often highly energetic, highly visibly Greek American community represents only a fraction of those who came to America during the Great Migration, and it remains to be seen how well the Second Wave immigrants pass on their Greek identity. But what happened to the Greeks who have disappeared?

The disappeared

Much of the first wave of the Great Migration consisted of men. Many of them hoped to make enough income in America to return home wealthy and to wed well. Some of them may also have stranded wives in Greece while trying to establish a family fortune abroad. All in all, some 25 percent of these males proved to be birds of passage who returned to Greece after a relatively short stay in America. This return rate is among the top five for European countries. Although the subject of many an anecdote, the subsequent social and economic impact these men made on Greece appears to be minimal. How the advent of World War II affected this phenomenon must remain a matter of sheer speculation.

What is not speculative is that the birds of passage were men who refused the social and economic conditions found in the United States. They are an integral part of the story of the Greeks in America, but they never became Greek Americans. Further clouding this aspect of the Greek saga are individuals who moved back and forth, some keeping wives and children in the old country. These men might be categorized as diaspora Greeks or Greeks living abroad. Studies which attempt to see why some men from a region or village stayed in America while others returned are lacking. Studies comparing the reasons for return of Greeks with those for Italians or others with high return rates are also lacking.

Other blocks of men were victims of early death, lived their entire lives as bachelors, or left the community when they outmarried. Although high early death rates among immigrants are not widely commented on in Greek ethnic histories, the thousands of young boys who worked as bootblacks are among the more obvious examples of this category. Many were literally wage slaves, as their transatlantic passage had been paid by an employer who held a mortgage on the home in Greece where the lad's parents lived as security the boy would not leave his job. The chemical fumes, inadequate food, and impossible living conditions the boys were subjected to have been well documented. Textile workers did not fare much better. The average life span for such workers in the 1910s and 1920s was under 30 years. Death or injury on the job and a short average life span were also the lot of most miners, whatever their ethnic background.

Greek men who went west had an almost impossible task in terms of forming a Greek family, because of the lack of Greek women in that region. Much has been written about the picture-card brides imported from Greece, but they were a relatively small number compared to the total number of eligible men. Greek men who remained in the West were likely to remain unwed or to outmarry. In the Southwest they often outmarried with Mexican women, and their children grew up with a Mexican identity. A typical situation in many outmarriages was that the father retained a lifelong identity as a Greek, but that identity was not passed on to the children.

Bachelors were Greektown fixtures as long as Greektowns existed, but they were never systematically studied. What little is known about them is that they were often distant from the church-going community and were often on the fringes of the underworld, a situation reflected in the high frequency of Greek characters in hard-boiled American detective fiction. An exact accounting of bachelors is clearly an impossible task. But the total count of bachelors, returnees, the early dead, and outmarried immigrants appears to be much larger than the total of immigrants who established Greek American families and identities.

Americanizing Greek American studies

The phenomenon of outmarriage is as American as apple pie. Any ethnic history that doesn't take that as a given simply doesn't relate to the basic experience of European immigrants in America. In the case of the Greeks, outmarriage has been massive since the marriages of New Smyrna Greeks with Italians and Minorcans. Massive outmarriage was the pattern in the cities of the East as well as in the mining and railroad centers of the West. Since the 1970s, outmarriages taking place within the Greek Orthodox Church have been in excess of 70 percent (Counelis 1989). The rate of outmarriages in civil ceremonies and the religious ceremonies of other denominations would probably come close to 100 percent.

Outmarriage within the Greek Orthodox Church need not be equated with cultural disintegration. One could argue that the non-Greek spouses of such unions are likely to raise their children with a Greek identity, thus increasing rather than decreasing the total number of Greek-identified Americans. Nonetheless, the massive outmarriage of Greeks has profound implications for how Greek American identity is defined. What the outmarriage numbers most definitely indicate is that the many studies of families faithfully passing on the customs and attitudes of their home villages are not dealing with the fundamental experience in America. The general experience has been an intensive assimilation that is often found in even the first generation and generally results in a total loss of ethnic identity by the third or fourth.

The Second Wave of immigration has masked some of these realities. Comparisons and contrasts between the new immigrants and the Greek American communities they encountered can be deceptive. They are valid for the time period and populations compared, but the Greek American component does not represent the collective experience of the Great Migration. The Greek Americans of the 1970s and 1980s constitute only one line of development. Particularly misleading are the educational and economic successes of that group. To project them backward to the immigrants is invalid back-formation projection of the worst sort.

Another problem arises from comparative studies of immigrants and second or third generations. A second-generation Greek American of Great Migration parents might have grown up during the Great Depression, World War II, or the 1950s. A second-generation Greek American of the Second Wave grew up in the Age of Reagan.

One second-generation Greek American could be 58 while another is 18. That each is a child of immigrants is likely to be less significant than the era into which each was born and the age at which both are questioned. Valid conclusions from such studies are dependent on the researcher's understanding that "the second generation" is a deceptive category that includes populations of significantly different cultural formation.

Another kind of research quicksand involves the comparison of Greeks who came to America with those who immigrated at the same time or in later periods to other lands. The assumption is that the immigrants have shared cultural values which are major determiners of their fate in the new land. There is certainly something to be gained from this approach, but the results to date indicate that the shape an immigrant Greek community takes in a new land has less to do with Greek culture than with the culture of the host country. In a nation such as Egypt, which did not demand religious, cultural, and political assimilation, Greek communities could endure for centuries. Similarly in a postcolonial nation like Zaire (now the Congo), the Greek community remained coherent and left en masse at a time of crisis. The experience in the United States is totally different.

The United States is in the process of continually reformulating its own national identity and expects immigrants to adopt that evolving identity even as they add their own ethnic contribution to the common culture. Historically, the time frame for assimilation of an immigrant group from Europe that does not have continuous immigration has been from two to four generations. In the case of sporadic new waves such as the Greek Second Wave, the Americanization pattern begins to work on the new cohort even as assimilation of the entire immigrant group momentarily slows. In the case of Greek immigrants to America the rapid Americanization of the Second Wave is evident in the disintegration in less than a generation of Second Wave enclaves in Chicago and New York. Even in the Astoria section of Queens, the Second Wave mecca and the largest Greek community in the United States, Greeks have become a dwindling minority.[12]

Comparisons with Greeks in Canada and Australia seem better bets for insights into the experiences in the United States. Each of those nations seeks to assimilate newcomers and each has English as an official language. A major difference is that these immigrations were primarily postwar and make better comparisons with the Second Wave than with the Great Migration communities. The different experiences, if any, of the Greeks in Ontario versus the Greeks in

Quebec would be of interest as would the differences between pre-war Greeks and postwar Greeks. How the Australian government's support of multilingualism affects the long-term retention of Greek is another open question. Fascinating as these ethnic experiences are, they are not likely to offer fundamental insights into the experiences of Greeks in the United States.

A richer area of investigation involves cross-cultural comparisons with other immigrant groups, particularly those of the Great Migration. Such work is still in its infancy. But the fabled success of the Greeks in the food industry may look different when compared with studies of German beer gardens and breweries (2,000 in New York City alone in 1900), Italian pizzerias, Chinese take-outs. Jewish delis, and the like. Such studies would quite likely show the Greeks are not unique, as community chauvinists would like to believe, but they might better identify just what traits are shared by immigrants who are successful in business.

Other work of this nature might try to see what factors link the four or five immigrant groups that have had the most success in America in terms of education, wealth, and prestige. In like manner what accounts for the differences between the least successful and most successful immigrant groups? Have some groups been more successful than Greeks in retaining cultural identity? If so, what are the critical factors? In categories where Greeks have been more successful than others, what accounts for the difference? Any such work requires familiarity with the complexities of both Greek and American culture and history.

The Americanization of the Greek Orthodox Church is already well advanced. Many of its practices which are similar to those of American religious bodies are quite different from those in Greece and other Orthodox jurisdictions. As the Orthodox Church deals with various challenges arising from outmarriage, biculturalism, and language, it could profit from knowing the experiences of other churches in America that have faced similar problems.

The American side of the immigrant equation is fundamental. Each immigrant group has its particular institutions, virtues, and shortcomings. How any group performs in the United States most certainly reflects its homeland culture, but without command of the American side of the dynamic, it is too easy to attribute successes and failures to ethnic culture when they are actually aspects of dominant American culture. Without a full grasp of other American ethnic experiences, it is impossible to sort out what is genuinely unique about an experience and what reflects a more general or universal pattern.

The United States encountered by the Great Migration immigrants was far different from the United States found by the Second Wave immigrants. Understanding the communities created by each wave necessitates understanding the United States of each wave as well as we understand the differing social contexts from which the immigrants departed. Comparisons with the experiences of Greek immigrants in other parts of the world have many rewards. Ultimately, however, the Greek American experience is not one to be correctly defined as Greeks living abroad or as a Greek diaspora in the sense that the culture remains essentially Greek. It does not. Greek Americans are Americans with a Greek cultural heritage, and Greek Americans are only one chapter in the story of the Greeks in America.

Notes

1. Rather than offer new data on the Greeks in America, this essay seeks to give a context to data now in hand. Many of my formulations have arisen from conversations and correspondence with Steve Frangos, one of the most creative and tireless thinkers about the history of the Greeks in America. Any errors are of my own making.
2. Unless otherwise cited, the factual material I employ in my arguments is not in dispute and forms the core of the standard works on Greek America, which are Moskos 1989; Papanikolas 1974; and Saloutos 1964.
3. The most comprehensive accounts of Greek working-class history in America are Georgakas 1994 and 1987.
4. Moskos 1989 covers this phenomenon well (62–66), but the outstanding authority is H. Papanikolas 1974. For copper miners see Z. Papanikolas 1982. For women in the Intermountain West see H. Papanikolas 1989.
5. Yavis [1944] 1987, 117–22, deals with fraternal groups, and 122–29, with the Greek-language press.
6. In my own home, my father read *Atlantis* on occasion, but he always read the American dailies and often bought an American newsweekly, such as *U.S. News and World Report*. We listened to the Greek hour for community news and to American radio and later television for political news. One *koumbaros*'s membership in AHEPA was no more commented or acted on more vigorously than another's membership in the United Auto Workers. My father belonged to a regional society which gave summer festivals notable for food and music. For years my grandfather went to American movies at least once a week. This pattern of merged American and Greek culture was typical of the Greeks I grew up with in Detroit from 1938 to 1963.

7. Constant 1946, 46, where he concludes, "For the first time since 1882, a great portion of the Greek-American population was reduced to the same financial status as when it entered the country as an immigrant population."

8. For discussion of such educational programs see Cantor 1996; for Hull House in Chicago see Kopan 1990.

9. This discussion does not deal with the pre-1880 Greeks in America, but they constitute yet another line of largely disappeared Greeks. This diverse group would include the Greeks who served with the conquistadores and other early explorers, settlers in the English colonies, the orphans of the War of Independence, and various adventurous individuals. Of an entirely different order would be speculations advanced that ancient Greeks may have reached the New World, a thesis sometimes associated with the myth of Atlantis.

10. Unlike the quotas established in 1924, various arrangements for refugees from Asia Minor and World War II, and the Hart-Celler Act of 1965, this was the first time in this century that the scale of Greek immigration was not primarily determined by American legislation.

11. An excellent analysis of the 1990 census and related population issues is found in Moskos 1993.

12. Many Second Wave Greeks who had made up the hard core of two areas of Astoria from the late 1960s to the 1980s have geographically dispersed to areas which do not have a Greek identity. The 1990 census for Astoria reveals that there are more Hindi-speakers than Greek-speakers and more foreign-born from Ireland than from Greece.

References

Dan Georgakas objects to this bibliographical format, imposed by the editors for consistency on all the papers in this book, despite its frequent use in certain disciplines, because he considers the capitalization employed to be at odds with the normal rules for titles and to yield no gain in comprehensibility or accessibility.

Cantor, Milton. 1996. Education and the nineteenth-century working class. In *Work, recreation, & culture: Essays in American labor history,* ed. Martin Blatt and Martha K. Norkunas. New York: Garland Publishing.

Constant, John. 1946. Employment and business of the Greeks in the U.S. *Athens* 7, no. 3: 28–29, 37–41, 46.

Counelis, James Steve. 1989. Greek Orthodox Church statistics of the United States, 1949–1989. *Journal of the Hellenic Diaspora* 16, no. 1–4 (special quadruple issue on the Greek American experience, 1989): 129–59.

Georgakas, Dan. 1994. Greek-American radicalism: The twentieth century. *Journal of the Hellenic Diaspora* 20, no. 1: 7–35.

_____. 1987. The Greeks in America. *Journal of the Hellenic Diaspora* 14, no. 1–2: 5–53.

Karanikas, Alexander. 1981. *Hellenes & hellions*. Urbana: University of Illinois Press.

Kopan, Andrew T. 1990. *Education and Greek immigrants in Chicago, 1892–1973*. New York: Garland Publishing.

Moskos, Charles [Jr.] 1989.*The Greek Americans, struggle and success*. 2nd ed. New Brunswick, N.J.: Transaction Press.

_____. 1993. Faith, language, and culture. In *Project for Orthodox renewal*, ed. Stephen D. Sfetkas and George E. Matsoukas. Chicago: Orthodox Laity Inc.

Papanikolas, Helen Zeese. 1974. *Toil and rage in a new land: The Greek immigrants in Utah*. Salt Lake City: Utah Historical Society.

_____. 1989. Greek immigrant women in the Intermountain West. *Journal of the Hellenic Diaspora* 16, no. 1–4.

_____. 1996. *The apple falls from the apple tree*. Athens, Ohio: Swallow Press and Ohio University Press.

Papanikolas, Zeese. 1982. *Buried unsung: Louis Tikas and the Ludlow Massacre*. Salt Lake City: University of Utah Press.

Petrakis, Harry Mark. 1963 *The odyssey of Kostas Volakis*. New York: McKay Company.

_____. 1987. *Collected stories*. Chicago: Lake View Press.

Saloutos, Theodore. 1964.*The Greeks in the United States*. Cambridge: Harvard University Press.

Yavis, Constantine G. [1944] 1987. Propaganda in the Greek American community. A report written for the Foreign Agents Section, War Division, Department of Justice, Washington D.C., April 21, 1944. Complete report in Poulos Collection, Tamiment Library, New York University. Excerpts in *Journal of the Hellenic Diaspora* 14, no. 1–2 (1987): 117–29.

Traditions: Historical perspectives

2. The Greek family in the Byzantine Empire

ALEXANDER P. KAZHDAN
Dumbarton Oaks

One feature of Byzantine society was the relative weakness of major social groupings and links (lineage, guild, hierarchy, and so on). The nuclear family was the major social unit. Accordingly, the Byzantine family had stronger internal links than the family in Western medieval societies. Women (especially widows) were relatively independent, and the Byzantines had no tradition of primogeniture, dividing—in theory—property in equal shares among the children of both sexes. Such an "individualistic" structure of the family had a significant impact on the political, ideological, and religious principles of Byzantine society.

THE SO-CALLED BYZANTINE EMPIRE (the scholarly name of the Kingdom of the Rhomaioi) was a vast state populated by diverse ethnic groups (besides the Greeks, it was inhabited by Italians, Armenians, Slavs, Vlachs, Jews, and others); it existed for many centuries (conventional dates are from the mid-7th to the mid-15th century). It is natural to assume that on such a territory and during such a long period the pattern of family organization was far from uniform. Unfortunately, the bureaucratic empire left behind sparse documentation, and we are unable to investigate local and ethnic particularities (as is possible, for instance, for medieval France). We can present only a general outline of family structure within the predominant— that is, Greek—population, basing ourselves primarily on narrative and legislative sources, documentary evidence being available only for restricted areas and restricted periods of time (mostly southeastern Macedonia in the first half of the 14th century). The picture, panoramic by necessity, will seem clear, but this "clarity out of poverty" is deceptive: the lack of knowledge is not a substitute for clarity; in fact it conceals the diversity of historical reality. Nevertheless, there is no other way to handle the problem.

The family in Byzantium was first and foremost a nuclear family, consisting of a married couple and their children. The extended family, although a less common form, was also known. An example of a vertically extended family is that of St. Philaretos the Merciful, described by his grandson Niketas in the early 9th century: it included Philaretos and his wife, their married children, and their children's children; all of them lived in a single house and had both common husbandry and common meals.[1] The vita of Philaretos is a literary text, but the rescript of the emperor Manuel I of 1156 provides more authoritative evidence, which confirms the existence of the vertically extended family: it ordains that the children of peasants dependent on the monastery of Theotokos the Merciful (in Macedonia) were allowed, if they wanted, not to detach themselves from their parents, not to run their own households, but rather to stay within the larger unit (Petit 1900). Some private documents also record extended families in the countryside. Thus the cartulary of the Latin church on Cephalonia compiled in 1264 itemizes numerous families of dependent Greek peasants, mostly nuclear units; among them we find the widow of a certain Strabangelos who lived with five sons and a daughter; three of her sons were married and had children.[2] Analysis of the monastic records of early 14th-century Macedonia led A. Laiou to the conclusion that the nuclear family was the predominant form of family organization, but that it was common for various relatives to live under one roof (Laiou 1977, 107). Her detailed study showed certain local differences in family structure: the "pure" nuclear family was obviously the norm in the region of Thessalonike (64–71 percent of households), while in the neighboring district ("theme") of Strymon, although substantial, it was proportionally less prevalent (49–58 percent; ibid., 80 and esp. 81, table III:1). To some extent the difference can be explained by the significant Slavicization of the basin of the Strymon river or by the "individualistic" impact of the big city (Thessalonike) on the surrounding area.

In Byzantine South Italy relatives *(consortes, sortifices,* or *consortifices)* frequently held land together *(communiter abuimus)* and sold it together; the Act of 962 describes a division of land among three brothers in which a part of the property remained in their common possession.[3] At the other end of the Byzantine world, in the region of Trebizond, common property of relatives could also be found: according to an act of the 13th century, five relatives *(syngo-nikarchioi)* held in common a property in the village of Choulion (Uspenskij and Beneshevich 1927, nos. 43 and 44).

The family was a social unit based on biological consanguinity and marital affinity and tied together by participation in ownership and inheritance. It coincided or at least overlapped with the household, an economic unit whose members resided and worked together; the Byzantine household could comprise biologically unrelated elements such as slaves, retainers, or hirelings *(misthioi)*. Certainly, these categories of household members were not common among the peasants, but we encounter them in the houses of urban craftsmen and particularly in aristocratic mansions. The "external" members of the household had no legal rights to ownership or inheritance; Byzantine social ethics, however, encouraged emancipation of slaves supplemented by grants of land or other properties, the so-called *legata*. The status of *misthios*, unlike that of slave, was temporary, but like the Western apprentice the *misthios* had private links and responsibilities within the household: while on the one hand the master could judge and punish his *misthios*, on the other hand marriage could open for him the way into family membership. Pseudo-Genesios, the 10th-century anonymous author of the *Book of kingdoms*, relates that the father of the future famous general Theophobos fled from Persia to Constantinople where he served as *misthios* to a woman running a small shop and eventually joined her in marriage or in cohabitation (Lesmüller-Werner and Thurn 1978, p. 39: 65–70). The situation is repeated, in a romantic guise, in the 13th-century fairy tale *Kallimachos and Chrysorrhoe* (Pichard 1956), the hero of which serves as *misthios* in the garden of the palace where his beloved dwells. It is difficult to determine to what extent such a situation was exceptional: at any rate, both Theophobos' father and Kallimachos were men of royal descent.

Lineage or kin was also a unit bound by consanguinity or affinity or both, but unlike the extended family it had no common residence or household. Accordingly, the limits of a lineage were ill defined; we may suggest that a Byzantine lineage *(genos)* was a more or less loose exogamous group of relatives connected by a common family name and the idea of common origin.

The use of the family (in fact, lineage) name, *nomen gentile*, typical of the Roman empire but fervently attacked by Christian authorities such as John Chrysostom (1972, 146.648–49; cf. Migne *PG* 53:179.25–27), became sporadic in the 5th and disappeared after the

6th century, as we may judge by the change in the character of epitaphs (Kajanto 1977, 421–28). On early Byzantine lead seals, created to certify documents and letters of both officials and private persons, we find the title, office, and single name of the owner, but only extremely infrequently his patronymic or rather sobriquet; the inclusion of family names on seals became common only after the 10th century.[4]

Family names in both historical texts (e.g., Theophanes the Confessor's *Chronography*) and letters (e.g., those by Theodore of Stoudios) of the 9th century were nonexistent or at least rare, whereas they are common in the works of the 12th century. Turning back to the authors of the 9th and 10th centuries we can see that they introduced their personages mostly by single names, indicating in some cases either the name of their fathers or mothers ("the son of X") or their personal, individual sobriquets, which denoted ethnic or local origin or certain qualities; some of these were often mocking or pejorative (such as "Swine" or "Large Head").[5] By the end of the 10th century some of these sobriquets started to be "inherited" and became the names of lineages. The transmission of the family name was not strictly patrilinear: thus the children of Nikephoros Bryennios and the famous princess Anna Komnena were called Alexios Komnenos, after his mother; Maria Bryennaina Komnene, after both parents; and John Doukas and Irene Doukaina, after their maternal grandmother (Barzos 1984, 197).

The change in the principle of naming imperial dynasties reflects the process of establishing appellations of lineages: the dynasties of the 8th through the 10th centuries were named after the place of the founder's origin: Isaurians, Amorians, Macedonians. From the 11th century on, dynasties were specified by the names of lineages: Doukai, Komnenoi, Angeloi, Laskarids, Palaiologoi, Kantakouzenoi. The most striking case is that of the imperial lineage of the Lekapenoi: the founder of the dynasty, Romanos I (920–44), is called Lekapenos only by the late 11th-century historian John Skylitzes (1973, 191.6, 204.18), whereas the chroniclers of the 10th century, including Theophanes Continuatus, Skylitzes's main source, designate him as Romanos the Elder.

Not only the manner of designation but the political role of the imperial lineage changed drastically from the 7th to the 12th century: in the 7th century, imperial relatives were considered a liability rather than an asset, and the successors of Heraklios (610–41) blinded and maimed their close relations to prevent them from claiming the imperial throne. In a reduced form this concept was still alive at the end of the 11th century, when the caesar John Doukas advised the emperor Nikephoros III Botaneiates (1078–81) to take as his spouse the Georgian princess Maria because she was a foreigner in the empire and had no relatives who could bother the emperor (Anna Komnena [Anne Comnène] 1937, vol. 1:107.25–26). Certainly, even before the reign of Nikephoros III some emperors tried to gain the support of their relatives and appoint them to high offices; Michael IV (1034–41) was one of the few who did so. But the system of the "ruling lineage" was created only by the Komnenoi when the "imperial relatives" formed the highest echelon of aristocracy, which practically monopolized the highest titles and the command of the army.[6]

The creation of fake genealogies can be seen as early as the 9th century, when the deposed patriarch Photios compiled a spectacular pedigree for Basil, the peasant from Macedonia who ascended to the throne of Constantinople—Photios made him a descendant of famous ancient dynasties. That, however, was an exceptional case and a harbinger of an incipient tendency. From the 11th century on, bogus genealogies became fashionable and were expanded from the emperor to aristocratic lineages: the historian Attaleiates counted 72 generations of the noble kin of the Phokades in which he included the "famous Fabii," both Scipiones, and Aemilius Paulus (1853, 217f.). No less ostentatious is Nikephoros Bryennios, who claims that the Doukai descended from Constantine the Great.[7] The 12th-century poet John Tzetzes addressed Nikephoros Serblios as the scion of the ancient Roman lineages of the Servilii (1972, 31.15–17). His contemporary Constantine Manasses extolled the aristocratic origin of Nikephoros Komnenos as a descendant of royal families, declaring that his mother was a descendant of Aeneas.[8] Some intellectuals found such a fashion ridiculous: thus, Michael Psellos listed Cyrus of Persia, Croesus, and Darius as ancestors of the hated patriarch Michael Keroullarios (Psellus 1936, 319). This tendency is rendered even more farcically by the 12th-century scholar and orator Michael Italikos, whose panegyric of the patriarch Michael Kourkouas announces that he could have traced the origin of his hero back to the Arsakids and have praised the successes, wealth, and titles of his ancestors, but he refuses to do so, for the patriarch's lineage descends from God (1972, 72.9–16). Accepted or rejected, the idea of noble origin was in the air.

The tendency toward exogamous restrictions was expressed in Byzantine canon law by defining grades of consanguinity or affinity and thereby also creating and defining incest;[9] beginning with the Tomos of the patriarch Sisinnios issued in 997, one can follow the struggle of the aristocracy to restrict the impediments and thus enlarge the possibilities of marital alliances between related lineages; in legal practice the tribunals oscillated between the sixth and seventh degree of relationship as the prohibited "distance" for marriage.

Even though the Byzantine lineage had neither common residence nor common husbandry, it obtained elementary rights to the property of individual families within the kin. A clause in a purchase deed of 1271 states that Michael Archontitzes, his wife Mary, and their children, together with "their entire lineage [genos] and party [meros] as well as their heirs and successors," sold their land to the monastery of Nea Petra in Thessaly (Miklosich and Müller 1871, 396.24–30). A clause certainly could be a sheer formality, but the agrarian legislation of the 10th century recognized the preemption right (protimesis) of the members of a lineage (relatives) possessing immovables in close proximity.[10]

The medieval West inherited the concept of lineage from barbarian societies and developed it as one of its major institutions.[11] Even though the forms of family and inheritance were multiple in Western Europe, the idea of lineage as the theoretical collective owner was stressed there by the system of primogeniture, but found no place in Byzantium. This difference becomes manifest when one analyzes the situation in the Peloponnese in the aftermath of the Crusade of 1204: the Latin conquerors treated their estates as family (i.e., clan or lineage) property, whereas the locals preserved the Byzantine or Mediterranean system of the division of land in equal parts among heirs, male and female alike (Jacoby 1971, 35).

The (predominantly nuclear) family was the most important unit among Byzantine microstructures (Kazhdan 1982 and 1991). The consolidation of its inner links is emphasized by the ritualization of marriage (Hunger 1973; Laiou 1992a; cf. also Ritzer [1962] 1982): instead of a simple, informal accord (as it was in the late Roman Empire) Byzantine marriage was concluded (from the late 6th century on) by an ecclesiastical ceremony. Accordingly, concubinage was (at least in theory) abolished by Basil I (867–86).[12] On the other hand, the "free" divorce permitted by the edict of Justin II of 566 was prohibited by the Ekloge, the "selection" of laws promulgated by Leo III in 741 (rather than 726).

Major political conflicts of the 8th through the 10th centuries were often connected with marital issues and concerns. Constantine V (741–75), a consistent Iconoclast, ridiculed monastic celibacy; he ordered monks to be led to the Hippodrome and paired off with women, whereupon the mob spat and jeered at them. His supporter Michael Lachanodrakon, governor of Thrakesion, summoned monks and nuns to the valley of Tzoukanisterin near Ephesus and forced monks to don white garb and take wives; those who dared to defy his command were blinded and exiled (Theophanes 1883, 437f., 445f.). Another Iconoclastic emperor, Theophilos (829–42), also issued a coercive regulation regarding marital status: all unmarried women and widows should be given in marriage to the *ethnikoi*, foreigners settled on Byzantine territory.[13] The divorce and second marriage of Constantine VI (780–97) became the focal point of a political battle (the so-called Moechian conflict) that outlived Constantine himself; similarly, the dispute over the Tetragamy, the fourth marriage of Leo VI (886–912), continued to rend Constantinople for many years, causing the deposition of the stubborn patriarch Nicholas Mystikos and quite probably the revolt of Andronikos Doukas.

The marriage rite consisted of two elements, usually separated in time: betrothal and "crowning,"[14] reinforced by nuptial blessing. Gradually, civil marriage (without a church ceremony) died out, and the only officially recognized marriage became the one that had received ecclesiastical blessing; in the 11th century, that form of marriage was extended to slaves. Betrothals with ecclesiastical blessing acquired traits similar although not identical to those of marriage. The minimum age for marriage (and for betrothal with ecclesiastical blessing) was established as 12 for girls and 14 for boys, but simple betrothal could be arranged much earlier (Laiou 1986, 381f.). Usually the groom was older than the bride, and widowhood was a frequent occurrence. Second marriage was permitted (but not for priests), a third was considered undesirable and required an ecclesiastical dispensation, and a fourth was completely prohibited.

The nuclear family appears as the strongest social unit, and family values took second place only to hermitic celibacy. From the 10th century on, a new type of saintly heroine was introduced. The earlier hagiographers depicted "wild" holy women—former prostitutes[15] or girls in male disguise (Patlagean 1981) who left their families and even entered male monasteries (where they fell into various predicaments, including being charged with siring illegitimate children). In contrast, writers of the 10th and succeeding centuries concentrated on married women, some of whom (like Theodora of Thessalonike), after having been widowed, entered convents, while others (notably Mary the Younger and Thomais of Lesbos, for whom see Laiou 1989 and Talbot 1996, 239–322) remained in the world coping with the problems of married life.

The peak of Greek pro-family writing is the panegyric of an obscure saint, Philotheos of Opsikion, written by one of the greatest Byzantine authors, Eustathios of Thessalonike, who died ca. 1195. Eustathios, who in general was very critical toward contemporary monks, insists in this vita that hermits care only about themselves and their own salvation; therefore they seek places of solitude and hide in caves and holes in the ground, trying to escape the throng of the marketplace. He contrasts them with those saints who fight the Devil in the full light of public attention and whose deeds therefore surpass the exploits of the hermit. Hermits run along a smooth course with no real obstacles, while the public contestants vie on a battlefield strewn with boulders and spikes. Philotheos did not emaciate his flesh; he lived in the world, raised a family, gathered various riches of the earth, sharing "the excess burden" with the poor (Kazhdan and Franklin 1984, 151f.). Eustathios extols the virtues of the family man over ascetic celibacy.

Despite insufficient archaeological research on urban and especially rural dwellings in Byzantine territory, it is possible to outline an evolution of the private house that corresponds with the tendency toward consolidation of the nuclear family. While the traditional Roman mansion with peristyle remained in use, new edifices of this type were no longer built after the middle of the 6th century; if we disregard the sumptuous "palaces" of the 6th-century aristocracy, the main type of habitation becomes a set of small rooms often built behind the façade of the old public construction (Ellis 1988 and 1993; cf. Sodini 1984). In the 12th century the poet John Tzetzes deplored the inconvenience of his housing in a many-storied building with many apartments (1972, 33.3–16), but such structures are exceptional. Roman *insulae* are known from the excavations in Ephesus, where they were being rebuilt up to the 7th century (Vetters 1978, 197f.); there is no evidence of them in the later archaeological layers. Excavations of medieval towns (Corinth, Athens, Cherson, and others) demonstrate that a small house, frequently connected with a shop, was the main type of urban dwelling (Bouras 1983, 22; cf. Jakobson 1959, 296f.); it was the "individual" building that best of all matched the needs and economic activity of a nuclear family. The locally and chronologically restricted observations about rural

dwellings (especially detailed for late Roman northern Syria) indicate a similar pattern of evolution—the superseding of relatively
vast, "latifundial" habitations by conglomerations of tiny houses.[16]
  The relative strength of the Byzantine family becomes apparent
especially in comparison with other microstructures. The solidarity
of the Byzantine village community was structured as the sum of distinct individual links of neighbors which primarily took the form of
rights in the next-door holdings, from *protimesis* to the entrance for
collecting chestnuts. Peasants could possess trees on other people's
land, and the principle of Roman law *superficies solo cedit* ceased to
be applicable despite the attempts of some commentators on the
Farmers' Law to restore it (Malafosse 1949, 47f.). In the same way,
Constantinopolitan guilds (we have practically no information about
the guilds in the provinces) appear to have been more individualistic
than the organized craftsmen in the medieval West: the individual
atelier was in Byzantium more or less independent of the community,
and control over the production of individual *ergasteria* was exercised not by the guild authorities but by the state apparatus. The
strict hierarchy of masters, journeymen, and apprentices typical of
Western guilds did not develop in Constantinople. The interrelations
between Byzantine tradesmen were regulated by personal contracts
rather than guild normative ethics or legislation, and Byzantine
"companies" *(koinoniai)* were associations of short duration, based
on the individual will of the partners.[17]
  Very little is known of local confraternities, organizations that
aimed at pious goals and mutual assistance among their members
(Nesbitt and Wiita 1975, 381); they seem to have been relatively loose
associations which would assemble at fixed intervals and access to
which was not regulated.
  The looseness of Byzantine microstructures had its counterpart in
the weakness of vertical links and the underdevelopment of hierarchy. As the Byzantines encountered the Crusaders, they noticed and
emphasized the difference between the two worlds. The 12th-cen-
tury historian John Kinnamos was astonished by the strict hierarchical structure of the crusading host, and his younger contemporary
Niketas Choniates ascribed to Frederick I Barbarossa the idea that
the Greeks failed to take into consideration men's differences in
virtues and nobility, and therefore they measured the whole population by the same yardstick, like a herdsman who drove all the hogs,
lean and fat alike, into the same pigsty.[18]
  Of all Byzantine microstructures, the monastery is the best

depicted in the available sources, and sources are particularly abundant from the 11th century on (Kazhdan 1971). There were two major types of monastic institutions in Byzantium: the solitary, family-like, "hesychastic" settlement run by a distinguished ascetic with one or two disciples, and the so-called *koinobion*, housing a community of monks or nuns (Papachryssanthou 1973–74). Even the Greek communal monastery was an individualistic institution. The famous 12th-century canonist Theodore Balsamon bluntly contrasted the contemporary Byzantine monastic community to both late Roman and Western institutions; he affirmed that *koinobia* of the type described in Novel CXXIII of Justinian I did not survive to his day, in sharp contrast to the West, where the monks would eat and sleep together.[19] The size of communities is more or less insignificant, and the mobility of monks striking. Even more striking is the monks' right to dispose of their own property (they would receive holdings *ad vitam*[20]) and even write wills, of which some examples are known (Herman 1941, 436f.; cf. Steinwenter 1932, 60).

On the other hand, monastic individualism is revealed in the weakness of intermonastery links and the absence of monastic orders. The 11th and 12th centuries witnessed the formation of monastic orders in the West; by the beginning of the 12th century the Cluniac monastic congregation encompassed approximately 200 communities, and eventually other orders were created. Nothing of this kind existed in Byzantium; here intermonastery links were either individual (based on a personal contract), or territorial (forming monastic confederations or "republics"), of which Mount Athos is the most renowned. Monastic confederations, however, consisted of independent entities, so that the unity of the Athonite monasteries remained superficial, and the *hegoumenoi* of many of the communities enjoyed more respect than the *protos* of the Holy Mountain. All in all the individualistic structure of Byzantine monasticism reflected the individualism of Byzantine society in which, as we have said, the nuclear family formed the seminal social cell.

The core element of the family was a couple (man and woman) united in marriage. Recently, a tendency has become fashionable to imagine Byzantine women as living under the oppression of "patriarchy," in a male-dominated society, a military society where men inevitably exercised power.[21] The reality, however, was ambivalent rather than disadvantageous for women.[22]

The Byzantine theoretical construct presupposed that women, especially while young and unmarried, were confined within the inner chambers of the house. Despite this construct, women could be seen abroad in the streets and marketplaces, took part in political conflicts, mounted the ramparts of besieged cities to defend them, and participated in public pageants; they were engaged in trade, crafts, and charitable activities, ascended the throne as empresses in their own right and as regents of minor princes, made their contribution to scholarship and literature, and did not abstain from extramarital love affairs.[23]

Were noble ladies actually confined to their quarters? A story of Andronikos Komnenos' incestuous affair with the niece of the emperor Manuel I, the young widow Eudokia (Choniates 1975, 104f.), allows us to question this presumption, at least for the 12th century: Eudokia, much to the indignation of her blood relations, followed her lover to the military camp at Pelagonia and stayed there in a tent, where Andronikos visited her at night.

The most detailed Byzantine description of an aristocratic mansion is probably that of the "palace" built by the epic hero Digenis Akritas on the Euphrates.[24] Not only is there no place for women's quarters in this description, but the author emphasizes the togetherness of the life of both sexes: Digenis' mother stayed with her son and daughter-in-law, and all three would sit together for their meals.

The 10th-century vita of Basil the Younger introduces us to a different world, that of ordinary people. One of them is Theodora, a maiden slave in a noble house in Constantinople; the master provided her with a tiny cell located in the vestibule of the mansion—not a proper place for women's quarters. Another female character of this vita is Melitine, the wife of a *misthios*. She obviously was not confined to a gynaeceum, since she slept with almost all the men in the neighborhood; she even tempted Gregory, the hagiographer, stalking him in the daytime (Vilinskij 1911, 301.5–6, 320f.).

A clear description of the physical environment of a girl's seclusion can be found only in the legend of St. Barbara, in the version written by John of Damascus (1988, 5:247–78). Barbara was a beautiful virgin confined by her cruel father to a tower from which she miraculously managed to escape. The exceptional, legendary character of the tower of the "Christian Danae" (as some scholars call Barbara) only emphasizes how shaky is the theory about the Byzantine harem or gynaeceum.

Archaeological study of Byzantine houses demonstrates that in ordinary Byzantine buildings, emphasis was laid on the privacy of the whole unit, separate from the street, and not on the privacy of individual sections within it which might have been assigned to women. Neither archaeology nor written texts confirm the existence of a Byzantine gynaeceum—they compel us neither to deny nor to accept its existence.[25]

The legal situation of women was not that of an oppressed sex. Daughters had a full right of succession, and widows ran the household and were listed as taxpayers in official records. There are some indications that Byzantine law, after the 8th century, acknowledged a certain expansion of women's property rights and strengthening of women's legal protection (Beaucamp 1977), and the everyday situation seems to have been a far cry from a patriarchal suppression. The first poem of the 12th-century poet Ptochoprodromos, picturing the henpecked husband, who had to come to his home disguised as a beggar in order to get some food from his despotic wife (1991, 99–107), is obviously a caricature, but there are more serious texts demonstrating the leading role of the mother within the family. Two great Byzantine writers, Theodore of Stoudios and Michael Psellos, devoted special panegyrics to their mothers (Migne *PG* 99:883–902; Sathas 1872–94, 5:3–61), whereas no similar eulogy of fathers is known. Fathers are usually shadowy figures in Byzantine texts; while Anna Komnena's *Alexiad*, in which she praises her parent, the emperor Alexios I (1081–1118), may be pointed to as an exception, one should note that Alexios is praised as a general and statesman rather than as a father. Saints are usually brought up by their mothers, as in the case of two patriarchs, Tarasios and Nikephoros, whose biographies Ignatios the Deacon wrote in the first half of the 9th century.

At the end of the 10th century Symeon Metaphrastes collected and revised numerous hagiographical discourses both for private and for liturgical reading;[26] the work is not original but it is significant for societal study, for it provides us with a hagiographical stereotype, the collective image of the Byzantine role model. The typical situation as handled by Metaphrastes is the close bond between the saintly hero and his Christian mother, whereas the father is either lukewarm toward the true religion or, even worse, pagan and anti-Christian.

A passage in the martyrion of St. Catherine, subsequently revised by Metaphrastes, reveals the ambivalence of Byzantine attitudes toward women: the heathen emperor of Rome Maxentius (306–12) is described as discussing the problems of faith with the well-read girl Catherine in Alexandria *(sic);* having failed to persuade her of the advantages of paganism, he organizes a theological debate between Catherine and 50 leading rhetoricians. The disputants gather, confident in their skill, and one of them exclaims: "What does a woman know about the art of rhetoric!"[27] The phrase could be interpreted as a patriarchal disdain of feminine lack of intelligence, but the case is not so simple. First of all, Symeon omits the boastful sentence of his original in which the rhetorician ridiculed Catherine's desire to overturn all rhetorical schooling, although she, in his view, was unaware even of the vocabulary of the rhetoricians. Then Metaphrastes inserts a crucial phrase: when Maxentius dispatched his encyclical summoning the disputants, he—according to the author—claimed that to argue with a woman was beneath his dignity. Symeon recognized that a Byzantine man would pretend that it was beneath his dignity to compete with a woman in a rhetorical disputation, but in fact neither Maxentius nor Metaphrastes himself thought so; moreover, it was Catherine who won the dispute and converted the 50 skillful rhetoricians to her faith.

There were in Byzantium periods of improvement and of decline in the social status of women, and it is noteworthy that one of the periods of their better situation was the most "military" Komnenian century: in Byzantium as in the West the chivalrous ideology led to a growing respect for women rather than a worsening of their status. Certainly, throughout the long history of Byzantium there were cases of male violence, of rape, of male sexual chauvinism, of misogyny—but there is no proof that Byzantine women lived in a harem and were physically and ideologically abused at every step as one would expect in a paradigmatic (but not a real) "patriarchal" and "military" society. Hypothetically, we may surmise that in rural conditions where cattle-breeding and ploughing were specifically male occupations and the role of women was limited to house chores, women's position was less respected than in the city, where they enjoyed more independence.

In Byzantine moral theory the purpose of marriage was defined as the suppression of promiscuous sexual drive and the direction of sex toward legitimate intercourse; celibacy being an ideal that not everybody was capable of achieving, marriage was instituted as a concession to the weakness of human nature. Socially, the major function of marriage was not carnal pleasure[28] but the reproduction of mankind, the procreation of posterity. The theme of barrenness as a sorrowful affliction permeates hagiographic and homiletic discourses, beginning with manifold sermons on St. Anne, the mother of the Virgin, who is said to have suffered not only because she wanted and could not conceive a child but also because she was scoffed at by neighbors as barren. Enormous sums were paid to doctors who promised to heal infertility, and the birth of a child (especially a male) was a cause for celebration.

Infants were nursed either by their mothers or wet nurses; the attitude of Byzantine society toward wet-nursing was equivocal (Beaucamp 1982). Despite the high rate of infant mortality, some families had many children: Laiou calculates that the household coefficient of children in the domain of the Athonite monastery of Iviron oscillated, in the first half of the 14th century, between 2.9 and 4.9, and in the villages of the Lavra of St. Athanasios between 4.1 and 4.9 (Laiou-Thomadakis 1977, 310).

Education started in the family, with the mother and maternal uncle playing the leading role in elementary schooling. Children, especially in rural areas, were involved in the work of the household at a young age; their typical occupation, if we go by the data of hagiographical texts, was herding geese, pigs, and sheep.

A law of Justinian I accepted the principle of Roman law that children were legally subordinate to their father, and the 9th-century law book *Procheiron* still required the formal emancipation of the son from his father's power. In fact, however, as soon as children assumed adulthood (at the age of 25) they became independent regardless of the formal procedure of emancipation; some of them, however, continued to stay with the family. Parents retained substantial rights with regard to their sons and daughters until they reached adulthood: parents could inflict corporal punishment, could castrate boys to make them eunuchs, and, in principle at least, could and did arrange their children's marriages. Despite these substantial rights, parents were prohibited from selling or abandoning their children.

Despite the strong parental authority over children, Byzantine literature reveals the affection of parents for their offspring. Thus Psellos was very fond not only of his mother but also of his daughter Styliane, whose death in childhood he lamented in a funerary oration (1988, 153–84; Vergari 1985), while maternal affection for a daughter is a crucial theme of the vita of Theodora of Thessalonike.[29] Conflicts between "fathers and sons," as described in literary texts, are connected either with attempts at elopement or with the desire to take monastic vows against the parents' will. The erotic romance *Hysmine and Hysminias* by Eustathios Makrembolites[30] revolved around the theme of elopement, whereas other 12th-century romances start with a different situation: the young couple taken captive by the barbarians, where the goal of the beautiful girl is to escape not the stern parents but the claims of the successful captor. Does it indicate that elopement was not a typical kind of Byzantine behavior? The epic of Digenis Akritas recounts how the hero encountered in a desert a girl who had eloped with a lover and been abandoned by him (Trapp 1971, ch. V). Digenis found the man and compelled him to marry his victim. But before Digenis delivered the girl to the safe haven of marriage, he urged her to sleep with him.

Flight to a monastery is a common theme of numerous hagiographical discourses: while some saints took this path to avoid marriage, others fled their homes after a short and virginal marital life. Upon entering a monastery the saintly person might completely sever his family ties. In the vita of the rigorist Symeon the Theologian, Niketas Stethatos narrates how the mother of the monk Arsenios (Symeon's disciple) came from Paphlagonia to Constantinople to see her son; for three days she waited at the gate of the monastery of St. Mamas, but Arsenios refused to see her (Hausherr and Horn 1928, ch. 46). A contrasting attitude is presented in the vita of three brothers from Mitylene, David, Symeon, and George (van den Gheyn 1899): when their mother decided to visit David in his *koinobion*, the saint received a divine sign predicting her arrival; immediately he dispatched one of his disciples to meet her at the seashore and escort her to the monastery. The vita of the three brothers extols family links and values in a general way and particularly stresses that all the brothers were buried in the same grave: "a single womb brought them into the world and a single wonder-working tomb received them after death" (ibid., 259). The contrast revealed in this comparison of two vitae is not an opposition of the public and the private but one of the extreme individualism of Symeon the Theologian's monastic community and the familial individualism of the hagiographer of the three brothers. We see again the same particularity of Greek medieval society—individualism, closely connected with the perception of the family as the major social unit.

The looseness of "public" social bonds and the strength of the family had momentous ideological and socio-psychological implications. Human relations outside the family were construed as a copy of or parallel to familial connections: Byzantine letter writers addressed their correspondents as brothers, sons, and nephews, regardless of their actual relationship. On the other hand, the Byzantine emperor, in addition to his supernatural and supertemporal epithets such as Shining Sun, image of Christ, or new Moses, was characterized by two important definitions drawn from the sphere of social relations:

he was the Lord of his subjects-slaves and the Father of his subjects-children.[31]

Extrafamilial personal relations took on both vertical and lateral forms. Vertical connections (spiritual father and son[s]) were especially common in a monastic milieu; Theodore of Stoudios, for one, was surrounded by *tekna* ready to follow their spiritual father into imprisonment and exile. The father-son spiritual relationship reached its peak in the cult created by Symeon the Theologian for his deceased spiritual father, Symeon the Stoudite or Eulabes ("Pious"; Rosenthal-Kamarinea 1952; cf. Turner 1990, 58–65). It is not accidental that when the official church became suspicious of this excessive veneration and tried to suppress it, a severe conflict ensued between Symeon the Theologian and Stephen of Nikomedeia—the latter representing the position of the patriarchate. Symeon was deposed and exiled to a small town near Chrysopolis. Father-son relations were a kind of Byzantine hierarchy but, unlike Western feudal hierarchy, it was a personal and individual rather than a public phenomenon.[32]

The classical form of lateral nonfamilial links was friendship. Like many social phenomena, Byzantine friendship was conceived ambivalently: on the one hand, we encounter the eulogy of intellectual friendship by Michael Psellos, "der Theoretiker der Freundschaft" (Tinnefeld 1973); on the other, we meet the wary position of Psellos' contemporary Kekaumenos, who asserted that he knew quite a few men who died because of their friends (Litavrin 1972, 218.26–27). Kekaumenos' book of advice and stories is consistently individualistic and antisocial: the author feels uncomfortable at emperors' banquets and does not want to sit at table with his equals; only within his family, surrounded by faithful spouse, obedient offspring, and loyal servants, would he discover relative security.

Some similarity in the theological views of Kekaumenos and Symeon the Theologian can be observed (Darrouzès 1964). The kinship of the two ideologues, however, is not restricted to sublime theological tenets: we find in the works of the Theologian the same Kekaumenian rejection of friendship. While Kekaumenos expanded his individualistic ethics into the sphere of socio-political relations, Symeon presented an individualistic theory of salvation—personal rather than public (ecclesiastical). Man should concern himself with his own salvation, repeats Symeon time and again, not with that of other people: "be careful not to destroy your own house in trying to build the house of another."[33] Without rejecting ecclesiastical sacraments, Symeon placed the personal vision of the divine light higher than baptism and the Eucharist. The individualistic content of Symeon's ethics and soteriology corresponded to the individualistic structure of Byzantine monasticism and moreover to the role of the nuclear family as the leading small social grouping.

The term "individualism" needs to be defined historically. Byzantine individualism differed radically from Renaissance or modern types of individualistic behavior. It was an individualism without freedom, since the Byzantine individual, as well as the Byzantine family, was subdued and suppressed by the powerful, "totalitarian" state, personified in the "king of the Rhomaioi," as the Byzantine emperor was officially called—not only the Father but also the Lord of his slaves. An average *homo Byzantinus*, bereft of any substantial vertical or horizontal social links (feudal hierarchy, lineage, guild associations, and so forth) and lacking the means of collective protection and assistance, looked for illusive comfort within the narrow circle of family and personal contracts; he felt alone and lonely in a threatening world of physical calamities, enemy assaults, demonic temptations, and particularly the arbitrary nature of the state: he stood naked before an incomprehensible metaphysical authority.

Notes

1. The vita of Philaretos has survived in two versions, those published by Vasiliev in 1900 and by Fourmy and Leroy in 1934.
2. Tzanetatos 1965, p. 68: 583–84. In the same survey (p. 67: 569–72), four sons of the late priest Lazarus form a laterally extended family: not only the married brothers and their children but two sons-in-law *(gambroi;* of the older brother?) belonged to the family.
3. *Codice diplomatico* 1897–, vol. IV, no. 1. For other cases see Abramson 1953, 166; Kazhdan 1960, 33f.
4. Kazhdan 1968. New publications of seals confirm this observation, made 30 years ago.
5. Winkelmann 1987, 146–80, gathered a great deal of information on the sobriquets *(Beinamen)* of the period before the 10th century; he does not draw a sufficient distinction, however, between personal sobriquets and family names.
6. The phenomenon was demonstrated by A. Hohlweg (1965), who interpreted it as a political reform. On the social nature of the change see Kazhdan 1974.
7. See on this Polemis 1968, 3.
8. Kurtz 1910, p. 308: 166–67. At the same time, Manasses rejects the idea that Nikephoros descended from Pelops or Kekrops, worthless men and false Hellenes (p. 305: 80–97).

9. The problem was examined by Laiou 1992d, 21–66.
10. Ostrogorskij 1947; cf. Alexakis 1995. The so-called Macedonian agrarian legislation has been the object of many studies—see a good survey of the edicts promulgated by Romanos I in Lemerle 1979, 91–97, and more recently Kaplan 1992, 414–26. The Greek term for the "relatives" is in the edict οἱ ἀνάμιξ συγκείμενοι συγγενεῖς, which Brand 1969, 79, renders "close relatives on either side [of the family]," and Geanakoplos 1984, 240, "close relatives, on both sides." The concept of "both sides," however, is absent from the original, and the participle συγκείμενοι is paralleled by οἱ οὕτως συμπεπλεγμένοι κοινονοί, "joint owners bound together *in the same manner.*" The legislator is speaking about territorial proximity. The correct interpretation had already been given by Vasil'evskij [1879] 1930, 268.
11. See, for instance, Le Goff 1988, 280–85.
12. Karabélias 1992, 739–48, and especially Laiou 1992b.
13. The edict of Theophilos is known from two hagiographical texts: the *Acts of the Forty-two Martyrs of Amorion* (Vasil'evskij and Nikitin 1905, 27.5–7), and the vita of Athanasia of Aegina (Halkin 1987, 181.7–9). Cf. Sherry 1996, 143, n. 22.
14. For the Akolouthia of nuptial crowning see Trempelas 1940, 139–74, and commentary 120–25. Cf. Walter 1979.
15. A classic example of the holy prostitute is Mary of Egypt; when, in the 10th century, Niketas Magistros reworked the legend and produced a similar vita of Theoktiste of Lesbos, the motif of "saintly whoredom" was eliminated—see Kazhdan 1985.
16. Tchalenko 1953, 399. More complex is the picture obtained by Tate (1992, 305–27): the number of houses per square kilometer increased substantially and the amount of land per house diminished as a result of the development of the *microfundium,* a form of small-size exploitation of land; at the same time, the houses grew larger, which implies the increasing wealth of the peasantry. Cf. Foss 1995, 220.
17. The role of *koinoniai* was emphasized by Sjuzjumov (1953, 20); cf. Oikonomides 1979, 68–83.
18. Kazhdan and Constable [1982] 1991, 24f.; Weiss (1969, 23–53) stressed the instability of the late Byzantine hierarchy.
19. Migne *PG* 138:176CD. The convents seem to have been less eremitical and more "communal" than male monasteries—see Talbot 1985, 16f.
20. Lefort 1973, 3.14–15 (the document appears to date from 1040–41); Lemerle, Dagron, and Ćirković 1982, 2.17–21. The formula of property is ἔχειν καὶ δεσπόζειν.
21. The formulations suggested by Herrin 1993, 167, and Galatariotou 1984–85, 56f.
22. Angold 1995, 433, speaks of "a discrepancy between stereotype and reality."
23. Laiou 1981–82, and 1992d.; Garland 1988. On the women involved in the textile industry, see Laiou 1992c.
24. On it see Xyngopoulos 1948; Andronikos 1969.
25. I examined this problem recently in a paper entitled "Women at home" presented at a Dumbarton Oaks colloquium. The paper is now in press

(*Dumbarton Oaks Papers* 52 [1998]), and I abstain from repeating the arguments used there.

26. There is no critical edition of Symeon's *Menologion;* the edition in the *Patrologia graeca* (vols. 114–16) not only omits a number of his works but contains some non-Metaphrastic vitae as well; quite a few Metaphrastic texts are dispersed in various editions. On the basis of ample manuscript material, Ehrhard (1936–39) established the composition of the "regular" Metaphrastic collection.

27. Migne, *PG* 116:284 C. The phrase is copied from an earlier martyrion.

28. Again we have to stress the ambivalence of Byzantine ethical views: *eros*, sexual desire, censured in the hagiographical stereotype (Kazhdan 1990) and usually relegated to illicit relations, was assumed, in "romantic" literature of the 11th and 12th centuries, to be a normal element of marital life; see Laiou 1992d, 91–111.

29. On this vita see the English translation and introduction in Talbot 1996, 159–237. The vita survived in two different versions, and it is not quite clear which of them is closer to the original.

30. On it see Poljakova 1979, and cf. Hunger 1978, 2: 137–42.

31. On the imperial father epithet see Hunger 1964, 93f.

32. The concept of hierarchy in Symeon was reconsidered by Golitzin (1994). In his words, Symeon's understanding of hierarchy was linked to the notion of charismatic (i.e. individual) ascetics. We shall leave aside the question, so dear to Golitzin, whether Symeon carried on a tradition inherited from pseudo-Dionysios the Areopagite.

33. Symeon the New Theologian 1957, 3: 13; cf. 1969–73, vol. 2, no. 22.117–21; vol. 3, no. 56.7–12; and 1963, vol. 1, no. 4.284–90. On Symeon's sociopolitical ideas see Kazhdan 1967.

References

Abramson, M. 1953. Krest'janstvo v vizantijskikh oblastjakh Juzhnoj Italii. *Vizantijskij vremennik*, n.s. 7: 161–93.

Alexakis, A. 1995. A ninth-century attestation of the neighbors' right of preemption in Byzantine Bithynia. *Erytheia* 16: 73–79.

Andronikos, M. 1969. To palati tou Digene Akrita. *Epistemonike epeteris tes philosophikes scholes Thessalonikes* 11: 7–15.

Angold, M. 1995. *Church and society in Byzantium under the Comneni.* Cambridge, England.

Anna Komnena [Anne Comnène]. 1937. *Alexiade.* Ed. B. Leib. Vol. 1. Paris.

————. 1945. Ibid. Vol. 3. Paris.

Attaleiates, Michael. 1853. *Michaelis Attaleiatis Historia.* Ed. B. Niebuhr. Bonn.

Barzos, K. 1984. *He genealogia ton Komnenon.* Vol. 1. Thessalonike.

Beaucamp, J. 1977. La Situation juridique de la femme à Byzance. *Cahiers de civilization médiévale* 20: 164–74.

————. 1982. L'Allaitement: Mère ou nourrice? *Jahrbuch der österreichischen Byzantinistik* 32 no. 2: 549–58.

Bouras, Ch. 1983. Houses in Byzantium, *Deltion tes Christianikes archaiologikes hetaireias* IV, no. 11.

Brand, Ch. 1969. *Icon and minaret.* Englewood Cliffs, N.J.

Choniates, Niketas. 1975. *Historia.* Ed. J. L. van Dieten. Berlin and New York.

Codice diplomatico Barese. 1897–. Bari.

Darrouzès, J. 1964. Kekaumenos et la mystique. *Revue des études byzantines* 21: 282–84.

Ehrhard, A. 1936–39. *Überlieferung und Bestand der hagiographischen und homiletischen Literatur der griechischen Kirche.* Leipzig.

Ellis, S. P. 1988. The end of the Roman house. *American Journal of Archaeology* 92: 565–76.

————. 1993. La casa. In *La civiltà bizantina: Oggetti e messaggio,* ed. A. Guillou. Rome.

Foss, C. 1995. The Near Eastern countryside in late antiquity. In *The Roman and Byzantine Near East,* ed. J. H. Humphrey. Ann Arbor, Mich.

Fourmy, M. H., and M. Leroy. 1934. La Vie de s. Philarète. *Byzantion* 9: 85–170.

Galatariotou, C. 1984–85. Holy women and witches: Aspects of Byzantine conceptions of gender. *Byzantine and Modern Greek Studies* 9: 55–94.

Garland, L. 1988. The life and ideology of Byzantine women. *Byzantion* 58: 361–93.

Geanakoplos, D. 1984. *Byzantium.* Chicago and London.

Golitzin, A. 1994. Hierarchy versus anarchy? *St. Vladimir's Theological Quarterly* 38: 131–79.

Halkin, F., ed. 1987. *Six inédits d'hagiologie byzantine.* Brussels.

Hausherr, J., and G. Horn. 1928. Un Grand Mystique byzantin. *Orientalia christiana* 12: 2–228.

Herman, E. 1941. Die Regelung der Armut in den byzantinischen Klöstern. *Orientalia Christiana periodica* 7: 406–60.

Herrin, J. 1993. In search of Byzantine women: Three avenues of approach. In *Images of women in antiquity,* ed. A. Cameron and A. Kuhrt. 2nd ed. Detroit.

Hohlweg, A. 1965. *Beiträge zur Verwaltungsgeschichte des oströmischen Reiches unter den Komnenen.* Munich.

Hunger, H. 1964. *Prooimion.* Vienna.

————. 1973. Christliches und Nichtchristliches im byzantinischen Eherecht. In *Byzantinische Grundlagenforschung.* Part XI. London. First published in *Österreichisches Archiv für Kirchenrecht* 18 (1967): 305–25.

————. 1978. *Die hochsprachliche profane Literatur der Byzantiner.* Munich.

Jacoby, D. 1971. *La Féodalité en Grèce médiévale.* Paris and The Hague.

Jakobson, A. 1959. *Rannesrednevekovyj Khersones.* Moscow and Leningrad.

John Chrysostom [Jean Chrysostome]. 1972. *Sur la vaine gloire et l'éducation des enfants.* Ed. A. Malingrey. Paris.

John of Damascus [Johannes von Damascus, John Damascene]. 1988. *Die Schriften des Johannes von Damascus.* Ed. B. Kotter. Vol. 5. Berlin and New York.

Kajanto, I. 1977. The emergence of the late single name system. In *L'Ono-mastique latine*, ed. H. G. Pflaum and N. Duval. Paris.

Kaplan, M. 1992. *Les Hommes et la terre à Byzance*. Paris.

Karabélias, E. 1992. Le Concubinat à Byzance. In *Le Droit de la famille en Europe*, ed. R. Ganghofer. Strassburg.

Kazhdan, A. 1960. *Derevnja i gorod v Vizantii. IX–X vv.* Moscow.

————. 1967. Predvaritel'nye zamechanija o mirovozzrenii vizantijskogo mistika X–XI vv. Simeona. *Byzantinoslavica* 28: 1–38.

————. 1968. Ob aristokratizacii Vizantijskogo obshchestva VIII–XII vv. *Zbornik Radova Vizantijskog instituta* 11: 52f.

————. 1971. Vizantijskij monastyr' XI–XII vv. kak social'naja gruppa. *Vizantijskij vremennik* 31: 48–70.

————. 1975. *Social'nyj sostav gospodstvujushchego klassa Vizantii XI–XII vv.* Moscow.

————. 1982. Small social groups (microstructures) in Byzantine society, *Jahrbuch der österreichischen Byzantinistik* 32, no. 2: 3–11

————. 1985. Hagiographical notes. *Byzantinische Zeitschrift* 78: 49f.

————. 1990. Byzantine hagiography and sex in the fifth to twelfth century. *Dumbarton Oaks Papers* 44: 131–43.

————. 1991. Mikrostruktury v Vizantii VIII–IX vv. In *XVIIIth International Congress of Byzantine Studies, Major Papers*, 84–101. Moscow.

Kazhdan, A., and G. Constable. [1982] 1991. *People and power in Byzantium*. Washington.

Kazhdan, A., and S. Franklin. 1984. *Studies on Byzantine literature of the eleventh and twelfth centuries*. Cambridge and Paris.

Kurtz, E. 1910. Evstafija Fessalonikijskogo i Konstantina Manassi monodii na konchinu Nikifora Komnina. *Vizantijskij vremennik* 17.

Laiou, A. 1981–82. The role of women in Byzantine society. *Jahrbuch der österreichischen Byzantinistik* 31, no. 1 (1981): 233–60. Addendum. Ibid. 32, no. 1 (1982): 198–204.

————. 1986. Ho thesmos tes mnesteias sto dekato trito aiona. In *Aphieroma ston Niko Sborono*, ed. V. Kremmydas, C. Maltezou, and N. M. Panagiotakes. Vol. 1. Rhethymno.

————. 1989. He historia henos gamou: Ho bios tes hagias Thomaidos tes Lesbias. In *He kathemerine zoe sto Byzantio*, ed. C. Angelide, 237–51. Athens.

————. 1992a. Consensus facit nuptias—et non. In *Gender, society, and economic life in Byzantium*. Part IV. Aldershot. Originally published in *Rechtshistorisches Journal* 4 (1985): 189–201.

————. 1992b. Contribution à l'étude de l'institution familiale en Épire au XIIIᵐᵉ siècle. In *Gender, society, and economic life in Byzantium*. Part V. Aldershot. Originally published in *Fontes minores* 6 (1984): 284–300.

————. 1992c. The festival of "Agathe." In *Gender, society, and economic life in Byzantium*. Part III. Aldershot. Originally published in *Byzantium: Tribute to A. N. Stratos*, 1: 111–22. Athens, 1986.

————. 1992d. *Mariage, amour, et parenté à Byzance aux XIᵉ-XIIᵉ siècles.* Paris.

————. 1992e. Observations on the life and ideology of Byzantine women. In *Gender, society, and economic life in Byzantium*. Parts I–II. Aldershot. Originally published in *Byzantinische Forschungen* 9 (1985): 59–102.

Laiou-Thomadakis, A. 1977. *Peasant society in the late Byzantine Empire.* Princeton, N.J.

Lefort, J., ed. 1973. *Actes d'Esphigménou.* Paris.

Le Goff, J. 1988. *Medieval civilization.* Trans. J. Barrow. Oxford.

Lemerle, P. 1979. *The agrarian history of Byzantium.* Galway.

Lemerle, P., G. Dagron, and S. Ćirković, ed. 1982. *Actes de Saint-Pantéléèmon.* Paris.

Lesmüller-Werner, A., and I. Thurn, ed. 1978. *Iosephi Genesii Regum libri quattuor.* Berlin and New York.

Litavrin, G., ed. 1972. *Sovety i rasskazy Kekavmena.* Moscow.

Malafosse, J. de. 1949. Les Lois agraires à l'époque byzantine. *Recueil de l'Académie de législation* 19.

Michael Italikos [Michel Italikos]. 1972. *Lettres et discours.* Ed. P. Gautier. Paris.

Migne, J. P., ed. *Patrologiae graecae cursus completus.* Paris, 1862.

Miklosich, F., and J. Müller, ed. 1871. *Acta et diplomata graeca medii aevi.* Vol. 4. Vienna.

Nesbitt, J., and J. Wiita. 1975. A confraternity of the Comnenian era. *Byzantinische Zeitschrift* 68: 360–84.

Oikonomides, N. 1979. *Hommes d'affaires grecs et latins à Constantinople.* Montreal and Paris.

Ostrogorskij [Ostrogorsky], G. 1947. The peasant's pre-emption right. *Journal of Roman Studies* 37: 117–26.

Papachryssanthou, D. 1973–74. La Vie monastique dans les campagnes byzantines du VIIIe au XIe siècle. *Byzantion* 43: 158–80.

Patlagean, E. 1981. L'Histoire de la femme déguisée en moine et l'évolution de la sainteté féminine à Byzance. In *Structure sociale, famille, chrétienté à Byzance.* Part XI. London. Originally published in *Studi medievali* 17 (1976): 597–623.

Petit, L. 1900. Le Monastère de Notre Dame de Pitié. *Izvestija Russkogo arkheologicheskogo instituta v Konstantinopole* 6, p. 32: 22–25.

Pichard, M. 1956. *Le Roman de Callimaque et de Chrysorrhoé.* Paris.

Polemis, D. 1968. *The Doukai.* London.

Poljakova, S. V. 1979. *Iz istorii vizantijskogo romana.* Moscow.

Psellos, Michael [Michael Psellus]. 1936. *Michaelis Pselli Scripta minora.* Ed. E. Kurtz and F. Drexl. Vol. 1. Milan.

———— [M. Psello]. 1988. Per la figlia Stiliana. In *Cultura e politica nell'XI secolo a Bisanzio*, ed. M. Solarino. Catania.

Ptochoprodromos. 1991. *Ptochoprodromos.* Ed. H. Eideneier. Cologne.

Ritzer, K. [1962] 1982. *Formen, Riten und religiöses Brauchtum der Eheschließung in den christlichen Kirchen des ersten Jahrtausends.* Münster.

Rosenthal-Kamarinea, I. 1952. Symeon der neue Theologe und Symeon Studites. *Oekumenische Einheit* 3: 103–20.

Sathas, K. 1872–94. *Mesaionike bibliotheke.* Athens, Venice, and Paris.

Sherry, L. 1996. Life of St. Athanasia of Aegina. In *Holy Women of Byzantium*, 137–58. Ed. A. M. Talbot. Washington.

Sjuzjumov, M. 1953. *Proizvodstvennye otnoshenija v vizantijskom gorode-emporii v period genezisa feodalizma.* Sverdlovsk.

Skylitzes, John [Johannes Scylitza]. 1973. *Joannis Scylitzae Synopsis historiarum.* Ed. H. Thurn. Berlin and New York.

Sodini, J. P. 1984. L'Habitat urbain en Grèce à la veille des invasions. In *Villes et peuplement dans l'Illyricum protobyzantin,* 341–97. Rome.

Steinwenter, A. 1932. Byzantinische Mönchstestamente. *Aegyptus* 12: 55–64.

Symeon the New Theologian [Syméon le Nouveau Théologien] 1957. *Chapitres théologiques, gnostiques, et pratiques.* Ed. J. Darrouzès. Paris.

————. 1963. *Catéchèses.* Ed. B. Krivochéine. Vol. 1. Paris.

————. 1969–73. *Hymnes.* Ed. J. Koder. Paris.

Talbot, A. M. 1985. A comparison of the monastic experience of Byzantine men and women. *Greek Orthodox Theological Review* 30: 1–20.

Talbot, A. M., ed. 1996. *Holy women of Byzantium.* Washington.

Tate, G. 1992. *Les Campagnes de la Syrie du nord du IIᵉ au VIIᵉ siècle.* Paris.

Tchalenko, G. 1953. *Villages antiques de la Syrie du nord.* Vol. 1. Paris.

Theophanes. 1883. *Chronographia.* Ed. C. de Boor. Vol. 1. Leipzig.

Tinnefeld, F. 1973. "Freundschaft" in den Briefen des Michael Psellos. *Jahrbuch der österreichischen Byzantinistik* 22: 151–68.

Trapp, E., ed. 1971. *Digenes Akrites.* Vienna.

Trempelas, P. N. 1940. He akolouthia ton mnestron kai tou gamou. *Theologia* 18: 101–96.

Turner, H. 1990. *St. Symeon the New Theologian and spiritual fatherhood.* Leiden.

Tzanetatos, Th. 1965. *To praktikon tes Latinikes episkopes Kefallenias tou 1264.* Athens.

Tzetzes, Ioannes. 1972. *Epistulae.* Ed. P. Leone. Leipzig.

Uspenskij, F., and V. Beneshevich. 1927. *Vazelonskie akty.* Leningrad.

Van den Gheyn, I. 1899. Acta graeca ss. Davidis, Symeonis, et Georgii Mitylenae in insula Lesbo. *Acta Bollandiana* 18: 217f.

Vasiliev, A. 1900. Zhitie Filareta Milostivogo. *Izvestija Russkogo arkheologicheskogo instituta v Konstantinopole* 5: 64–86.

Vasil'evskij, V. [1879] 1930. Materialy dlja vnutrennej istorii Vizantijskogo gosudarstva. In *Trudy.* Vol. 4. Leningrad.

Vasil'evskij, V., and P. Nikitin, ed. 1905. *Skazanija o 42 amorijskikh muchenikakh.* St. Petersburg.

Vergari, G. 1985. Sull'epitafio pselliano per la figlia Stiliana. In *Studi di filologia bizantina* 3: 69–76.

Vetters, H. 1978. Die Insulabauten in Ephesos. In *Wohnungsbau im Altertum.* Berlin.

Vilinskij, S. G., ed. 1911. *Zhitie sv. Vasilija Novogo v russkoj literature.* Odessa.

Walter, Ch. 1979. Marriage crowns in Byzantine iconography. *Zograf* 10: 83–91.

Weiss, G. 1969. *Joannes Kantakuzenos—Aristokrat, Staatsmann, Kaiser, und Mönch—in der Gesellschaftsentwicklung von Byzanz im 14. Jahrhundert.* Wiesbaden.

Winkelmann, F. 1987. *Quellenstudien zur herrschenden Klasse von Byzanz im 8. und 9. Jahrhundert.* Berlin.

Xyngopoulos, A. 1948. To anaktoron tou Digene Akrita. *Laographia* 12: 547–88.

3. The evolution of the family and marriage in modern Greece[1]

PAUL SANT CASSIA

Department of Anthropology

University of Durham

The late 18th and early 19th century was a critical period in the development of the modern Greek family. During this period certain social developments emerged in Athens that were to shape, inform, and ultimately dominate regional variations in family forms throughout the society. These included an emphasis on the mobility of dowry goods; neolocality; the massive endowment of daughters as a means of achieving social mobility; the primacy of the matrimonial contract as a legal agreement to establish trust and security in an uncertain and changing world; the use of godparenthood as a means to lure powerful non-kin as potential allies; and the cult of motherhood and women's seclusion within the home as a means to reinforce the emerging distinction between the "public" and the "private." Crucial to an understanding of this process was the reluctant and precarious urbanization of country folk. The chapter concludes by placing the available data on marriage and the family in Greece within wider discussions on the "Western European marriage pattern," and suggests that we need to look at both culture and structure in understanding family and kinship.

Introduction: The city is the key to everything

THE KEY ISSUE this chapter addresses is the evolution of the modern Greek family in the 19th century, a critical period in the development of modern Greek society. Its central theme is that during this period certain features of the modern Greek family evolved among certain emerging social groups under specific conditions in Athens; and that backed by the political and cultural primacy of the new capital, these features were to shape, inform, and ultimately dominate regional variations in family forms throughout the society. These included an emphasis on the mobility of dowry goods; neolocality; the massive endowment of daughters as a means of achieving social mobility; the primacy of the matrimonial contract, a legal agreement to establish trust and security in an uncertain and changing world; the use of godparenthood as a means to lure powerful non-kin into potential allies; and the cult of motherhood and women's seclusion within the home as a means to reinforce the emerging distinction between the "public" and the "private." Crucial to an understanding of this process was the reluctant and precarious urbanization of country folk.

Of all the Mediterranean countries in the modern era, Greece was perhaps the earliest and the most heavily exposed to the transformative effects of urbanization coupled with massive dislocation in the countryside (through the wars of independence, the various Balkan wars, the Second World War, and the civil war, as well as through the incorporation of Greek agriculture in the modern world economy). The combination of its mountainous terrain, poor soils, small-scale farming (with the exception of the large Thessalian estates), lack of credit, and low productivity, together with the general insecurity prevailing in the countryside, meant that Greek peasants were, in the words of the 19th-century French observer and novelist Edmond About, always thinking of abandoning their holdings for the city. For most of the last 150 years modernity, security, and "culture" *(politismos)* in Greece were coterminous with the city; "backwardness," insecurity, and boorishness with the countryside. The role of Athens as the center of national Greek culture, the site of government employment, and the ultimate destination of peasants for *mia kalliteri zoi* (a better life) is unparalleled by other Mediterranean cities. Athens' population grew spectacularly from approximately 10,000 in 1834 to 180,000 in 1896 to 3 million in 1976 (McNeill 1978). In spite of the rediscovery of Greece in classicism and classical ruins (Tsigakou 1981), modern Greece was spawned in the city, and urbanization was its cultural matrix. We should look there for an understanding of the making of the modern Greek family. In this chapter I look at some essential features of the emergence of the modern Greek family, basing the discussion on some earlier research I conducted with Constantina Bada[2]. I then relate and situate this within current debates on the history and evolution of the Western family.

Traditional patterns

Although there has been a great deal of regional variation in domestic organization and property-transmission patterns in Greece, such differences have tended to decrease in the modern nation-state. Couroucli (1987, 329) has identified four different systems of domestic organization with corresponding distinctions in property transmission. The first were pastoralists with extended families and a trousseau given to daughters at marriage (as for example the Sarakatsani studied by Campbell [1964]). Among transhumant pastoralists in the latter 19th century, larger and more complex household forms were relatively common. Caftanzoglou (1994) has provided a picture for the Vlach community of Syrrako in Epiros in the latter 19th century. Marriage ages for women were low (40.8 percent of women in the 20–24 age group were married), and the age gap between spouses fluctuated between 5.6 and 7.5 years. This made it closer to the Mediterranean family pattern. Settlement was patri-virilocal. Daughters were excluded from inheriting land, houses, and animals from the parental estate, and claimed their share as dowries in the form of housekeeping utensils, a trousseau, jewelry, and money.

The second group comprised mainland farmers with nuclear families, patri-virilocality, and land and trousseaux given to daughters as dowries (as studied by Friedl [1962] and du Boulay [1974]). A third group consisted of neolocal island farmers who gave mainly trousseaux as dowries. The fourth group was made up of fishermen with uxorilocality and a bias towards heavy daughter endowment (Papataxiarchis 1985; Kasdagli 1988; Skouteri-Didaskalou 1976). Large islands such as Crete (Herzfeld 1985), Cyprus (Loizos 1975), and Corfu (Couroucli 1985) tended to be agnatically oriented, although the situation was complex and varied and changed over time (Sant Cassia 1982).

Islands had varied family and household patterns, reflecting the complexity and progression of occupations, with individuals moving from fishing (at the bottom of the scale), to sailoring, and finally to large landholding and farming. We could say that (medium to small) island communities (such as Mykonos) almost represent the mirror image of transhumance. For the patrilineal bias of transhumant pastoralism, we have the matrilineal orientation of the island communities. For a predominance of male household headship in transhumant communities, we find a significant number of households headed by women. In 1861 in Mykonos, 23 percent of households were headed by women (Hionidou 1995, 73). For the relatively common extended household (at least at a particular stage of the developmental cycle) among transhumants, in island communities the dominant household was generally nuclear or even indeed headed by a single woman, as the men were often away. In Mykonos according to the 1861 census the household was "overwhelmingly nuclear with 70 percent of the households comprised exclusively of conjugal families" (ibid., 71). In contrast to transhumant practice, "the inheritance was shared equally by all children irrespective of age and sex" (ibid., 78), but dowries were also considered the daughter's share of the inheritance. And whilst among transhumants settlement at marriage was patri-virilocal, neolocality was the rule among islanders (ibid.). What seems to be common to both transhumants and islanders in the 19th century was young age at marriage for females, the near universality of marriage for both sexes, and a wider gap in ages at marriage between spouses than the Western European pattern. This places these communities with the Mediterranean family pattern. Finally, islands such as Mykonos were different from other port societies (such as Valletta in Malta) in that they had very low levels of illegitimacy and even lower rates of prenuptial pregnancies (ibid., 92).

In cities, by contrast, which were often settled by refugees displaced either by war (such as the 1922 Asia Minor catastrophe; cf. Hirschon 1983 and 1989), or by the more peaceful but equally pernicious ravages of modern capitalism in the countryside, residence is often uxorilocal, affinal ties are strong, and the mother-daughter link is the basis for future additions. These patterns had emerged in Athens in the 19th century. Thus the contemporary pattern of investing daughters with large dowries, especially of urban real estate, to attract suitable grooms; the tendency towards uxorilocality; the emphasis on the nuclear family rather than on lineage ties, on affinity rather than agnation, on *koumbaria* rather than adoption or fosterage, are specifically urban in their genesis, especially among an emerging Athenian middle class in the 19th century. Because Athens came to dominate Greek society in the new small nation-state politically, economically, and culturally, and because Greece was a society consisting mainly of peasants with small landholdings, the family models that permeated the rest of Greek society were heavily influenced by Athenian urban patterns.

Athens under Ottoman rule

Under Ottoman rule the population in Athens was divided into four distinct taxation groups, reflected in sumptuary laws: the *arkhontes* (ruling group of notables), *noikokyreoi* (household gentlemen), *bazarides* (market traders), and *ksotarides* (migrants to the city). The *arkhontes*, originally traders who had emerged during the Venetian occupation, had like most elites elsewhere managed to make themselves indispensable to the ruling Ottomans. They drew up the taxation lists, collected taxes, and settled civil cases within the Christian community (Benizelos 1902, 275). They were major landowners. They also supplied the higher echelons of the clergy. They thus wielded immense power, straddling the polity, the economy, and the Church. Inevitably they developed strong and mutually beneficial (but ultimately compromising) links with highly placed Ottoman officials. The *noikokyros* chronicler P. Skouzes (1975, 65–66) scathingly referred to them as sycophants.

Although accumulating capital (primarily land) in 17th- and 18th-century Greece was generally precarious, and the capital, once acquired, was liable to arbitrarily imposed sequestration, it seems clear that there was generally a movement towards a rigidification in land ownership. By 1760, Athens had become fully incorporated in the prebendal regime (*mulikame*—holdings leased for life). Ottomans amassed land given over to cereal production, pushing out the peasant-owners, who become cultivators or pastoralists. Conditions appear to have been worse in the city than in the countryside. During most of the 18th century, Athens lacked the necessary might to commercially dominate the countryside, to which townsmen regularly fled to escape oppressive taxation, and there are references in 1775 to a sizable group of paupers (*ftokhon*) in Athens who worked as seasonal mobile agricultural workers (Andrews 1979, 118). *Arkhontic* control of trade became increasingly threatened by the new, up-and-coming class of *noikokyreoi* traders. By 1765, Chandler observed that "the *arkhons* are now mere names" (Andrews 1979, 113). Tension between the *arkhontes* and *noikokyreoi* was exacerbated by political differences, the former being identified as *kotzabashides* who "in all else imitated the Turks, in clothing, in external manners and in [their] house" (Clogg 1976, 21).

Tension between the two groups was not restricted to trade and the concomitant issues of political representation. It was pursued through the transmission of goods and the endowment of daughters at marriage.

From an analysis of 523 marriage contracts drawn up in Athens between 1788 and 1834 (Sant Cassia and Bada, 1992), it appears that some 30 percent of all brides had both parents dead and another 30 per cent had widowed mothers. Most parents did not share houses with their married daughters. Only 30 percent of all living parents endowed a daughter with a house or part of a house (usually associated with an agreement to care for the elderly parent), whilst nearly 75.8 percent of all parents, jointly or singly, lived with their married sons or their sons remained in the parental home at marriage. This was not a function of wealth: titled parents were even more unlikely to supply their daughters with houses. Some 60 percent of all brides were fatherless; one may therefore surmise that the proportion of fatherless grooms may have been larger, although we have no figures for marriage ages. This parallels Corfu during this period, where some 27 percent of all grooms married with their father alive (Couroucli 1985, 53 n. 2). In practice, therefore, paternal power was likely to be weak and of short duration. Of more significance appears to have been maternal power or the links between brothers.

Approximately 37 percent of brides in our sample received houses or parts of houses, whilst 58 percent of all couples do not appear to have been formally endowed with a house at marriage. It is clear therefore that the nuclear family and neolocality were far from the cultural norm at least at marriage in the early 19th century. The majority of house transmissions to both sons and daughters were explicitly linked to old-age care of an elder parent. The general rule was that daughters moved and sons remained at marriage. Most couples started their conjugal careers in complex households, either extended (containing the widowed mother) or to a lesser extent in a multiple household made up of two couples linked by consanguinity (Laslett and Wall 1972). Children were thus brought up in extended households. Because death dissolved unions early, it is more likely in practice that it was matriarchal power rather than patriarchal power that dominated.

At the top of Athenian society during this period we find a small elite of *arkhontes*. This was a tightly knit and intermarried group who settled patri-virilocally at marriage. The family homes so formed were known as houses *(oikoi)* or hearths *(tzakia)*, a usage similar to that of the Tuscan *case* (Klapisch Zuber 1985). Much of their parental property was retained intact and was referred to as *intrigada;* this term, from the Italian, means "full of intrigues," and was used of property that was inherited as a whole, because the terms of the inheritance inhibited its easy division. Their households included family retainers and foster children. They identified with their native city, of which they were traditional patrons. At the bottom end were the large group of migrants and seasonal workers. Among them uxorilocal residence at marriage was much more common, and the central dyad was the link between the elderly widow and her coresiding married daughter or daughters. This pattern was consistent with a traditional horizontally stratified society in a preindustrial agrarian age, and was paralleled in other parts of the Mediterranean. Klapisch Zuber (1985, 19) notes that in Renaissance Tuscany, "among the poor, each new couple founded its own household, but many households were not based on a new union. Among the rich, the independent 'establishment' of the children does not follow their marriage either, since the sons continued to live under the parental roof. Unlike families in northern Europe, marriage and the establishment of a household did not go hand in hand in Tuscany."

In Athens, daughters were less excluded from property than Tuscan women, who were excluded from inheriting landed property. In Athens, women inherited property, including landed property, mainly through dowries.

Marriages tended to be class-endogamous. Some 56.5 percent of *noikokyreoi* grooms took titled brides. But whereas titled women tended to marry in their own status group (65.5 percent), titled grooms were more likely to take brides from lower social groups. The dominant pattern was isogamy for high-status women and hypergamy for lower-status women, to a statistically less significant extent.

Titled brides received major cash-producing resources. The olive tree was the most important resource and was clearly associated with titled families, as were cash settlements apart from their bridal costumes. But it is clear that the relatively modest amounts of basic resources transmitted at marriage (land and livestock) implied that most couples expected to rely on wider kin networks for access to land, from both the groom's and the bride's family.

In the late 18th century, dowry inflation appeared in Athens and other parts of Greece. This was not just a matter of the relationship between the supply of spouses and the increase of goods transmitted at marriage. Rather it appears to have been due to major changes in the economy and the emergence of a new class that employed new strategies in the matrimonial market that had political implications.

Marriages and class tensions

The old system of property transmission within the family was largely homeostatic, so long as it reflected the preexisting distribution of power. New changes were afoot. Among the Athenian *arkhontes* class a system of unequal, and eventually partible, inheritance prevailed, which was nevertheless *intrigada*. In Lesbos (Papataxiarchis 1985) and Karpathos (Vernier 1984) a de facto form of unigeniture obtained. In Chios according to Lord Charlemont, an 18th-century visitor, it appears that Sunni (Ottoman) law was followed, with daughters receiving half the share of their brothers. Younger sons of the *arkhontes* either joined the clergy (Kampouroglous 1896, 176) or remained as cadet members of the household, although we do not know how the problem of keeping them under control and not unruly was addressed. Daughters, by contrast, inherited goods at their marriages, both movables and immovables, and circulated endogamously within the *arkhontes* group or married into the *noikokyreoi* below. But when in the late 18th century the *noikokyreoi* started massively endowing their daughters, partly to reflect their growing economic might and anticipate their political aspirations, the members of the *arkhontes* class were obliged to increase their daughters' dowries. Such increases had the unfortunate consequence from the perspective of *arkhontes* elders of also attracting young *arkhontes* men, especially the younger sons, and thus subverted *arkhontes'* agnatic solidarity. The *arkhontes* class was much less a unified group than other Mediterranean elites, which had a more stable and hierarchical class structure, based upon control over land. In Catalonia, for example, the bulk of the parental estate devolved upon the single designated heir (usually male; McDonough 1986, 148). The wealth of the *arkhontes* depended less upon tangibles such as land, and more upon administrative and political prerogatives. They were therefore much more susceptible to changes both from below and from above.

During the Turkokratia a complex interplay existed between customary practices and Church-imposed guidelines, which varied from region to region. When practices were codified into national law (civil code) in the mid-19th century, this tended to reflect the interests and cultural perspectives of the urban and middle-class legislators.

Dowry inflation had been troubling Greek society since the early 18th century. In 1737, Patriarch Neophytos wrote to the metropolitan bishop of Athens complaining that parents were giving cash, land, olive trees, vineyards, gold, pearls, and clothing to their daughters. He continued "because this evil is increasing all the time, parents are obliged to give all their wealth to their daughters, thus leaving their sons improvident and ungoverned" (Vretos 1864, 233–34). The letter referred to the response of the *arkhontes* class to the increasing tendency of the *noikokyreoi* to heavily endow their daughters. This had the effect of obliging *arkhontes* parents to increase their daughters' dowries, and thus deflect resources from sons. Such practices alienated resources from the family. They also threatened to subvert the distribution of power within the agnatic household. Second or younger sons who had previously accepted a lower profile within the patrilineal household were now tempted to break the ranks of agnatic solidarity by the promise of large dowries. The *noikokyreoi* had greater access to cash, a scarce resource, which facilitated the circulation of daughters to a greater extent as they were not tied to the land. The effects were far-reaching, for the increase in daughters' dowries among both classes facilitated the breakdown of traditional localized groups of elites and the integration of a new class that had geographically varied origins.

Similar processes were also present in late medieval urban Italy. The pattern seems to have emerged in contexts where new social classes were emerging. In Tivoli nobles and commoners were crushed by "the enormous and unusual dowries that they must pay for their daughters, nieces, or sisters"—a practice characterized as an "evil custom and abuse" (quoted in Klapisch Zuber 1985, 243). In the Greek countryside the introduction of cash was feared just as strongly. In Skopelos in 1824 "villagers threatened to burn down houses of those from a neighboring village who gave their daughters more than a certain customary amount" (Skouteri-Didaskalou 1976, 124). This parallels Bohannon's observation that in times of social change such as the introduction of money or new resources, it is always the elders who deplore the situation (Parry and Bloch 1989, 14).

In response to this situation the Church in Athens attempted to fix the dowries into three classes in 1737. This was largely ineffective or subverted, and the Church felt obliged to repeat the encyclical in 1760, widening and increasing the thresholds (Valetas 1848, 76). The encyclicals refer to the "accidental *[atykhima]* growth of the dowry" and said that "all want to become equal," that such practices are rowdy and loud *(thorivodhes)* and "cause sadness." The Church also feared that girls would remain unmarried or enter into other forms of marriage, such as *kepin* marriage, which was recognized by the Ottomans (and thus had the force of superior law recognizing it), but which the Church considered concubinage. Indeed for many, especially the poor, *kepin* marriage appeared to be considered legitimate, and was resorted to as a remarriage strategy because of the rising cost of the dowry (Zolotas 1926, 277). Appeals could be made to the Turkish judge, or cadi, and his decision could subvert the decisions of the committee of elders and the bishop over the endowments (Charlemont 1984, 113).

The rulings extended to matrimonial costumes. But by the late 1830s the old social order had been effectively superseded; costumes that were repositories of wealth lost importance to cash dowries, and rather than attempt to control the movement of women by concentrating on their dowries, and prevent the breakdown of the system, the Church changed direction. It concentrated instead on pegging the bride's dowry to the social origins of her future spouse. This was a capitulation. Costumes had been associated with different social and geographical groups, representing in a tangible form the *ancien régime* of permanent and formalized social differences. A single type of matrimonial costume now began to symbolize not just a common synchronic ethnicity, but also a common diachronic set of customs.

Whereas the previous system had encouraged group endogamy and the lateral circulation of spouses, the new system heralded cash as the major dowry component and permitted gradual but definite social mobility. It signified the change, well brought out by Skouteri-Didaskalou (1984, 158), from the equation "good groom → wealthy dowry" of the old system to the equation "wealthy dowry → good groom" of the 19th century. Signifiers became signifieds and vice versa.

By the end of the 1820s the old *arkhontes* class of *signori* had merged with the *noikokyreoi* through greater intermarriage. Social mobility became increasingly common as the city began losing its agricultural base and became the capital of the new Greek kingdom. Land previously held by the Turks was released for purchase at low prices. Numerous merchants settled in the city and intermarried. They are recognizable in the contracts by their pledges of large amounts of cash as dowers, as a means to ensure acceptability. The state bureaucracy was already beginning to become attractive. These attractions were to increase in the future. Urban-oriented dowries began to make their appearance (Friedl 1962). By 1890, Peloponnesian villagers were already building houses in Athens to attract government employees—and prospective grooms; they were, in the words of Kalpourtzi (1987, 94), "a completely different matter to rural house transfers."

While the agricultural component of the dowry decreased in the post-1830 period, its monetary component increased. Before 1830 only 17 percent of brides were endowed with over 300 groshia at marriage. After 1830 this increased to 24.1 percent. The figures are even greater for endowments of over 600 groshia (from 5.1 to 20.7 percent). The introduction of cash as a major component of the dowry held far-reaching implications to which I now turn.

Gifts, trousseaux, and commodities

Both cash and trousseaux lent themselves to a greater strategic manipulation than land. They were ideal as semiotic markers. You cannot do much with land. But you can signify a great deal with cash, and moreover it has certain associations that are more manipulable than those of land. Cash figured both as dowry and as dower. Bridal costumes, which formed a significant part of the trousseaux, reflected socially recognized claims to preeminence in a way titles did not. Yet it is important to note that cash did not correspond to capital and "commodities," nor trousseaux to symbolic items and "gifts." In the period we are dealing with cash possessed a heavy symbolic and ultimately ambiguous significance, while trousseaux had a strong economic value.

That women tended to receive movables raises important questions whether this marks their exclusion from receiving immovables, which went to sons. Logically one would expect land to go to daughters because they can provide greater continuity. An alternative would be to see a property-transmission system in terms of a cultural logic that assigned certain goods to daughters and others to sons. Ultimately a question about "equality" in the transmission of resources may be useful to pose but absurd to answer seriously, especially for precapitalist semi-gift, semi-commoditized "transitional" economies such as this one. To begin with, whose notion of equality are we to apply? If we were to apply ours, then some of our presumptions might be shown to be grievously wrong. Whilst women were excluded from receiving land in Athens, the capital value of what they received (cash and trousseaux) was far greater than that of the land that went to their brothers. Nor would such an approach tackle how people of the period saw matters. In early-19th-century Athens, the dowry was linked in a performative sense to inheritance. Individuals inherited their status and a specific position within society; consequently they inherited certain goods which enabled them to enter status-specific types of marriage. Daughters' marriages were viewed in a collective corporate sense rather than as a series of discrete individual strategies. Similar patterns (the exclusion of daughters from postmortem inheritance) were found in other parts of Greece in the 19th century (Caftanzoglou 1994; Hionidou 1995).

By the 1830s a new form of marriage had emerged. Dowries increasingly became conceptually separable from inheritance. They began to be seen as an "obligation" imposed by "society" which men had to "satisfy," rather than as the expression of a right which individuals possessed as members of a determinate status group and which gave them claims to a specific type of marriage. Dowries became disembedded from (inherited) status, becoming much more a means to acquire prestige by a series of individual cumulative and negotiable steps, or to paraphrase Simmel (1971), as an expression of a "rationally calculated [matrimonial] egoism."

Cash endowments at marriage

Money figured in many areas of matrimonial, literary, and national life in 19th-century Athens. Parents donated large sums to daughters at marriage; husbands promised it to their wives as dowers; popular literature dwelt on the contrast between fabulous wealth and abject poverty; peasants recounted stories of buried treasures of gold coins, often contrasting them to "useless statues [achrista agalmata]"; and national political debates revolved around the national debt.

Money marked both the beginning and the termination of marriage. Athenian women received cash at the commencement and termination of their marriages in the form of cash dowries from parents and dowers from the husband's male kin. Some 60 percent of brides received some cash at marriage. Cash was also a restricted resource. To an even greater extent than the olive tree, cash was the prerogative of the Athenian aristocracy in the late 18th century. As Kolokotronis recounts, "in my time commerce was very limited, money was scarce" (1969, 128). By the late 19th century, cash had made its appearance as a significant component of women's dowries even in the villages (Kalpourtzi 1987, 96). Cash was also required for the dower (*progamiaia dhorea*—the premarriage gift), probably of Byzantine origin (Skouteri-Didaskalou 1976, 119). The dower in Athens consisted of the specification of a sum of money by the groom and his kin at the drawing up of the contract, which was to be handed over to the bride in the case of divorce or dishonoring of the matrimonial contract, or in the event of the husband's predeceasing his wife. There was some variation in Greece in its manner of transfer and terminology (Couroucli 1987; Skouteri-Didaskalou 1984, 225). The dower held brothers together in a series of mutual obligations. Sisters were excluded from these obligations just as they were excluded de facto from sharing in the residue of the parental estate once they received their dowries. Indeed a sister's dowry was often considered her *meridhio* ("share") of the inheritance, which in Athens could be considerable. The greater the social gap between the bride and groom (i.e., the higher the bride's status), the greater the tendency and requirement for the groom to pledge a large dower.

Dowers almost always consisted of cash rather than land (Vernikos 1979) throughout Greece, and were a virtual requirement for a man's marriage. They also suggest late marriage ages for men or significant differences in marriage ages for men and women, or both. The dower's significance depended upon its matrimonial context. Among titled Athenians it was a symbol and index of wealth and of the "family's" (i.e., the men's) *axioprepia* (self-esteem). It was part and parcel of Church-approved marriage, which excluded cohabitation prior to the signing of the *proikosymfono* and made material provision for widows. It institutionalized and symbolized relations between a bride and her affines. Among the uxorilocal urban poor and where cohabitation often preceded the signing of the *proikosymfono*, dowers were less in evidence. The death of a husband in a wife's household was clearly less disruptive to domestic arrangements than in a virilocal settlement, where the widow might have to move. The dower and dowry were complementary. While the dowry was a type of premortem endowment of women as sisters by men (fathers and brothers), the dower was a type of postmortem settlement upon the widow as an affine by the husband's male kin. Indeed the amount of cash promised as dower was much higher than that actually given as dowry.

It seems clear that this society was using money not in its fully commoditized and commoditizing sense. Cash linked groups, not individuals; the "exchange" was not immediate, but delayed; and a "counterpayment" (the dower) was only demanded if the "spirit" of the initial gift (cash dowry to establish a marriage) was not honored. Something similar seems to have occurred in Renaissance Tuscany, where Klapisch Zuber (1985, 233) suggests that marriage gifts represented a "clandestine counterdowry."

Cash and gender

There were various reasons why dowers consisted of cash. One was that men desired to retain control over the residue of the parental estate. By expressing obligations in cash, brothers could ensure that the death of one of them would not followed by an alienation of holdings (i.e. property would not be put on the market by the widow, which would disrupt arrangements among them). A second reason was that dowers were often due when a husband predeceased a wife who had borne him no children. Cash dowers enabled women to pursue a relatively untroubled widowhood. In cases of separation, dowers were often not paid, and women who did not retain rights in their parental household were obliged to rely on their own wits to survive, as Georghios Psilla, an early-19th-century politician recorded (1974, 6): "We had family problems and my mother was obliged to remove herself from our father's house and several times to reside in the rooms of the church [set aside to provide shelter to the poor and homeless]."

But another reason is related to the symbolic associations of cash and trousseaux. Here the traditional anthropological distinction between gifts and commodities has limited explanatory validity. In early-19th-century Greece cash was not a full commodity, and it was often used between kin almost as much as between unrelated free-acting agents in society. It functioned more as a gift, establishing relations between people, rather than between things.

The possession of cash and its pledging to women also held symbolic associations. Cash and trousseaux complemented each other in their circulation and in their associated significance. Apart from the dowers promised by their husbands, women also brought trousseaux, which were essential for their married life. Whilst women received modest amounts of immovables, they received much larger amounts of movables. Wealthy men (as fathers and brothers) endowed women (as daughters and sisters) with cash dowries, necessary qualifications for marriage. Grooms and their agnates endowed women (as wives and widows) with the cash *progamiaia dhorea.* Cash was thus a valuable dominated by men, but funnelled by them to women. In modern Greece, cash remains gender-specific. Hirschon notes (1989, 100) that it is "seen as an integral aspect of male competence." In Piraeus, husbands made over most of their cash to their wives, a situation paralleled in Malta as well as in Cairo (Watson, 1989).

Women were, however, also heavily involved in the exchange system, in what Marilyn Strathern (1984, 166) has called the "genderizing of valuables." The production of trousseaux established relations of support and solidarity among women, in contrast to the divisive and differentiating exchange world of cash dominated by men. Trousseaux can also be seen as women's response to men's domination of cash. The "subversive stitch" also contributed to the production of wealth in a material sense. In matrimonial contracts costumes and jewelry as the trousseaux held pride of place, always heading the list of a bride's goods, to be followed by the groom's pledging of the dower, a counterposition of equal status. Costume and jewelry represented and embodied a considerable portion of the value of a bride's direct or indirect dowry. They could also be pawned as security against a loan. In 1787, during the tyrannical rule of Adji Ali, Panayis Skouzes disgustedly records that in order to save the lives of their husbands, Athenian women were obliged to give up their dowries: "And they went weeping to the *arkhons* who told them, 'Give whatever you have—everything to save your husbands'. . . . They thus sold their jewellery and their farmlands and paid up" (Andrews 1979, 121–22). Similar patterns emerged among refugees from Asia Minor who settled in the island of Amouliani in 1926. Such ritual wealth "considered as capital just as was land or gold, was sold by families, painfully piece by piece, as they struggled to survive the years of exile during the Graeco-Turkish war" (Salamone and Stanton 1986, 109).

Trousseaux were also highly symbolic. The higher up the social scale, the greater was the tendency to restrict their realization as productive capital. They were not just "treasure," as Jane Schneider (1980) aptly describes them. They were invested in for the purposes of social mobility. They functioned both as gifts circulating between kin and affines, and as commodities sold on the market between strangers. Although they could be sold for cash, cash itself was hoarded as a scarce resource. Trousseaux were halfway between "gifts" and "commodities." They were never fully "gifts," because they were given a monetary value which entered calculations on the size of the dowry, and because they could be sold on the market. They were never fully "commodities," because they were often transmitted from mother to daughter, and because their sale on the market indicated an "emergency conversion" (Herskovits 1962). Significantly, the trousseau decreased in importance when the economy became fully commoditized; it became, in J. Davis's words (1973, 36), "a poor sort of investment; it does not carry interest, nor does it have great liquidity; it is hard to sell it and impossible to secure a loan with it."

The investment of the *noikokyreoi* and wealthy families in trousseaux is an expression of the desire to maintain women in the leisure and safety of the home. Trousseaux were also not subject to taxation, as was land under the Ottomans. By the 1830s a new type of costume had emerged, modeled on Western fashions. As J. du Boulay has noted (1983, 259), the function of the traditional dowry was "not so much to confer, as to reveal, wealth."

Goods thus given and received at marriage had a specific gender identity and valuation. Crucially, these valuables could function both as gifts and as commodities. Cash, which was male-dominated, achieved its fullest significance not so much in deployment in capitalist production, but in expressing kinship obligations and in the establishment of a new conjugal unit. It was also rare enough in this imperfectly monetized economy to have the symbolic nuances of a gift, and it was given by men to women. Conversely, trousseaux represented and embodied the productive use of time by wives and daughters which the possession of cash permitted. A *noikokyra* was mistress of her own household because she was mistress of her own time. This was time spent in the production of goods that embodied and glorified the use of leisure time in the seclusion and safety of the home. As Jane Schneider has suggested (1980, 338), there was a strong connection between the production of textiles in the home and restrained sexuality, a connection encouraged by Christianity. A *noikokyra* was like the *casalinga*: "a housewife who 'loves to stay in the house,' living in the bosom of her own family, occupying herself with domestic affairs, with the education of children, seeking refuge from rowdy entertainment."

Such views found ready expression in texts (originally French but later Greek) which began circulating in early-19th-century Athens. As Kitromilides has noted (1983, 48), such texts enjoined women to be "reserved and avoid laughter and noisy company." These are models of behavior that can find their fullest expression in urban contexts, and that are oriented towards self-control, the interiorization of norms, and an increasing separation of the public and private domains. Such models increasingly came to influence behavior and gender construction in Greece. Trousseaux were seen as the physical and symbolic embodiment of virtue, and schooling of girls was, in the words of a popular journal of the time, designed to "educate them as virgins, mothers and wives."

Here a distinction drawn by M. Strathern (1984, 165) may be useful. She distinguishes between the metaphoric and metonymic symbolism of valuables. In the former, "wealth or assets . . . stand for an aspect of intrinsic identity, for agnatic status or 'name' for example. They cannot be disposed of, or withdrawn from the exchange system without compromising that identity." Within this class of goods we can locate land and houses for men and trousseaux for women. In metonymic symbolism, by contrast, "people express proprietorship to the extent that they have personal rights of disposal" (ibid.). Within this class we can locate cash gifts as dowries and the *progamiaia dhorea*. With the passage of time the metaphoric identities of valuables in 19th-century Greece became progressively subverted. Land ceased to have a strong linkage with men, houses were increasingly given to daughters, and trousseaux became increasingly commoditized. All these resources became increasingly "metonymic" in their symbolism—"although disposable they are not 'alienable' in the way that commodities are alienable" (ibid.).

Conversely, the metonymic symbolization of valuables such as cash has become progressively "metaphorical." Cash has become an aspect of the "intrinsic identity" of a family's worth which cannot be "withdrawn from the exchange system [the dowry] without compromising that identity." As Strathern observes, "the same valuables may operate as now one type, and now the other" (ibid.).

The relationship between cash and trousseaux changed across time. By the early 1830s trousseaux had begun to decline in importance and a new bridal costume had begun to replace previous costumes, which had been tied to social classes. Conversely, cash endowments increased in value. A growing homogenization of national culture in the nation-state, shaped mainly by the *noikokyreoi* group, was reflected in the adoption of a new style of bridal costume, which became universal throughout Athens.

The Family and emotional life

Although matrimonial contracts give very little insight into the nature of emotional life in the family, we can turn to other accounts such as travellers' accounts, memoirs, and the like. Matrimonial contracts, the *proikosymfona*, were themselves very ambiguous, representing very different things to various social actors and institutions, and changing in significance across time. For the Church the *proikosymfono* was an instrument to control a "custom"—the "scandalous" practice of cohabitation among the urban poor. For the higher social strata it was important as a "rite" of literacy in a context of restricted literacy. Finally the *proikosymfono* assumed the function of a secular contract as a means to achieve trust, and became both law and custom. Thus writing and social organization can be seen to have a dialectical relationship across time: whilst the use of written formulas reflects changes in the organization of family life, these formulas themselves influence the way that emotions within the family are expressed and perceived.

In the context of restricted literacy and uncertain land tenure as in the latter years of the Turkokratia, the *proikosymfono* was as much a claim to ownership of property on the part of the "donor" as a claim to its receipt by the recipient. As McGrew has pointed out (1985, 28–29), Christians during this period were enabled to acquire property: "where Turkish authority was weak or indifferent Greeks found ways to circumvent Ottoman legal procedures. They might trade previously issued deeds, or in transactions among Christians, rely on sales documents signed before bishops or village elders." *Proikosymfona* thus possessed the institutional preconditions necessary to camouflage the steady increase of private property during this period: the transfer of property to another person which thus ratified *possessio;* registration in a reliable form recognized by the authorities; and "reliable" witnesses. *Proikosymfona* thus had as much to do with the accumulation of property as with its devolution.[3]

Proikosymfona were also religious artifacts. They were an expression of formality between members of the elite, and they established and regularized a set of obligations between the two contracting parties. They were entered into because of the popular significance of marriage (not necessarily in the Church's sense as a sacrament), but also because marriage through the matrimonial contract of the *proikosymfono* was a means to achieve full adulthood and to satisfy the social and moral imperative of marriage. They were rituals of literacy as much as legal safeguards, as popular among the poor as among the wealthy.

Some indication can be obtained from the timing and significance of the *proikosymfono*, which varied with different groups. Among wealthy and titled Athenians it was signed immediately prior to the church ceremony, and it formally celebrated an alliance between two groups. Among the poor it was often signed quite some time after the couple had begun to cohabit, even after the father had died. As in Lesbos (Papataxiarchis 1985), the poor appear to have entered into long and unofficial periods of cohabitation, before the signing of the *proikosymfono;* and as in many parts of Europe (e.g. in 18th-century France; see Segalen 1986, 131), they appear to have viewed their engagement as a virtual marriage, anticipating their conjugal rights. About noted (1855, 134) that the custom was prevalent in the Greek countryside: "In certain districts . . . the betrothed enjoys all the privileges of a husband. Before celebrating the marriage they wait until it gives promise of the first fruits. If the bridegroom, after having conscientiously performed the betrothal withdrew from the 'sacrament' his refusal would cost him his life."

In the new state the Church, long concerned with such grassroots practices, attempted to tighten control. A Holy Synod decree of 1835 aimed at rooting out simony, "as the right time has come to stop this evil wherever it exists" (Frazee 1969, 128), together with a whole raft of other changes. Engagements *(mnisties)*, which until 1835 had taken place in the church and were accompanied both by ritual and by the exchange of gifts, were banned from taking place in the church. The Church thus hoped to eradicate the practice whereby the poorer members of society viewed such rituals as tantamount to marriage.

With the development of a more complex civil society the *proikosymfono* became increasingly important not just to legitimate cohabitation in the eyes of the Church (as among the poorer classes), nor merely as a means of reducing ambiguity between heirs and of retaining control of the bulk of the parental estate in male hands (as among the wealthy and titled); it became socially required. Indeed with the progressive dismantling of the dowry regulations, marriage became one of the main means of social mobility in a monetarized economy. Matrimonial alliances and the accompanying extension of spiritual kinship became one of the main avenues for the accumulation of political capital in the form of votes, clients, and contacts in the vastly expanding state bureaucracy. Legally, the dowry and the matrimonial contract moved from the domain of custom to national law, and the Ottonian regent L. G. Maurer (1835), in true German *Völk-erkunde* fashion, expanded professorial energy codifying local customs in anticipation of their recognition in national law. One of the first laws passed by the revolutionary government was to place the registration of notaries on a sounder footing (Dimakopoulos 1966, 89). Whereas previously the drawing up of the *proikosymfono* was the culmination of a process of the achievement of trust and alliance and its ratification through a ritual of literacy, it now became the precondition to a marriage. The previous equation of alliance → dowry/marriage → *proikosymfono* was transformed into *proikosymfono* → dowry → alliance/marriage. No class was more insistent on this transformation of the *proikosymfono* into a private contract backed by state law than the *noikokyreoi*.

In a dominant viri-patrilocal settlement pattern at marriage, women must have initially found it hard to gain full acceptance by affines. Yet the position of brides must have differed considerably according to social group. Among the small, tightly knit Athenian aristocracy, brides were sufficiently endowed to be somewhat isolated from the awkwardness of their situation. J. A. Buchon, an observer of the mid-19th century, noted the cosmopolitan orientations of the members of the Athenian aristocracy, the suspicion that surrounded them after independence, their tendency to isolate themselves from the rest of the population, and finally their intermarriage with the new political class of ex-Klephts (Andrews 1979, 211).

By contrast, among the rising middle class the position of brides was complex and varied. For those who married within their own social group, marriage tended to separate the bride from her natal family to a greater extent than among the tightly knit aristocracy and the neighborhood-bound ex-peasants and migrants. The tendency towards neolocality and more monetarized cash dowries was to a large extent an urban middle-class phenomenon. There were various reasons for this. This was a much larger group consisting of wealthy merchants and the like, who were attracted to Athens from other regions of the Greek kingdom, and after 1870 from Greek-speaking Ottoman provinces. Trust was more difficult to achieve among such a diverse group unless backed by law. In the new Greek state, land became a full commodity, and it began to be supplanted by cash as the main dowry component. Its very liquidity made parental concern more acute.

The family was home-oriented; daughters were more homebound

than those of migrants, virtuously producing embroidery and other items for their trousseaux. In contrast to the circumstances of traditional elites elsewhere, resources were not in the hands of the older generation but were monopolized by the young in the vastly expanding Athens-based state administration. Neolocality was the "modern" solution, a feature encouraged by the Church.

With the opening up of the matrimonial market and the spread of a cash economy, the urban middle class increasingly came to perceive marriage in economic terms. This does not just mean that the marriage of a daughter involved considerable expense. It also suggests that the urban middle classes perceived the successful marriage of daughters as the satisfaction of a debt imposed by society and as a means to acquire salvation. Their matrimonial ethic structured the way fathers worked, accumulated wealth, and retired once their daughters were married, and the concerns of mothers and comportment of daughters. For daughters this involved an emphasis on urban chastity and its exploration through the production of *kendimata* within the safety of the home—not the "utilitarian" goods of countrywomen, but "symbolic" items for home decoration.

The concern with security and with symbolic manifestations of purity in an urban context was heavily grounded in the life-chances of the city. About perceptively noted how employment by the state could make all the difference between security and despair: "Toute cette bourgeoisie est triste et souffrante. La difficulté de vivre, le manque du nécessaire, l'amour-propre éternellement froissé, et surtout l'incertitude de l'avenir, empêcheront longtemps encore la naissance de cette intimité sans laquelle nous ne concevons pas la famille" (Andrews 1979, 252). Preachers such as Kosmas O Aetolos emphasized homogamy and the suitable imbuing of brides with a sense of *pudeur*. Such concerns were brought out in popular literature.

Ithografia and the family

Popular literature, or *ithografia*, has received much interest from literary scholars, and readers wishing to explore the material could profitably look at Vitti 1988, Politi 1988, Beaton 1982, Holton 1992. Together with Constantina Bada I have also explored (Sant Cassia and Bada 1992, 178ff.) some of the issues insofar as they relate to the tension between *ithografia* and anthropology. Here I wish to summarize some of our arguments relating to the matrimonial and family ethic in Athens. In a number of popular novels of the period unmarried daughters are metaphorically likened to *grammateia* (promissory notes or IOUs). In Andreas Karkavitsas's novella *I Lygeri*, a father's predicament is somewhat artlessly, but perhaps ironically, brought out:

> The father of Vasiliki felt like a debtor with a heavy mortgage. Pantellis had of course other bills of exchange *[synallagmata]*, his five other daughters, but Vasiliki was the only one falling due to the present. A seventeen-year-old daughter, my friend! (1978, 121)

If daughters' marriages were perceived as an economic problem, they also ideally required a political, or status-oriented, solution. Daughters are also viewed metaphorically as "bills of exchange *[synallagmata]*" to establish alliances—the word is also used for "foreign exchange." So, too, if marrying off a daughter or sister is viewed as satisfying an obligation imposed by society, then one's sons are expected to "collect" at a later stage, a situation cunningly highlighted by Edmond About:

> If marriages are contracted rather hastily in the country, it is not always so in the town. A residence in Athens accustoms the mind towards speculation; there are more wants to be supplied, more resources to be sought for. A young man looks not only for a wife but for a portion. Unfortunately marriage portions are rarer than brides. A girl with six thousand Francs ready money, and who is accustomed to wear feathers, is not a bad match. (1855, 136–37)

In such contexts it is hardly surprising that the *proikosymfono* became purely and simply a contract wrought between two sets of unrelated men. For the groom it became the means to extract the greatest possible wealth to accompany his bride. For the father it signified both that he had honorably redeemed his debt to society, and that the groom was now obliged to marry his daughter. The theme of the dowry-hunter *(proikothiras)* was already present in mid-19th-century Athens and received attention in Papadiamantis's novel *I fonissa* (The murderess).

Other colorful accounts, such as Theotokis's *Sklavi sta desma tous*, reveal the concerns and fears of petit bourgeois culture ("today money is everything"): an "unjust society" *(adyki koinonia)*, faceless and oppressive, whose problems can only be resolved by recourse to the law *(me nomos);* a fear of social upstarts who may well reflect their own origins, but who threaten to subvert the order of power and authority in the home; cautionary tales about incorporating "outsiders" into the family, and the obligation of young girls to sacrifice their affections and sentiments to uphold the family honor—that is, the honor of their fathers. Many of these authors, influenced in some way by foreign novelists such as Hugo, were nevertheless critical of such values. Popular literature betrayed the apprehension of the middle class at having to come face to face in an urban milieu with the very symbols of the countryside and of their own social origins, which they were eager to leave behind.

Among the ex-peasants attracted to the city, it appears that migrant girls worked as maids and in other jobs to amass their dowries. Migrant girls often married migrant grooms, and settlement was often uxorilocal. This was a more commensal arrangement, and women were less secluded within the home. The number of young men and women from poorer strata in employment outside the home appears to have grown in the 19th century. Kampouroglous (1896) reports figures of 2,000 maids, 2,000 male servants, and 3,200 female shop attendants in Piraeus in 1882. Service in a household appears to have replaced the more long-term fosterage that was more common in the past. Petrinioti-Konsta (1981, 51) gives the following figures:

DISTRIBUTION OF MAIDS IN THE TOTAL FEMALE
WORKING POPULATION OF ATHENS, 1856–79

Year	1856	1861	1870	1879
Maids	?	7,724	10,808	15,593
Total Employed Female Population	1,300	8,556	12,037	21,774

Finally it is important to discuss widowhood. At least 30 percent of our sample of mothers of brides were widows. This suggests significant differences in marriage ages between men and women or particularly high rates of adult mortality possibly affecting men differentially—rather likely, given that we dealt with a period that also included the revolutionary uprising. Men were apparently in short supply, and that must have further contributed to dowry inflation, perhaps heightened too by emigration. One would expect there to have been differences in marriage ages between town and country, although the distinction in the case of Athens during the 18th century may have been less pronounced. Some figures may be useful. Todorova writes (1993, 41) that in the Bulgarian Catholic village of Baltadzhi for 1834–86 the average age for men at first marriage was 20.1 (median and mode being 20) and for women 18.8 (median 19 and mode 20). Towns were different. There higher marriage ages were the norm, as noted by Herlihy and Klapisch Zuber (1985) for Florence, where men married about the age of 28 and women about the age of 19. Todorova observes (1993, 45) that great age differences between spouses were also typical of Bulgarian towns. She attributes this to the need by men to obtain a living and training (apprenticeships and the like)—a not unreasonable hypothesis.

By the late 19th and early 20th centuries, Athens had begun to exhibit many features of the "modern marriage pattern." Men were apparently marrying late, and there were two unsuccessful parliamentary attempts in 1887 and 1928 to tax unmarried males (Kairophilas 1982, 157).

Finally we ought to ask about the nature of emotions between husbands and wives. About noted that urban life in Athens "accustoms the mind towards speculation" (1855, 136), and that "a young man looks not only for a wife but for a portion" (ibid., 137). Although there were some basic differences between rich and poor, there was nevertheless a degree of homogeneity in morals. There seems to have been little of the complex illicit emotional entanglements so well documented by Balzac for French society. Instead the peccadillos appear to have been political and financial:

> High society has, as everywhere else, morals of its own. The chronicle of scandal in Athens is rich enough to supply a little Brantôme. But these intrigues have a peculiar character; love has little to do with them, all depends on vanity and interest. (Ibid., 144)

The main reason, he suggests, is that "the sacredness of the conjugal ties is sufficiently respected in Greece. The reason is very simple. Love is luxury, especially if illicit. There are also very few who have a desire for it" (ibid., 143).

About seems to be suggesting not so much that love was absent as an emotion in Athens, or even that with his French background he expected to find it *outside* marriage rather than in it. Rather, he seems to imply that the intermeshing of interest and emotion in the structures of everyday life in Athens rendered love superfluous as a motive for peccadillos. One should not necessarily presume, according to Macfarlane (1986), that this is a suitable demonstration that such emotions were found just among the English and nowhere else. Rather it suggests that we should look at the structures that help frame the expression of emotions:

> The Greeks marry young. Marriage is a subject of conversation among young people of sixteen; they often marry rashly and without any certainty as to the future. (About 1855, 134)

One may be inclined to see this as not inimical to "love," but rather as love of a particular sort, one that tends to be found in traditional contexts where people marry or cohabit young, or indeed in modern societies where people marry young out of love (or lust), but also separate young—a feature absent in 19th-century Greece. One would expect different types of love with later marriage ages and the mobility of the young. About was also struck by the equality between sons and fathers, as well as between husbands and wives, such patterns being very different from those obtaining among the bourgeois culture that he knew:

> Marriages are contracted and broken off freely; woman is neither a slave, nor shut up; unions are fertile, and that is the principal, if not the sole object of marriage; the brothers are equal among one another and to their father; relations give one another help and assistance, whatever may be the difference of their conditions of life; the husband and the wife herself, are jealous of their rights and defend energetically the sacredness of marriage. (1855, 148)

Patterns of marriage and divorce puzzled About, coming as he did from a French Catholic background:

> If it be difficult to break off a marriage [i.e., an engagement considered tantamount to a marriage], nothing is easier to undo it when it has been performed [in contrast to Roman Catholic practice]. The papas . . . are by no means incorruptible, and, if one only knows how to set about it he will discover in the most regular union 5 or 6 irregularities which necessitate the nullity of the marriage. (ibid., 134–35)

Yet he noted that, especially in the city, "divorce is a luxury which middle class people never allow themselves; the country is peopled with exemplary couples" (ibid., 135).

National school curricula and the social role of popular novels also upheld the sacredness of motherhood and its critical role for the *ethnos*. Periodicals specifically designed for women began circulating in Athens from the 1870s onwards (*Ephimeris ton kyrion*, 1887; *Thaleia*, 1867; *Evridikhe*, 1870–73; *I oikogenia*, 1897–98; *I pleias*, 1899–1900). A main concern was with the relative placement of men and women in society and the home, the sacred quality of child rearing, and the fear of exposure to Western influences that could "weaken" the *ethnos* and the national character. Women were a critical symbolic shield in the defense of the *ethnos*, and marriage was the central means for the transcendence of their natures. As in Papadiamantis's work, salvation for women was visualized through *engarterisis*—"a combination of patience, endurance and forbearance" (Constantinides 1987, xvi) very similar to the virtues of Mary, a theme that du Boulay (1986) brought out in her discussion of women's natures and destinies in Greece.

Conclusion: The Greek family within a European perspective

> Flee the wife who seeks to rule by virtue
> of her dowry.
>
> —Cato

Although differences among the various Athenian social strata in ways of transmitting property clearly existed in the early 19th century, by the 1830s a relatively uniform property-transmission system had emerged. This included a more egalitarian division of property among children, with a heavy bias towards the endowment of daughters at marriage, an increasing tendency towards cash dowries, the de facto exclusion of daughters from inheritance, a tendency towards neolocality among the upper strata or uxorilocality if they could not afford to do so, dowers by husbands to which widows had usufructuary rights, and the increasing seclusion of women in the home among families aspiring to an urban middle-class lifestyle. Throughout the latter 19th century and increasingly in the 20th, regional and urban-rural differences have tended to disappear in Greece, and although differences in emphasis remain, the "modern" form of property transmission in Greece is now relatively uniform. Some anthropologists such as Friedl (1963) have even seen the dowry as a mechanism for the integration of town and country, and there certainly is something to this, although I would argue that the nature of the modern dowry itself (in contrast to the traditional one that Cato warned men against) was shaped within the crucible of the city. Similar processes seem to have occurred in other parts of southern Europe, such as early Renaissance Italy. In Savona "families with new fortunes used the dowry as a mechanism for alliance and the acquisition of status" (Hughes 1985, 43).

In spite of their indubitable differences, both societies have nevertheless certain common features. Both Athens and Renaissance Italy were urban environments and were heavily involved in trade; new social groups were emerging, and their wealth was threatening the old social order of ascribed and permanent hierarchies. As the new up-and-coming civic class viewed marriage as the most available and attractive means of social mobility, its rise was accompanied by dowry inflation, which was strongly resisted by the old aristocracy. The increase in the value of dowries in both societies had the effect of pushing up marriage ages for men. In both Athens and the Italian communities, conflicts over the political spoils of office and their accompanying administrative privileges emerged between the old aristocracy and the new civic class.

Many observers now correctly question the validity of the rural-urban distinction for the Mediterranean and assert that "the development of urban anthropological theory must be founded on a conceptualization of the 'urban' which goes beyond the margins of a place we call a city or town into the very complexities of Mediterranean society at large" (Kenny and Kertzer 1983, 10–11). In Greece, partly because the ruralization of the city and the urbanization of the countryside were roughly simultaneous and recent processes, some of the customs we now identify as "rural" (such as the dowry) evolved within the city as a response to a particular urban way of life, and they eventually went on to fashion, dominate, and transform rural customs. What seems to have occurred in Athens and in other Mediterranean cities (e.g. Seville, cf. Press 1979) is not so much the retention of rural customs, nor their reinforcement, but rather the elaboration and "rationalization" of practices that were themselves urban in origin and had been adapted to the countryside.

The growth of the dowry in Greece and Athens in the 19th and 20th centuries, and its puzzling persistence—even recently its ambiguity was recognized as that of "an institution between persistence and decline" (Lambiri-Dimaki 1985)—should alert us to the fact that it disappeared elsewhere. Nazzari has devoted a book (1991) to explaining the "disappearance of the dowry" in São Paulo, Brazil, between the 17th and early 20th centuries, especially among the propertied classes. She suggests that it disappeared because it "was among the many fetters to the development of capitalism, such as entail, monopolies, and the privileges of the nobility...."[4] As a result women were relegated to the domestic sphere, "where they became economically dependent on their husbands and lost the status and bargaining power in marriage that their role as producers had assured them" (ibid., 166), a point that Friedl (1986) made when discussing the "appearance and reality" of power among Greek women. Nevertheless, dowries in urban contexts do not necessarily result in greater power for women, especially where they tend to be secluded.

It remains to relate this material on the Greek family to a long-standing debate on approaches to the history of the Western family. How does the Greek material relate to our knowledge of the family in Western Europe? The material presented here would not necessarily correspond to what certain historians of the family—such as Laslett (1972, 1977), Hajnal (1965), and the Cambridge History of Population and Social Structure Group—would have us concentrate on, but matrimonial contracts nevertheless give us different insights into the family. For example the Cambridge Group has concentrated on the following four areas: (1) marriage rates and ages; (2) patterns of child-rearing; (3) extramarital conceptions; (4) size and membership of the household. We do not know the marriage ages of Athenian spouses, but it would appear from About's observations that the Greeks married young, especially in rural areas, certainly among women. This made the age at marriage different from the that in the typical Western European pattern, which had late marriage ages and substantial agamy (Hajnal 1965). "Typical mean ages of marriage in rural areas were 27 or 28 for men, and 25 or 26 for women" (Smith 1977; cf. Gaskin 1978). The figures for Mykonos were a mean real age of 19.7 and a median real age of 20 at first marriage for brides for the period 1848–52 (Hionidou 1995, 8, table 3) and 24.6 and 24 respectively for grooms for the period 1889–93 (ibid., 82, table 4). In the pastoral community studied by Caftanzoglou "the average age at marriage for men in the 19th century was 25.7" (1994, 86).

On the other hand there is some evidence that marriage ages tended to increase in the towns. By the late 19th century late marriage ages for men in the towns were relatively widespread. The "problem" for urban fathers of marrying off daughters at a young age remained, as Karkavitsas's novel indicated. By the latter part of the 19th century such problems were also being experienced in the periphery. Hionidou has noted the higher marriage ages in Mykonos for professionals and the wealthiest groups who were participating in the national economy centered in Athens: "An additional reason for the delayed marriage among the professionals was the substantial dowry given to the daughters. This seems to have been markedly big compared to those provided by farmers or sailors. Thus it was in the interest of the parental household to retain for as long as possible the property that would be transferred to the daughter as dowry upon her marriage, but not long enough to jeopardize her marriage opportunities" (1995, 85).

The Cambridge Group's concentration on extramarital conceptions is problematical. Whose concept of marriage is being employed here? It has been suggested that almost everywhere in Western Europe the 18th and early 19th centuries were periods of steady rise in both illegitimate births and prenuptial conceptions. The problem here, from the perspective of Greece, is that different social groups had different concepts of what constituted a marriage (as indeed is the case in present-day Britain). Poorer Athenians considered an engagement a marriage to all intents and purposes, and they anticipated the fruits of marriage. There is no reason to reject such perspectives and adopt the Church's. As anthropologists we should be aware that the recorder may have had different views and interpretations of an observed fact than the people whose behavior he is recording. Categories are never neutral; they reflect the institutions that produce them.

A good example is provided by the first national census in Mykonos. As Hionidou notes (1995, 70), "No definition was given in any of the known sources as to what the 'household' or 'family' represented," and the persons conducting the survey also enumerated "the persons who were away from their usual place of residence for less than a month" (ibid., 71). As a result we get very little information about the fluidity of household arrangements. She notes (perhaps with tongue in cheek) that "the number of Mykoniati sailors reported as being away at the census time [which lasted two months] was zero" (ibid., 71). What this means is that some censuses, rather than documenting the actual state of affairs, are more the working-out and expression of what nationally charged enumerators expected to find in their communities according to their criteria of what constituted the implicit norm locally and nationally. Similarly, there are problems when estimating prenuptial pregnancies or even "illegitimacy," for whose categories are we adopting here—the Church's or popular ones? The two are not necessarily identical. For example, Hionidou comes to the conclusion that illegitimacy was low and prenuptial pregnancies were even lower in 19th-century Mykonos (ibid., 92). Yet what is a prenuptial pregnancy? One where conception takes place before the engagement or before the actual marriage celebration in church officiated at by the priest? We know from Athens that the Church was concerned about the widespread custom of couples' anticipating their matrimonial rights after engagements rather than after a church-celebrated marriage. Such practices were probably the case among the poor then and now. Hionidou also admits that up to 1929 the person registering marriages was the village priest, but village priests were in many cases more inclined to subscribe to local moral codes than impose strict nationally derived regulations, and may well have registered engagements as marriages, as their parishioners considered them; but they were not from the perspective of the law and the official Church. Clearly, then, all Mykoniati were models of temperance.

Similarly too, the Athenian family, at least among the elite, would seem to have have been of the type that Le Play would have called the stem family (European peasant), which had a patriarchal element but usually had one son and his wife and his descendants living together with his parents. This renders it different from what the Cambridge Group has noted, namely that most households in northwest Europe were small. Laslett (1972) has demonstrated that the mean household size in England (including servants) remained at about 4.75 from the 16th to the 19th century, after which it declined further to 3. Laslett showed that the nuclear family form was more widespread and had a far longer history than is normally assumed. Yet in Athens whilst the ideology may have been of hearths (tzakia), in practice many fathers were dead at the time of the marriages of their children. The presentation of the English material often makes it seem as if small households were the result of a *conscious* cultural choice. Might it not be the case that in practice small households were the norm not so much because of choice but because of shorter life expectancy? It is possible to envisage that the statistical norm of the small nuclear family may have a great deal of continuity across time, whilst the prescriptive model may be different and change. Furthermore, one should take patterns of property transmission into account, as Goody (et al. 1976) has pointed out. In the Peloponnese, where small-scale peasant farming and partible inheritance were the norm, households tended to be small. Panayiotopoulos (1983, 7), who worked on the Venetian census of the Peloponnese for the late 17th and early 18th century, shows that the household as such was small. The average family size was 4.04 members.

Census-type data, on which the conjectures of those who take a demographic approach depend, risk not distinguishing between households and organization. Such conjectures do not take into account that census data capture a household at a particular point in time, which may be at an early or a late stage in the developmental cycle of the domestic group. Thus whilst no stem household may appear in a census, the stem-family organization may remain. Flandrin (1979) called this the Meaningless Mean. As Anderson (1980, 31) pointed out, household size is as much sensitive to varying fertility and mortality patterns as to rules of household formation and is thus "almost useless as an indicator of family processes." Such data do not take differences between socioeconomic groups into account. Separate social groups living in the same communities could often exhibit different family systems (Kertzer 1989). In Italy, for example, Douglass (1991) has suggested that multiple-family households, especially the patrilineally extended joint family wherein the adult sons continue to reside with the father, were the cultural ideal in southern Italy, in the Molise region in the Kingdom of Naples, in the 18th century. Kertzer (1989) also found a durable joint-family household pattern in Emilia, and suggested that this was due to the need for labor in a sharecropping economy.[5] Similarly different ideals were present among different groups in Athens. For example, the *arkhontes* group inclined toward a system of impartible inheritance with dowries for daughters, which resulted in stemlike families, whilst the *noikokyreoi* were oriented toward nuclear families and partible inheritance, which increasingly tended toward the preferential endowment of daughters. As Viazzo observed (1989, 224), "impartible inheritance will produce low levels of nuptiality and a predominance of stem-family households, whereas partibility should result in early marriage, moderate rates of permanent celibacy and a high proportion of nuclear families."

Athens also offers interesting angles on the issue of servants. Northern European rural families often included young unmarried servants who had left their own rural homes in their early teens to spend some 10 to 15 years in domestic service. Towns had lodgers, many of whom were young people who had migrated there to obtain their dowries. In Athens by contrast, during a period when that city was both simultaneously urban and rural (late 18th and early 19th centuries), we find the phenomenon of adoption *(niothesia)* and fosterage. Many such young people were taken in as family retainers at a young age, and their adoptive parents contributed to their dowries. Different societies have different solutions to similar problems, and we should be sensitive to that variability and not privilege certain categories or classifications or one possible solution (e.g. servants) above others (e.g. foster children). At a later stage we also find the growth of domestic service in Athens, but this was a means of labor recruitment and social mobility suited to the times.

Finally, we should be cautious in moving too facilely from structure to culture. As Anderson has pointed out (1980, 34), there is a "constant and natural temptation to make inferences from demographic behaviour to attitudes which may—or may not—have underlain it." For example Laslett's notion (1977) that a narrow age gap between spouses (and late marriage) may have tended towards compassionate marriage, a point later elaborated by Macfarlane (1986), is dubious. There were compassionate marriages in Athens and between spouses with large age differences. Sometimes it seems from the reading of family historians that "compassionate" means "apassionate"—lacking in passion. Todorova (1993, 171) makes a telling comment: "In refuting certain myths, family history paves the way for the introduction of others. Thus, the myth of the extended family in Western Europe being abandoned, two others set in and have since been dominant: the myth of the small nuclear family, and the myth of the individualistic European (also called English, Northwest European or Western) *Sonderweg*."

In this paper I have tried to steer a middle road between the demographic approach and the "sentiments" approach to the Athenian and Greek family. According to the latter approach, "family" is a culture not a structure. The family is perceived not "as a reality but . . . as an idea" (Ariès 1972, 7). Flandrin (1979, 9) asserted that "the concept of the family . . . as it is most commonly defined today, has only existed in western culture since a comparatively recent date." Historians of sentiments have been primarily concerned with demonstrating the emergence of the modern world, "modern" social relationships, and the like. But whilst they have been very good at identifying the many hidden assumptions underlying what we mean

by "home," "privacy," and even the "family" itself, they suffer from
an equally grave problem. They are good at raising questions and
provoking uncertainty but perhaps less at demonstrating what
exactly people meant or felt. Attitudes also do not change overnight.
This chapter has tried to demonstrate the complex and sometimes
dialectically tense relationship between structure (transmission of
property, matrimonial contracts, and similar phenomena) and senti-
ment (attitudes of men toward women and vice versa), and how they
changed over time.

Nevertheless, some insights of the sentiments approach seem convincing, especially when applied to Greece. An important one relates
to the embeddedness of individuals: individuals were embedded in
households, and households within the wider community. The notion
of a nuclear family only began to emerge late in the 18th century, primarily among the *noikokyreoi*, and they equally made use of kinship
and spiritual kinship *(koumbaria)* in a "contractual," patronage
mode, somewhat different from the patrimonial ethic of the *arkhontes*, which made use of adoption, large households, redistribution
of resources, and the like. It was this ethic that led to Capodistrias's
assassination. In Greece well into contemporary times the individual's rights and expectations have been subject to the wider kin-
dred's. Yet in contrast to what the historians of sentiments suggest,
affection was present within the Greek family. Shorter (1976) points
out that in France peasant couples stopped using the *tu* form on their
wedding day and began using the *vous* form. Marriage was not an
emotional relationship but a means for transmitting property from
one generation to another. Greece provides a good example that the
two (transmission of property and affection) should not be seen as
opposed. Indeed affection was often expressed and realized through
such material symbols, for resources and property of all sorts are as
much symbolic as material, although tension is always present
between these two modes of seeing and evaluating them.

Finally the historians of sentiments seem to be correct in suggesting that there was a growing emphasis on domesticity. Nineteenth-century Greece certainly complements their observations.
Privacy became increasingly appreciated; the conjugal family was
isolated and "became an object of veneration as did the culture of
'true domestic womanhood'"(Anderson 1980, 47). Men began working away from the home, and the home came to be seen as a haven,
opposed to work in a capitalist society (Lasch 1977, 88). In Greece
particularly so, where an *adiki koinonia* (unjust society) was not only

counterposed to the security of the home, the *spiti*, but was also seen to threaten it and at the same time sustain its ideality—an attitude that further reinforced the *pessimismo naturalistico* that the Fall is a necessary precondition for the attainment of Grace.

Notes

1. Paper submitted on December 10, 1997, for a collective work on the family in modern Greece. Copyright © Paul Sant Cassia. Not to be quoted without the author's permission.
2. This chapter is based upon many of the ideas first explored in Sant Cassia and Bada 1992. For purposes of brevity many themes have been left out of this chapter—for example, the evolution of adoption and godparenthood, spiritual kinship, the role of the cult of the Panayia and of the linkage between motherhood and the nation. On the other hand, this chapter tries to locate the Greek family more firmly within debates on the evolution of the "Western family."
3. Similar practices seem to have been common throughout the Ottoman world. Todorova notes (1993, 127) that in 19th-century Bulgaria, questions regarding inheritance were referred to the competence of local elders "as a means of avoiding the Ottoman court."
4. Nazzari 1991, xix. Her suggestion is not too convincing to my mind, however. Capitalism can take many forms, not necessarily inimical to the dowry.
5. In the community studied by Douglass, however, sharecropping was rare.

References

About, E. 1855. *Greece and the Greeks of the present day.* Vol. 9 of *Constable's miscellany of foreign literature.* Edinburgh. Originally published in French in 1854.

Anderson, M. 1980. *Approaches to the history of the Western family, 1500–1914.* London: Macmillan.

Andrews, K., ed. 1979. *Athens alive.* Athens: Hermes.

Ariès, P. 1972. *Centuries of Childhood.* London: Johathan Cape.

Barbagli, M. 1991. Three household formation systems in eighteenth- and nineteenth-century Italy. In *The family in Italy: From antiquity to the present,* ed. D. Kerzer and R. Saller. New Haven: Yale University Press.

Barthélemy, D. 1988. The use of private space. In *Revelations of the medieval world.* Vol. 2 of *A history of private life,* ed. P. Ariès and G. Duby. Cambridge: Harvard University Press, Belknap Press.

Beaton, R. 1982. Realism and folklore in nineteenth-century Greek fiction. *Byzantine and modern Greek studies* 8: 103–22.

Benizelos, I. 1902. Istoria ton Athinon ipo Athinaiou dhidhaskalou Ionnou Benizelou. In *History of Athens*, ed. T. N. Philadelfeus. Vol 2. Athens: K. Eleftheroudakis.

Boswell, J. 1980. *Christianity, social toleration, and homosexuality*. Chicago: University of Chicago Press.

Bresc, H. 1996. Europe: Town and country. In *A history of the family*, ed. A. Burguiere et al. Cambridge: Harvard University Press, Belknap Press.

Caftanzoglou, R. 1994. The household formation pattern of a Vlach mountain community of Greece: Syrrako 1898–1929. *Journal of Family History* 19, no. 1: 79–98.

Campbell, J. K. 1964. *Honour, family, and patronage*. Oxford: Oxford University Press.

Charlemont, Lord. 1984. *The Travels of Charlemont in Greece and Turkey*. Ed. W. B. Standford and E. J. Finopoulos. London: Trigraph.

Clogg, R., ed. 1976. *The movement for Greek independence, 1770–1821: A collection of documents*. London: Macmillan.

Constantinides, E. 1987. Introduction to *Tales from a Greek island*, by A. Papadiamantis. Baltimore: John Hopkins University Press.

Couroucli, M. 1985. *Les Oliviers du lignage*. Paris: Maisonneuve et Larose.

―――――. 1987. Dot et société en Grèce moderne. In *Femmes et patrimoine dans les sociétés rurales de l'Europe Méditerranée*, ed. G. Ravis Giordani. Paris: Éditions du Centre National du Recherche Scientifique.

Davis, J. 1973. *Land and family in Pisticci*. London: Athlone Press.

Dimakopoulos, J. D. 1966. *O kodix ton nomon tis ellenikis epanavtavtos, 1822–1828*. Athens.

Douglass, W. A. 1991. The joint-family household in eighteenth-century southern Italian society. In *The family in Italy: From antiquity to the present*, ed. D. Kertzer and R. Saller. New Haven: Yale University Press.

du Boulay, J. 1974. *Portrait of a Greek mountain village*. Oxford: Oxford University Press.

―――――. 1983. The meaning of dowry: Changing values in rural Greece. *Journal of Modern Greek Studies* 1, no. 1: 243–70.

―――――. 1986. Women—Images of their nature and destiny in rural Greece. In *Gender and power in rural Greece*, ed J. Dubisch. Princeton: Princeton University Press.

Duby, G. 1978. *Medieval marriage*. Baltimore: John Hopkins University Press.

―――――. 1983. *The knight, the lady, and the priest: The making of modern marriage in medieval France*. London: Allen Lane.

―――――. 1988. Introduction to *Revelations of the medieval world*. Vol. 2 of *A history of private life*, ed. P. Ariès and G. Duby. Cambridge: Harvard University Press, Belknap Press.

Flandrin, J. L. 1979. *Families in former times*. Cambridge: Cambridge University Press.

Frazee, C. 1969. *The Orthodox Church and independent Greece, 1821–1825*. Cambridge: Cambridge University Press.

Friedl, E. 1962. *Vasilika: A village in modern Greece*. New York: Holt, Rinehart and Winston.

―――――. 1963. Some aspects of dowry and inheritance in Boeotia. In

Mediterranean Countrymen, ed. J. Pitt-Rivers. Paris: Mouton.
————. 1986. The position of women: Appearance and reality. In *Gender and power in rural Greece*, ed. J. Dubisch. Princeton: Princeton University Press.

Gaskin, K. 1978. Age at first marriage in Europe before 1850. *Journal of Family History* 3.

Goody, J., et al. 1976. *Family and inheritance: Rural society in Western Europe, 1200–1800* Cambridge: Cambridge University Press.

Hajnal, J. 1965. European marriage patterns in perspective. In *Population in history*, ed. D. V. Glass and D. E. C. Eversley. London: Arnold.

Herlihy, D., and C. Klapisch Zuber. 1985. *Tuscans and their families: A study of the Florentine catastato of 1427*. New Haven: Yale University Press.

Herskovits, M. J. 1962. Preface to *Markets in Africa*, ed. P. Bohannon and G. Dalton. Evanston, Ill.: Northwestern University Press.

Herzfeld, M. 1985. *The poetics of manhood: Contest and identity in a Cretan mountain village*. Princeton: Princeton University Press.

Hionidou, V. 1995. Nuptiality patterns and household structure on the Greek island of Mykonos, 1848–1959. *Journal of Family History* 20, no. 1: 67–102.

Hirschon, R. 1983. Under one roof: Marriage, dowry, and family relations in Piraeus. In Kenny and Kertzer 1983.

————. 1989. *Heirs of the Greek catastrophe*. Oxford: Oxford University Press.

Holton, D., ed. 1992. The backward glance: Place and time in modern Greek literature. *Journal of Mediterranean Studies* 2, no. 2 (special issue on modern Greek literature).

Hughes, D. 1985. From brideprice to dowry in Mediterranean Europe. In *The marriage bargain: Women and dowries in European history*, ed. M. Kaplan. New York: The Institute for Research in History and the Haworth Press. Originally published in *Journal of Family History* 3, no. 3 (1978).

Kairophilas, J. 1982. *I Athina kai oi Athinaies*. Athens: Philippotis.

Kalpourtzi, E. 1987. Ina pragmatopoiithi i dhia tou gamou sizevxis. *Greek Society* 1: 81–86.

Kampouroglous, D. 1896. *Tourkokratia*. Vol. 3 of *Istoria ton Athinaion*. Athens: G. D. Papadimitriou.

Karkavitsas, A. 1978. *I Lygeri*. Athens: Estia.

Kasdagli, A. 1988. Family and household in 17th-century Naxos: Paper presented to the Special Lectures on Greek Themes, Cambridge.

Kenny, M., and D. Kertzer, ed. 1983. *Urban life in Mediterranean Europe: Anthropological perspectives*. Urbana: University of Illinois Press.

Kertzer, D. 1989. The joint family household revisited: Demographic constraints and household complexity in the European past. *Journal of Family History* 14: 1–15.

Kitromilides, P. 1983. The Enlightenment and womanhood: Cultural change and the politics of exclusion. *Journal of Modern Greek Studies* 1, no. 1: 39–62.

Klapisch Zuber, C. 1985. *Women, family, and ritual in Renaissance Italy*. Chicago: University of Chicago Press.

Kolokotronis, Th. 1960. *Th. Kolokotronis: Memoirs from the Greek War of Independence, 1821–1833*. Ed. E. M. Edmonds. Chicago: Argonaut.

Lambiri Dimaki, J. 1985. Dowry in modern Greece: An institution at the crossroads between persistence and decline. In *The marriage bargain: Women and dowries in European history*, ed. M. Kaplan. Binghamton, N.Y.: The Institute for Research in History and the Haworth Press.

Lasch, C. 1977. *Haven in a Heartless World*. New York: Basic Books.

Laslett, P. 1972. Introduction to *Household and family in past time*, by P. Laslett and R. Wall. Cambridge: Cambridge University Press.

Laslett, P., ed. 1977. *Family life and illicit love in earlier generations*. Cambridge: Cambridge University Press.

Laslett, P., and R. Wall. 1972. *Household and family in past time*. Cambridge: Cambridge University Press.

Loizos, P. 1975. Changes in property transfers among Greek Cypriot villages. *Man*, n.s., 10: 502–23.

McDonough, C. W. 1986. *Good families of Barcelona*. Princeton: Princeton University Press.

Macfarlane, A. 1986. *Marriage and love in England: Modes of reproduction, 1300–1840*. Oxford: Basil Blackwell.

McGrew, W. 1985. *Land and revolution in modern Greece, 1821 to 1871*. Kent: Ohio State University Press.

McNeill, W. 1978. *The Metamorphosis of Greece since World War II*. Chicago: University of Chicago Press.

Maurer, L. G. 1835. *Das griechische Volk*. Heidelberg: privately printed.

Nazzari, Muriel. 1991. *Disappearance of the dowry: Women, families, and social change in São Paulo, Brazil, 1600–1900*. Stanford, Calif.: Stanford University Press.

Panayiotopoulos, V. 1983. Meyethos kai synthesi tis oikoyenias stin Peloponniso yiro sta 1700. In *Ta istorika*. Vol. 1. Athens.

Papataxiarchis, E. 1985. The values of the household: Social class, marriage strategies and ecclesiastical law in 19th-century Lesbos. Paper presented to the 1985 Lesbos Conference on the Social Anthropology of Greece.

Parry, J., and M. Bloch, ed. 1989. *Money and the morality of exchange*. Cambridge: Cambridge University Press.

Patlagean, E. 1996. Families and kinships in Byzantium. In *A history of the family*, ed. A. Burguiere et al. Cambridge: Harvard University Press, Belknap Press.

Petrinioti-Konsta, X. 1981. Oi prosdhioristoikoi paragontes tis yinaikias simmetokhis sto ergatiko dhinamiko stin Elladha, 1961, 1971. Ph.D. diss., Law Faculty of the University of Athens.

Politi, J. 1988. The tongue and the pen: A reading of Karkavitsas' *O arkhaiologos*. In *The Greek novel AD 1–1985*, ed. R. Beaton. London: Croom Helm.

Press, I. 1979. *The City as context: Urbanism and behavioural constraints in Seville*. Urbana: University of Illinois Press.

Psilla, G. 1974. *Apomnimonevmata tou viou mou*. Monuments of Greek History. Athens: Athens Academy.

Sant Cassia, P. 1982. Property in Greek Cypriot marriage strategies, 1920–1980. *Man*, n.s., 17: 643–63.

Sant Cassia, P., and C. Bada. 1992. *The making of the modern Greek family:*

Marriage and exchange in nineteenth-century Athens. Cambridge: Cambridge University Press.

Salamone S. D., and B. Stanton. 1986. Introducing the nikokyra: Ideality and reality in social process. In *Gender and power in rural Greece,* ed. J. Dubisch. Princeton: Princeton University Press.

Schneider, J. 1980. Trousseau as treasure: Some contradictions of late nineteenth-century change in Sicily. In *Beyond the myths of culture: Essays in cultural materialism,* ed. E. B. Ross. London: Academic Press.

Segalen, M. 1986. *Historical anthropology of the family.* Cambridge: Cambridge University Press; Paris: Édition de la Maison de les Sciences de l'Homme.

Shorter, E. 1976. *The making of the modern family.* London: Collins.

Simmel, G. 1971. *On individuality and social forms.* Chicago: University of Chicago Press.

Skouteri-Didaskalou, N. 1976. On Greek dowry: Spatio-temporal transformations. Post-graduate diploma thesis, University of London.

————. 1984. *Anthropoloyika yia to yinaikio zitima.* Athens: Kedros.

Skouzes, P. 1975. *Apomnimonevmata: I tyrannia tou Khatzi-Ali Khaseki stin Tourkokratoumeni Athina, 1772–1796.* Athens: Kedros.

Smith, D. S. 1977. A homeostatic demographic regime: Patterns in west European family reconstitution studies. In *Population patterns in the past,* ed. R. D. Lee. Cambridge: Cambridge University Press.

Strathern, M. 1984. Subject or object? Women and circulation of valuables in highlands New Guinea. In *Women and property—Women as property,* ed. R. Hirschon. London: Croom Helm.

Todorova, M. 1993. *Balkan family structure and the European pattern.* Washington, D.C.: The American University Press.

Tsigakou, F. M. 1981. *The Rediscovery of Greece.* London: Thames and Hudson.

Valetas, G. 1948. *Samouil Khantzeri: Logoi patriarkhikoi.* Athens: privately printed.

Vernier, B. 1984. Putting kin and kinship to good use: The circulation of goods, labour and names on Karpathos (Greece). In *Interest and emotion,* ed. H. Medick and D. H. Sabean. Cambridge: Cambridge University Press.

Vernikos, N. 1979. Proikosymfona kai i progamiaia dhorea. In *Proceedings of the 3rd folklore symposium of northern Greece.* Thessaloniki: Institute for Balkan Studies.

Vitti, M. 1988. The inadequate tradition: Prose narrative during the first half of the nineteenth century. In *The Greek novel, AD 1–1985,* ed. R. Beaton. London: Croom Helm.

Vretos, M. 1864. *Ithnikon imeroloyion.* Athens.

Watson, H. 1989. Women in the city of the dead: Migration, money, marriage. Ph.D. diss., University of Cambridge.

Zolotas, I. G. 1926. *Istoria tis Khiou.* Athens: privately printed.

4. Family ties: Marriage, migration, and community in 19th- and 20th-century Greece

Department of Anthropology, Indiana University
Purdue University at Indianapolis

Recent scholarship on the historical dynamics of families in modern Greece is assessed for its relevance in understanding Greek American family life. Research on Greek families has moved from assuming a generic peasant type to delineating how family form and practices have been shaped by regional variation, persistent migration, and economic circumstance. This is illustrated by the household shifts accompanying the 19th-century growth of Nemea and the 20th-century migration of Amorgians to Athens. Such studies suggest that Greek American family structures reflect the conditions of American life as much as they do the maintenance of unbroken tradition.

THE IMPORTANCE OF THE family is a theme that permeates the discussion of modern Greek life, a theme stated as strongly by family members as by the scholars and writers who portray them. Taking such statements simply at face value, however, can mask the texture and variability which Greek family life has historically displayed. Research on the family in Greece has increasingly moved from normative pronouncements to delineation of the ways in which family form and practice have been shaped by time, place, and circumstance. Depictions of the essential nature of a single family type have been replaced by investigation into the reasoning and forces behind such depictions in the first place.

This essay pulls together such recent work on families in the

Greek nation in ways that may have meaning for similar endeavors in Greek American studies. I approached it with considerable trepidation about finding points of connection with a set of scholarly concerns with which I have been only marginally conversant. As I delved more deeply into the literature on Greek Americans than I had for some time, however, I found more than I had anticipated. The way family life has unfolded among Greek immigrants to the United States sheds new light on changing family structures in the Hellenic Republic. I should not have been surprised, of course, for a major tenet of this paper is that the practice, construction, and community affiliation of Greek families reflect particular conditions and specific moments in time. The evolving nature of Greek families in the United States stands alongside the evolving nature of those in Greece in building a nuanced understanding of this process.

Three themes concerning family life seem, to my eyes, most prominent in the well-known and readily accessible writings on Greek Americans. The first, present even in the early works of Fairchild (1911) and Burgess (1913), asserts the significance of the family as a support mechanism for immigrants (e.g., Monos 1988; Moskos 1980; Saloutos 1964; Scourby 1984). The second, arising later and voiced by several other contributors to this volume, examines the strains produced in Greek American families when patriarchy stifles aspirations of daughters and wives (e.g., Callinicos 1991; Chock 1995; Scourby 1984, 123). The third, running widely throughout this literature, glosses the family base which Greek immigrants brought with them as an unplumbed, generic peasant type (e.g., Collins 1991, 105; Costantakos 1980, 290; Moskos 1980, 90; Saloutos 1964, 87; Scourby 1984, 10). The first two themes parallel and shed light on similar work done in Greece. The last, however, might be modified by looking more closely at family life in the Greek nation throughout the period for which large-scale immigration to the United States occurred, a task I here undertake by summarizing existing research on this issue and presenting an illustrative example from my own work.

In so doing, I also bring together several strands in the anthropology of domestic groups in general. Much recent work explores the relationship between household form, local conditions, and global economies (e.g., Maclachlan 1987; Netting 1993; Smith and Wallerstein 1992; Wilk 1991). Along such lines, for example, Kertzer has developed an intricate understanding of the interaction of family structure, sharecropping, and wage labor in northern Italy over the last century (Kertzer 1984; Kertzer and Hogan 1989; Kertzer and

Saller 1991). Moving in a different, but complementary, direction, Yanagisako has led the way in rethinking the boundaries of kinship and exploring relations of gender, power, and economy that crosscut this domain (e.g., Yanagisako 1991; Collier and Yanagisako 1987; Yanagisako and Delaney 1995). Taken together, these studies view family life as historically variable, reflecting specific cultural conceptions and economic contingencies, at the same time that idealized statements of family relations mask such processes. They recommend moving beyond definitions of the essential Greek family to ask what a family is at any particular moment, and they suggest that broad typologies have as much to tell us about the typology makers as the people being classified.

Such a contingent view of family life contributes to the present discussion by identifying a heterogeneous family base for Greek immigrants and suggesting that Greek American families, even in their earliest forms, arose at least partly from the circumstances of American life, a conclusion which can be extended to the particular ways in which patriarchy has been defined and experienced in the United States. This approach also indicates that while families are indeed a good site for discussing gender differentiation, they are also an appropriate place from which to examine political and economic life. These are points to which I return after developing some sense of the diversity of families in 19th- and 20th-century Greece.

Family life in 19th- and 20th-century Greece

There are problems, of course, in assuming that the term *family* has always meant the same thing. Several writings on Greek nationals and Greek Americans leave this issue undiscussed, an omission implying that all Greek families have been shaped and conceived in the same way, and that this form is obvious and beyond analysis. The word *oikoyenia* is, however, tellingly ambiguous. It is composed of two terms, *oikos*, meaning "house," and *yenos*, meaning "birth" or "lineage." In antiquity *oikoyenia* referred to a social unit including not only those born, adopted, or marrying into a particular household, but also the slaves and the dogs and other animals attached thereto. At present, the word is used in different ways in different contexts, variously signifying all members of a nuclear family whether or not they live together, all relatives residing in the same home whether or not they are from the same nuclear family, and even a much wider network of kin beyond the household level (e.g., Campbell 1964, 52). This ambiguity both reflects and advances the flexible deployment of kin relationships under disparate circumstances. The resulting variability of Greek families has been documented in several ways.

It has been documented by recognizing regional differences in the construction and workings of Greek families. For example, even though parental property has most often passed to children bilaterally, certain islands of the eastern Aegean have stressed matrilineal inheritance while some shepherd groups of northern Greece have emphasized patrilineal (Handman 1989). Postmarital residence patterns have also varied. In the Cyclades, houses have generally been transferred from mothers to daughters, a situation yielding an uxorilocal (matrilineally based) residence pattern in that region (e.g., Casselberry and Valvanes 1976; Kenna 1976; Sutton 1986), while the reverse has obtained on much of the mainland (e.g., Allen 1976; Aschenbrenner 1986; Clark 1995; Friedl 1962). While loose networks of relatives have been the most common larger kinship structures,[1] more corporate, lineage-type formations have recently existed in Mani, the Ionian Islands, and parts of Crete (Couroucli 1985; Herzfeld 1985; Seremetakis 1991).

The multiple meanings of *family* have also reflected adjustments and transformations which people have made to these regional forms in response to historical conditions and life situations. Sant Cassia and Bada (1992), for example, have examined patterns of adoption and fosterage in 19th-century Athens, demonstrating the widespread use of such practices to bring young villagers into the city as servants for the families which sponsored them. In parallel fashion, Hirschon (1989) has revealed the different household forms emerging among refugees from Asia Minor who came to Athens in the 1920s, while Handman (1989) and Skouteri-Didaskalou (1976) have documented many types of female inheritance in addition to dowry.

Working in yet another vein, several studies have explored statements asserting that primary bonds of trust and cooperation should remain within the family. They have come to see these as but one side of an ongoing discussion which emerges as Greeks balance family ties with other allegiances, a discussion in which people renegotiate their positions over time (Hart 1992). Along these lines, Just (1991) has shown that Ionian Islanders emphasize skill over kinship in assembling work crews despite normative statements to the contrary; Koster (forthcoming) has demonstrated the economic importance of

cooperative relations among neighbors for shepherds in the Ermion-
idha; and others have investigated the adult friendships that crosscut family ties (Kennedy 1986; Papataxiarchis 1991).
The relations of gender and authority which characterize Greek
families have also drawn attention, just as they have in the United
States. Much of this work has identified ways in which Greek women
reject or rework conceptions of male authority. It has also detailed
Greek women's own sources of power and self-definition deriving
from child rearing, ownership of land and housing, and participation
in religious activities, both sanctioned and unsanctioned (Danforth
1989; Dubisch 1986, 1995; Friedl 1967; Hart 1992; Seremetakis 1991).
Others have examined the significant, and not always straightfor-
ward, shifts in familial gender relations accompanying the urbanization and marketization of Greek life over the last century (Cavounidis
1983; Cowan 1990; Galani-Moutafi 1993–94; Lambiri-Dimaki 1965;
Salamone and Stanton 1986; Sutton 1985, 1986).
Yet another focus of Greek family studies is the one to which my
own work belongs, and from which I draw the illustrative example
occupying the rest of this essay. Studies of household economy have
explored the ways in which domestic groups function as units of production and consumption. Those of us pursuing such questions in
Greece have investigated ways in which family form and practice
reflect and even sometimes alter broader political and economic systems.[2] Such work has tended to focus on households, those relatives
pooling economic resources and living space (Goody 1976; Plakans
1984; Segalen 1986).
While a persistent myth of European peasant life is its presumed
detachment from national and international systems of political economy, nothing could be further from the truth (Macfarlane 1977; Netting 1993; Sutton 1994). The small settlements and hand technology of
most Greek smallholders in the 19th century, and of some even at the
end of the 20th century, reflect particular patterns of articulation with
broader systems, not isolation. The flaw in Chayanov's well-known
family-based model of peasant economy was its assumption that
household financial decisions were made only by looking inward
(Chayanov 1986; Maclachlan 1987). This has been proven wrong for
many parts of Europe (e.g., Hareven 1977; Kertzer 1984; Segalen
1986), and parallel work in Greece (e.g., Bennett 1988; Beopoulou 1981;
Clark 1995; Costa 1988; Karakasidou 1993; Petronoti 1985; Vermeulen
1976) has shown that, even in the most seemingly remote villages,
household strategies have long been responsive to more distant forces.

My own examination of such household tactics has been animated by a growing recognition of the repeated migrations undertaken by Greek families as they negotiated the shifting economic and political systems in which they have long been involved. Migration may be added to the factors already mentioned as a persistent, formative influence on both rural and urban Greek households. This observation may, of course, have particular resonance for studies of Greek American life, a product of one of the most extensive of these migrations. It is also one which some may find surprising, since many images of Greek peasants fix them to a timeless soil, and many discussions of village and region in Greece imply demographic stasis until recent times.[3]

Recent scholarship, however, has shown Greek families to have been in motion for centuries. Demographic studies (e.g., Baxevanis 1972; Damianakos 1981; Kayser 1963; McGrew 1985; Panayiotopoulos 1985; Wagstaff 1982) have revealed not only the 20th-century urbanization of Greece, but also a 19th-century movement from upland to lowland areas, and an even earlier 18th-century mobilization in other directions. Full-coverage archaeological surveys (e.g., Cherry, Davis, and Mantzourani 1991; Jameson, Runnels, and van Andel 1994) have extended these repetitive population shifts back into antiquity, as has much Byzantine historiography (e.g., Laiou-Thomadakis 1977). My own scrutiny of 25 well-known works on the contemporary Greek countryside reveals that over half the villages discussed were either founded or grew greatly during the 19th century, before losing population to emigration and urbanization in the 20th century (Sutton 1988). This conclusion is also supported by several ethnohistorical studies which document such newly formed villages (Aschenbrenner 1986; Beuermann 1954; Bialor 1976; Burgel 1965). In short, whether responding to the feudal systems of the Ottoman Empire or the developing capitalist systems of the modern Greek state, Greek farmers and shepherds have repeatedly changed residence over the centuries. Migration to Athens and emigration to the United States fit within long-standing patterns of mobility.

Such an understanding places statements on the abiding significance of the Greek family in a new context. The recognition of persistent mobility frees such statements from the implication of lineal continuity in an area, but also raises questions concerning the formation and interconnections of such movable households. It was this issue which led to the case studies which follow. In this discussion, I examine family history for two rural Greek communities, each somewhat differently involved in the migratory patterns of recent history.[4] In each case, I combine local birth and death records with family histories to develop some understanding of changing household composition and location over the last 150 years. Both instances suggest a connection between household structure and migration and reveal the play and variation in Greek family life.

Case one: Building villages in the Nemea Valley

The Nemea Valley is located slightly west of the main road from Corinth to Argos in the Peloponnesos.[5] Once the site of ancient athletic games, and later a prosperous Byzantine farming region, the valley was only sparsely settled toward the end of the period of Turkish domination in the 18th century. At that time, two small settlements which housed 140 people, or 34 families, nestled high on the valley's western ridge (Bory de Saint-Vincent 1834–46, 68; Clarke 1814, 714; Panayiotopoulos 1985, 240; Pouqueville 1826, 182). Lekosi was a small cluster of houses whose inhabitants worked a Turkish farming estate, while Koutsoumadhi was a free village closely tied to the market town of Ayios Yeorgos in the next valley westward. The inhabitants of both supplied their own subsistence needs, kept some sheep and goats, and cultivated vineyards which yielded a small surplus sold in both Ayios Yeorgos and Argos as wine must *(mousto)*. These residents were joined in the colder months by transhumant shepherd families who wintered their flocks on the valley floor. On the whole, the valley's residents were oriented more toward the market towns and mountain roads to its west than to the strongly Ottoman-controlled areas around Corinth. The valley floor and its eastern hills stood as a virtually uninhabited buffer between these areas.

Greek independence changed this situation. Vacant areas of the Nemea Valley became part of the government-controlled National Lands, fitfully transferred to smallholder ownership during the 19th century (McGrew 1985, 114–213). Despite the lack of immediate title to such lands, families from several areas began moving into the valley soon after the Revolution. Lekosi, the former Turkish-controlled hamlet, was taken over by a single cluster of patrilineally related households from the Argolid, while Koutsoumadhi received in-migrants from the mountainous areas of the Peloponnesos and several as yet unliberated areas of central and island Greece. Many families expanded their vineyards onto the valley floor, built new vats for producing wine, and also began cultivating the small raisins known as currants *(mavri stafidha)*, which were quickly becoming the major export of Greece. The high quality of currants produced in the Corinthia enabled the area to withstand the economic crisis of the late 19th century when a French boycott and declining English market sent many Peloponnesian farmers to seek their fortunes in the United States.

Nemea was thus one of many rural areas which attracted inmigration in post-Revolutionary Greece. Its population reached 490 by 1907.[6] By mid-19th century, the valley contained not only the former hamlet of Lekosi, now renamed for the family which lived there, and the growing village of Koutsoumadhi, but also scattered compounds housing small clusters of newly arrived families, some living in the area year round, and some continuing to migrate with their flocks between the valley and more upland summer homes. By my estimate, over half the valley's families in 1879 lived in these outlying compounds, each of which contained several patrilineally related households.

Events of the late 19th century altered this settlement pattern yet again. By this time, the National Lands had been officially distributed, Athens had become the economic and political hub of the nation, foreign investors were constructing the roads, canals, and railroads that fed this hub, and a national reorganization of the countryside emphasized and established the smaller municipal units known as *koinotites* in place of the original, much larger *demoi*. There was increasing impetus to locate near the emerging national transportation network and to create what elderly residents now recall were considered "true villages," which could become the basis of independent *koinotites*.

After an earthquake leveled Koutsoumadhi in 1876, half its inhabitants resettled outside the area, while the rest moved down to two new settlements which were developing along the main east-west road through the valley. Other families from outlying compounds also began moving into these two communities, which soon acquired churches and small general stores. Residence in these growing settlements was given added impetus as marriage patterns became more locally based. Both bride and groom were native to the valley in 37 percent of all newly married couples between 1870 and 1900, a strategy which gave such families a greater concentration of land in the valley than they might otherwise have had. Bilateral inheritance practices presented these families with fields located in several different areas, however, making centrally located settlements more attractive.[7] Many shepherds also effected a switch to farming at this time by marrying someone in one of these communities. The then-prevailing maxim that a man should chose a "bride from a good family rather than a sheepfold *[nifi apo soi okhi apo mandhri]*" can be understood in multiple ways, one of which related to this move away from pastoralism.

Thus it was that by the early 20th century, the two older, hillside villages had been completely abandoned, while two new villages on the valley floor had been founded. The larger, named Iraklio, had fifteen core patrilines, while the smaller, called Linos, had five. Less than half these family lines had been present in the valley at the start of the 19th century. In 1912, the two new villages were officially separated from the former *demos* of Ayios Yeorgos, and designated as the new *koinotis* of Iraklio (renamed Arkhaia Nemea in 1958).

These founding families have remained influential to the present day. Although many people moved into the two villages during the 20th century, raising their population to 871 by 1961, only 3.2 percent of the newcomers settled without marrying someone already living there. All others were spouses, most often from a group of nearby villages. Residence patterns were most often virilocal (patrilineally based), and the majority of these in-moving spouses were thus wives.[8] Parents and those married sons who stayed in the villages often lived close to each other, forming named, patrilineal neighborhoods where child care, household duties, and farming activities were shared.

The situation at Nemea is currently transforming itself once again. Despite the area's success in commercial farming, the valley's drop in population to 704 in 1991 reflects the out-migration of many young Nemeans. Spouses are now sought much more widely, and preference is given to those who have Athenian connections or property on the very fertile plain near Argos. The virilocal household groups are thus breaking up due to out-migration, just as others elsewhere had previously disbanded to form the valley's 19th-century population. Modern communications allow more frequent contact among such geographically dispersed kin than in the past, but actual return migration is beginning to resemble the low rates of the second case now to be discussed.

Case two: Amorgian migrants in Athens

While at first seeming quite different from Nemea, this second case both picks up where Nemea leaves off and reveals the same underlying principles of household dynamics. At the start of the 19th century, the village of Langadha on the Cycladic island of Amorgos stood in some contrast to Nemea. Langadha had been in existence for at least two centuries,[9] and its population of 640 individuals (125 families) represented a demographically mature settlement.[10] Marriage patterns were generally endogamous among Langadha and three neighboring villages which circled the small northern plain of Amorgos. Much land was owned by the large monastery, the Moni Khozoviotisa, in the central part of the island, an institution whose power had secured Amorgos from direct Turkish influence (Vacalopoulos 1976, 90–92). Villagers worked monastic lands, providing for themselves and contributing to the monastery. Unlike the practice in Nemea, houses were generally given to daughters, and husbands moved to live with their wives; this resulted in a series of matrilineally based neighborhoods.[11]

After Greek independence, monastery lands were transferred to peasant ownership (Kolodny 1974, 186). Despite some initial in-migration from Greek lands still under Ottoman control, however, the island lost much population. Amorgos was the kind of area that emptied out while Nemea expanded. As Kolodny has argued (1974, 194–99), the Aegean islands commanded great importance through their participation in sea trade during the Turkokratia but were ill-equipped to enter the emerging systems of the new Greek state. Too small for large-scale agriculture, they lost even their shipping functions when Piraeus was developed. Thus it was that almost 100 Langadhians had moved to Athens by the end of the century, and the village's population had dropped to 591.[12] Interestingly, those who left were generally less connected to the village's core family lines than those who stayed.[13]

Migration from Langadha to Athens gained momentum in the 20th century and came to affect all strata of the population. Less than half of each cohort born after 1870 stayed in the village. In establishing themselves in Athens, these migrants followed patterns of adaptation common for newcomers to the city (Allen 1976; Dubisch 1977; Friedl 1976; Kenna 1976; Mendras 1962; Moustaka 1964; Sandis 1973). A full two-thirds lived with relatives for anywhere between six months and several years after they first arrived in Athens.[14] Such composite households diverged significantly from those in the village, containing a wide variety of kin, collateral as well as lineal. The most common time for Langadhian migrants to move away from these initial households was at marriage. It is striking that two-thirds of these migrants, throughout the 20th century, chose non-Amorgian spouses, something in considerable contrast with the 95 percent local-area endogamy practiced on the island.[15] Most also chose a non-Amorgian wedding sponsor *(koumbaros)*. This pattern had the effect of strengthening ties to the general Athenian community. It also led to an increase in arranged marriages over the number on the island, since many migrants felt this practice became more important when marrying outside a known community.

The fact that Langadhian migrants generally married spouses from other regions also engendered variation in residence patterns. Negotiations concerning where a couple should live have been complex and even contentious as virilocal and uxorilocal traditions have played against each other. The decision has generally rested on the quality of housing obtained from various options, as well as the proximity of relatives with whom the couple could participate in cooperative household clusters (see also Moustaka 1964, 14). The giving of apartments as dowry or patrimony has remained a very common pattern and one of the major determinants of where a young couple lives. It is not unusual for parents, upon the marriage of their adult children, to give such a child an apartment in the same building where they themselves live. When both sets of parents make such an offer, the couple must negotiate the situation with some delicacy.

The movement of so many Langadhians to Athens also affected kinship structures on the island. The village population had declined to 216 by 1991, heavily concentrated in older cohorts and less than one-third its 19th-century size. Two-thirds of Langadha's houses are unoccupied but cared for by relatives of the migrants who own them. These structures are used for storage and occasional visits to the island. Migrants' fields are also sometimes worked by relatives according to various arrangements for sharing the proceeds. While kindreds thus maintain some contact even when geographically spread between village and city, one should guard against overstating this situation. The rate of return migration to the island has dwindled to almost zero, while second- and third-generation migrants maintain their connection to the island much more weakly than their migrant parents.

Change, variability, and Greek family life

In sum, the repeated migrations of Greek history have been accompanied by much flexibility in household form and practice. Family allegiance has in some ways been more durable than community affiliation. Households have been major units of mobility under the very changeable conditions of Greek history, units that supported their members in the move from settlement to settlement, units that negotiated concepts of self and identity in unknown situations. The adaptive utility of households in meeting these functions, however, has rested on the ease with which household composition could be altered in response to the different circumstances of each migratory movement. Household groups have expanded and contracted as people moved from one location to another, while the size of local kindreds has come to reflect longevity in an area. Marriage has variously established connections to a new area or consolidated a family's position in an old one. That newcomers to Nemea and Amorgians in Athens sought spouses who would integrate them with their new communities underscores this point, and seconds Kalafati-Papagalani's view (1989) of Greek marriage as a matter of social strategy (see also Costantakos 1980, 259; Monos 1988, 80).

The diversity of households resulting from migration adds to the other forms of family variability mentioned earlier in this paper. Together, they undercut images of a single, essential Greek family. The full implications of this conclusion for Greek American studies are best explored by those working directly in this area. I will, however, close with several possibilities, some of which apply equally well to the Greek national situation.

On one level, images of a single, generic family reflect a desire to see the past and the countryside as simpler, to render them into ahistorical abstractions by which viewers judge their own situations as good or bad, depending on personal philosophy and political belief (Macfarlane 1977, 1). When a monolithic form of patriarchy is enshrined in this generalized rural family, the situation sometimes takes on dimensions of what Yanagisako and Delaney (1995) call "naturalizing power." Gender differentiation is thus legitimated as longstanding, pervasive, and perhaps even inevitable. Even when the writer's intent is to challenge patriarchy, however, assumptions of a uniform and constant past for the practice can obscure the way in which present forms of patriarchy reflect present conditions. Chock (1995, 245) observed that conflicts over paternal authority in Greek

American families are often discussed in terms of "custom" or "the past."

This paper suggests more variation for this "customary past," however, than is generally conceived in such discussions. The flexible nature of Greek households supports the position of Seremetakis (1993) that gender differentiation has been reworked in each phase of Greek history, so that even when older practices continue they take on new meaning (see also Kertzer and Saller 1991, 13). From Lambiri-Dimaki's assessment (1965) of the value shifts leading young Megara women to factory work in the 1950s, to Galani-Moutafi's recent study (1993–94) of the ways tourism has enhanced the role of women on Samos, to my own work (1985) on the involvement of women in family businesses in 1920s Nafplio, it would appear that the issues of home, work, and gender in modern Greece have been renegotiated time and again. Regional variations in postmarital residence and inheritance have mixed with shifting modes of production to create multiple practices, and hence diverse experiences which Greek immigrants brought to the United States.

This also suggests, as Scourby (1984, 12, 123) anticipated some time ago and Karpathakis details in her contribution to this volume, that the particular forms of patriarchy at issue for Greek American families reflect American conditions as much as Greek traditions. Chock (1995) and Callinicos (1991, 166) have both observed that Greek American women are often left out of male-inflected stories of immigrant economic success. This situation resonates with that of many Amorgian women in Athens, who while experiencing some aspects of their move as modernizing and hence liberating, found other aspects to entail a loss of power and status (Sutton 1986). Many initially worked for wages; but most of those who were not in great financial need ceased doing so at the birth of their first child. The kinds of jobs available and the separation of home and work found in Athens led them to focus on child rearing, housework, and what is often called cultural work, such as participating in church activities. In a paradoxical shift, the bargaining position they had held within their families on Amorgos when they actively worked in the fields was thus diminished. As long as patriarchy is only discussed under the headings of custom and interpersonal relations, the economic and political circumstances which also shape gender relations are masked. There is much to be gained by viewing Greek American families in terms of such issues as the labor markets which Georgakas explores elsewhere in this volume (see also Georgakas and Moskos 1991).

This, in an odd way, returns us to the oft-stated thesis on the importance of the Greek family with which I began this essay. When I teach this to non-Greek Americans in my classes, it elicits a very positive response toward Greek life for which I am grateful in my perpetual campaign against ethnocentrism. Inevitably, however, some non-Greek students remark that their families are important to them, too. This is, of course, true, and has led me to puzzle over why the statement is made so often and so emphatically about Greek families. Some of this reflects a process of romanticized othering, whereby Greek families, particularly rural ones or ancestral ones, are held to be of a different, more primeval sort than the people writing about them (see Herzfeld 1987). Some of it also reflects, however, the recognition, sometimes explicit, sometimes vague, that Greek families have historically performed many different functions, functions which in other situations are distributed among different social groups. This is not, of course, unique to Greek families; it is also, however, not universal to all families. When exploring the nature of Greek families, it is important to recognize that they have long operated in political and economic realms as well as those more conventionally considered under the heading of kinship.

Whatever light this discussion of family processes in modern Greece has shed on issues of concern to this conference, my own thinking on the ways families strategically use migration has been altered by taking a new look at the literature on Greek American families. I have been chastened by the clear message from these narratives that not all members of a family may agree with or experience migration the same way. What appears to be unitary family strategy when viewed from the perspective of aggregate statistics and decades of change is rife with struggle and disagreement when viewed more closely. Men and women, old and young, may have very different levels of commitment to the projects being pursued (Yanagisako 1991, 323). Perhaps we might all proceed better if we remember that Greek families are neither as generic nor as unified as we sometimes tend to portray them.

Notes

1. Known in anthropology as bilateral or cognatic kindreds.
2. In line with the general theoretical work of Maclachlan (1987), Netting (1993), Smith and Wallerstein (1992), and Wilk (1991).

3. For discussions of this tendency, see Herzfeld 1982; Lagopoulos and Boklund-Lagopoulou 1992; Leontis 1995; and Sutton 1988.

4. My investigation of the Nemea area was part of the larger Nemea Valley Archaeological Project, which involved field study during seven summers from 1984 to 1994. This project was funded by the National Endowment for the Humanities, the National Geographic Society, and the Society for Aegean Prehistory. Research on Amorgos was carried out during 18 months of fieldwork in 1974–75, and a follow-up study during the summer of 1980, as well as periodic contact with various residents and migrants since that time. This work was funded by grants from the National Science Foundation, the National Institute of Child Health and Human Development, and Indiana University. I was greatly aided in both projects by the gracious cooperation of village presidents and secretaries, as well as the libraries and services of the National Statistical Service, the Ministry of Agriculture, and the Gennadius Library in Athens.

5. I here use the term "Nemea Valley" to refer to the area occupied by the present-day *koinotis* of Arkhaia Nemea. The *demos* of Nemea (formerly known as Ayios Yeorgos) is in the next valley westward. That *demos* was given the name after Greek independence, when it also encompassed what is here called the Nemea Valley; the name was given as part of a national move to give most *demoi* the names of the most prominent ancient sites near them. Even when the *koinotis* split from the *demos* in 1912, the Nemea name stayed with the *demos*, a situation only partially clarified in 1958, when the *koinotis* was renamed Arkhaia Nemea and the main town of the *demos* officially named Nea Nemea.

6. All post-Revolutionary population figures given in this paper derive from the de facto population statistics reported from the periodic national Greek censuses.

7. The advent of centrally located settlements at Nemea also affirms the general principle advanced by Goody (1976, 12) and Segalen (1986, 120–24) that the practice of equal inheritance among European peasants supports local endogamy, but also places this principle in a historical context which shows both the development and then the dissolution of such endogamy.

8. Such in-marrying brides often still received fields in their natal villages as part of their dowries, a circumstance which caused other kinds of adjustments. In some cases, the new couple would periodically travel to the bride's village to work those fields. In others, they would ask relatives or day laborers to attend to them. In still others, they would sell or trade the fields for land closer to Nemea.

9. Miller ([1908] 1964, 473) mentions that the entire island of Amorgos was abandoned for a lengthy period during the 14th and 15th centuries, thus indicating that the village of Langadha could possibly be as recent as the island's repopulation about 1600. In any event, when Tournefort visited the island in 1700, he found it "at present well improved" and that its "fertility invites thither the ships of Provence" (1741, 249).

10. This figure is based on extrapolation from the overall population figure for the island of Amorgos at that time (Houliarakis 1975).

11. Typically, an Amorgian woman's dowry consisted of such a house plus nearby fields. Her husband also eventually brought fields to the family, but usually at a later stage of the life cycle when he received his patrimony upon his parents' retirement or death. In the case of grooms who came from distant villages, the receipt of lands at such a distance from the new family's home base required the same kinds of adjustments as were made in Nemea for in-marrying brides.

12. This figure is derived from calculations of the net migration from Langadha for each intercensal period, using what demographers refer to as residual methods and national rates of natural increase (Valaoras 1960; Willigen and Lynch 1982).

13. This conclusion is derived from a detailed set of data compiled from local records and family interviews, and analyzed through a kin-linking genealogical computer program written specifically for this study.

14. This figure is derived from interviews conducted among a random sample of 73 Langadhian migrant households.

15. This parallels the marriage patterns identified by Moustaka for other groups (1964, 10).

References

Allen, Peter. 1976. Aspida: A depopulated Maniat community. In Dimen and Friedl, 168–98.

Aschenbrenner, Stanley. 1986. *Life in a changing Greek village.* Publications in Ancient Studies, no. 2. Minneapolis: University of Minnesota.

Baxevanis, John J. 1972. *Economy and population movements in the Peloponnesos of Greece.* Athens: National Centre for Social Research.

Bennett, Diane. 1988. "The poor have much more money:" Changing socioeconomic relations in a Greek village. *Journal of Modern Greek Studies* 6: 217–44.

Beopoulou, Ioanna. 1981. Trikeri: Mobilité et rapports d'appartenance. In Damianakos, 191–99.

Beuermann, Arnold. 1954. Kalyviendorfer im Peloponnes. In *Ergebnisse und Probleme moderner geographischer Forschung,* by the scholars, friends, and colleagues of Hans Mortensen and the Akademie für Raumforschung und Landesplanung, 229–38. Bremen: Walter Dorn.

Bialor, Perry A. 1976. The northwestern corner of the Peloponnesos: Mavrikion and its region. In Dimen and Friedl, 222–35.

Bory de Saint-Vincent, J. B. G. M. 1834–36. *Expédition scientifique de Morée: Travaux de la Section des sciences physiques.* Paris: F. G. Levrault.

Burgel, Guy. 1965. *Pobia.* Athens: National Centre for Social Research.

Burgess, Thomas. 1913. *Greeks in America.* Boston: Sherman, French.

Callinicos, Constance. 1991. Arranged marriage in Greek America: The modern picture bride. In Georgakas and Moskos, 161–79.

Campbell, John K. 1964. *Honour, family, and patronage: A study of institutions and moral values in a Greek mountain village.* Oxford: Oxford University Press.

Casselberry, Samuel, and Nancy Valvanes. 1976. "Matrilocal" Greek peasants and a reconsideration of residence terminology. *American Ethnologist* 3: 215–26.

Cavounidis, Jennifer. 1983. Capitalist development and women's work in Greece. *Journal of Modern Greek Studies* 1: 321–38.

Chayanov, A. V. 1986. *The theory of peasant economy*. Ed. D. Thorner, B. Kerblay, and R. E. F. Smith. Madison: University of Wisconsin.

Cherry, J. F., J. L. Davis, and E. Mantzourani, ed. 1991. *Landscape archaeology as long-term history: Northern Keos in the Cycladic Islands*. Monumenta Archaeologogica, no. 16. Los Angeles: University of California at Los Angeles, Institute of Archaeology.

Chock, Phyllis Pease. 1995. "The self-made woman": Gender and the success story in Greek-American family histories. In Yanagisako and Delaney, 239–55.

Clark, Mari H. 1995. From shelters to villas: changing house and settlement form on Methana, 1880–1987. *Yearbook of Modern Greek Studies* 10–11: 511–36.

Clarke, Edward Daniel. 1814. *Travels in various countries of Europe, Asia, and Africa*. London: Cadell and Davies.

Collier, J. F., and Sylvia Junko Yanagisako, ed. 1987. *Gender and kinship: Essays toward a unified analysis*. Stanford: Stanford University Press.

Collins, Donna Misner. 1991. *Ethnic identification: The Greek Americans of Houston, Texas*. New York: AMS Press.

Costa, Janeen Arnold. 1988. The history of migration and political economy in rural Greece: A case study. *Journal of Modern Greek Studies* 6: 159–86.

Costantakos, Chrysie Mamalakis. 1980. *The Greek-American subculture*. New York: Arno Press.

Couroucli, Maria. 1985. *Les Oliviers du lignage*. Paris: Maisonneuve et Larose.

Cowan, Jane K. 1990. *Dance and the body politic in northern Greece.* Princeton: Princeton University Press.

Damianakos, Stathis, ed. 1981. *Aspects du changement social dans la campagne grecque*. Athens: National Centre for Social Research.

Danforth, Loring M. 1989. *Firewalking and religious healing: The Anastenaria of Greece and the American firewalking movement*. Princeton: Princeton University Press.

Dimen, Muriel, and Ernestine Friedl, ed. 1976. *Regional variation in modern Greece and Cyprus: Toward a perspective on the ethnography of Greece*. Annals of the New York Academy of Sciences, vol. 268.

Dubisch, Jill. 1977. The city as resource: Migration from a Greek island village. *Urban Anthropology* 6: 65–82.

————. 1995. *In a different place: Pilgrimage, gender, and politics at a Greek island shrine*. Princeton: Princeton University Press.

————, ed. 1986. *Gender and power in rural Greece*. Princeton: Princeton University Press.

Fairchild, Henry P. 1911. *Greek immigration to the United States*. New Haven: Yale University Press.

Friedl, Ernestine. 1962. *Vasilika: A village in modern Greece*. New York: Holt, Rinehart, Winston.

————. 1967. The position of women: Appearance and reality. *Anthropological Quarterly* 47: 97–108.

————. 1976. Kinship, class, and selective migration. In *Mediterranean Family Structures*, ed. John Peristiany, 363–88. Cambridge: Cambridge University Press.

Galani-Moutafi, Vasiliki. 1993–94. From agriculture to tourism: Property, labor, gender, and kinship in a Greek island village. *Journal of Modern Greek Studies* 11: 241–70, 12: 113–31.

Georgakas, Dan, and Charles C. Moskos, ed. 1991. *New directions in Greek American studies*. New York: Pella.

Goody, Jack. 1976. Inheritance, property, and women: Some comparative considerations. In *Family and inheritance*, ed. J. Goody, J. Thirsk, and E. P. Thompson, 10–36. Cambridge: Cambridge University Press.

Handman, Marie-Élisabeth. 1989. Les Prestations matrimoniales en Grèce: Vaste champ en friche. In Peristiany and Handman, 293–310.

Hareven, Tamara. 1977. Family time and historical time. In *The family*, ed. A. Rossi, J. Kagan, and T. Hareven, 57–70. New York: W. W. Norton.

Hart, Laurie Kain. 1992. *Time, religion, and social experience in rural Greece*. Lanham, Md.: Rowman and Littlefield.

Herzfeld, Michael. 1982. *Ours once more: Folklore, ideology, and the making of modern Greece*. Austin: University of Texas Press.

————. 1985. *The poetics of manhood: Contest and identity in a Cretan mountain village*. Princeton: Princeton University Press.

————. 1987. *Anthropology through the looking-glass: Critical ethnography in the margins of Europe*. Cambridge: Cambridge University Press.

————. 1991. *A place in history: Social and monumental time in a Cretan town*. Princeton: Princeton University Press.

Hirschon, Renee. 1989. *Heirs of the Greek catastrophe: The social life of Asia Minor refugees in Piraeus*. Oxford: Oxford University Press.

Houliarakis, Michail. 1975. *Geografiki, dhioikitiki kai plithismiaki exelixis tis Elladhos, 1821–1971*. Athens: National Centre for Social Research.

Jameson, Michael H., Curtis N. Runnels, and Tjeerd H. van Andel. 1994. *A Greek countryside: The southern Argolid from prehistory to the present day*. Stanford: Stanford University Press.

Just, Roger. 1991. The limits of kinship. In Loizos and Papataxiarchis, 114–32.

Kalafati-Papagalani, Irini. 1989. Femme sujet, femme objet: Se marier à Aghios Petros de Leucade. In Peristiany and Handman, 355–78.

Karakasidou, Anastasia. 1993. Politicizing culture: Negating ethnic identity in Greek Macedonia. *Journal of Modern Greek Studies* 11: 1–28.

Kayser, Bernard. 1963. Les Migrations interierures en Grèce. In *Contributions to Mediterranean sociology*, ed. John G. Peristiany, 192–200. The Hague: Mouton.

Kenna, Margaret. 1976. Houses, fields, and graves: Property and ritual obligation on a Greek island. *Ethnology* 15: 21–34.

Kennedy, Robinette. 1986. Women's friendships on Crete: A psychological perspective. In Dubisch, 121–38.

Kertzer, David I. 1984. *Family life in central Italy, 1880–1910: Sharecropping, wage labor, and coresidence*. New Brunswick: Rutgers University Press.

Kertzer, David I., and Dennis P. Hogan. 1989. *Family, political economy, and demographic change: The transformation of life in Casalecchio, Italy, 1861–1921.* Madison: University of Wisconsin Press.

Kertzer, David I., and Richard P. Saller, ed. 1991. *The family in Italy from antiquity to the present.* New Haven: Yale University Press.

Kolodny, Émile Y. 1974. *La Population des îles de la Grèce.* Aix-en-Provence: EDISUD.

Koster, Harold A. Forthcoming. Neighbors and pastures: Reciprocity and access to pasture. In *Contingent countryside: Settlement, economy, and land use in the southern Argolid since 1700,* ed. Susan Buck Sutton. Stanford: Stanford University Press.

Lagopoulos, Alexandros Ph., and Karin Boklund-Lagopoulou. 1992. *Meaning and geography: The social conception of the region in northern Greece.* New York: Mouton de Gruyter.

Laiou-Thomadakis, Angeliki E. 1977. *Peasant society in the late Byzantine Empire.* Princeton: Princeton University Press.

Lambiri-Dimaki, Ioanna. 1965. *Social change in a Greek country town.* Athens: Centre of Planning and Economic Research.

Leontis, Artemis. 1995. *Topographies of Hellenism: Mapping the homeland.* Ithaca: Cornell University Press.

Loizos, Peter, and Evthymios Papataxiarchis, ed. 1991. *Contested identities: Gender and kinship in modern Greece.* Princeton: Princeton University Press.

Macfarlane, Alan. 1977. *Reconstructing historical communities.* Cambridge: Cambridge University Press.

McGrew, William W. 1985. *Land and revolution in modern Greece, 1800–1881.* Kent, Ohio: Kent State University Press.

Maclachlan, Morgan D. 1987. From intensification to proletarianization. In *Household economies and their transformations,* ed. M. Maclachlan. Monographs in Economic Anthropology, no. 3. Lanham, Md.: University Press of America.

Mendras, Henri. 1962. *Six Villages d'Épire.* Paris: UNESCO.

Miller, William. [1908] 1964. *The Latins in the Levant.* Reprint, New York: Barnes and Noble.

Monos, Dimitris. 1988. *The Greek Americans.* New York: Chelsea House.

Moskos, Charles C. 1980. *Greek Americans: Struggle and success.* Englewood Cliffs, N.J.: Prentice-Hall.

Moustaka, Calliope. 1964. *The internal migrant.* Athens: National Centre for Social Research.

Netting, Robert McC. 1993. *Smallholders, householders: Farm families and the ecology of intensive, sustainable agriculture.* Stanford: Stanford University Press.

Panayiotopoulos, Vasilis. 1985. *Plithysmos kai oikismoi tis Peloponnisou 13os–18os aionas.* Athens: Commercial Bank of Greece.

Papataxiarchis, Evthymios. 1991. Friends of the heart: Male commensal solidarity, gender, and kinship in Aegean Greece. In Loizos and Papataxiarchis, 156–79.

Peristiany, John, and Marie-Élisabeth Handman, ed. 1989. *Le Prix de l'alliance en Méditerranée.* Paris: Éditions du Centre National de la

Recherche Scientifique.
Petronoti, Marina. 1985. *Skediasma yia ti meleti ton oikonomikon kai koinonikon skimatismon sto Kranidhi, 1821–1981.* Athens: Greek Review of Social Research, no. 57.
Plakans, Andrejs. 1984. *Kinship in the past: An anthropology of European family life, 1500–1900.* Oxford: Basil Blackwell.
Pouqueville, F. C. H. L. 1826. *Voyage de la Grèce.* 2nd ed. Paris: Firman Didot.
Salamone, S. D., and J. B. Stanton. 1986. Introducing the "nikokyra": Ideality and reality in social process. In Dubisch, 97–120.
Saloutos, Theodore. 1964. *The Greeks in the United States.* Cambridge: Harvard University Press.
Sandis, Eva. 1973. *Refugees and economic migrants in Greater Athens.* Athens: National Centre for Social Research.
Sant Cassia, Paul, and Constantina Bada. 1992. *The making of the modern Greek family: Marriage and exchange in nineteenth-century Athens.* Cambridge: Cambridge University Press.
Scourby, Alice. 1984. *The Greek Americans.* Boston: Twayne Pubs.
Segalen, Martine. 1986. *The historical anthropology of the family.* Trans. J. C. Whitehouse and Sarah Matthews. Cambridge: Cambridge University Press.
Seremetakis, C. Nadia. 1991. *The last word: Women, death, and divination in Inner Mani.* Chicago: University of Chicago Press.
_____. 1993. Gender, culture, and history: On the anthropologies of ancient and modern Greece. In *Ritual, power, and the body: Historical perspectives on the representation of Greek women,* 11–34. New York: Pella.
Skouteri-Didaskalou, N. 1976. *On Greek dowry: Spatio-temporal transformations.* Post-graduate diploma thesis, University of London.
Smith, Joan, and Immanuel Wallerstein, ed. 1992. *Creating and transforming households: The constraints of the world-economy.* Cambridge: Cambridge University Press.
Sutton, Susan Buck. 1985. Women's work in Nafplio, 1920–1940. *Ethnohistory* 32: 343–62.
_____. 1986. Family and work: New patterns for village women in Athens. *Journal of Modern Greek Studies* 4: 33–49.
_____. 1988. What is a village in a nation of migrants? *Journal of Modern Greek Studies* 6: 187–215.
_____. 1994. Settlement patterns, settlement perceptions: Rethinking the Greek village. In *Beyond the site: Regional studies in the Aegean area,* ed. P. Nick Kardulias, 313–35. Lanham, Md.: University Press of America.
Tournefort, M. 1741. *A voyage into the Levant.* London: Midwinter, Ware, Rivington.
Valaoras, Vasilios G. 1960. A reconstruction of the demographic history of modern Greece. *Milbank Memorial Fund Quarterly* 38: 115–39.
Vacalopoulos, Apostolos. 1976. *The Greek nation.* New Brunswick: Rutgers University Press.
Vermeulen, Cornelis J. J. 1976. Development and migration in the Serres

basin. In Dimen and Friedl, 59–70.

Wagstaff, J. Malcolm. 1982. *The development of rural settlements.* Avebury: Avebury Press.

Wilk, Richard. 1991. *Household ecology: Economic change and domestic life among the Kekchi Maya in Belize.* Tucson: University of Arizona Press.

Willigen, J. Dennis, and Katherine Lynch. 1982. *Sources and methods of historical demography.* New York: Academic Press.

Yanagisako, Sylvia Junko. 1991. Capital and gendered interest in Italian family firms. In Kertzer and Saller, 321–39.

Yanagisako, Sylvia Junko, and Carol Delaney, ed. 1995. *Naturalizing power: Essays in feminist cultural analysis.* London: Routledge.

Transformations: Intermarriage, social roles, and personal identity

5. Church and family in Greek Orthodox society from the Byzantine era to the present-day United States: Problems and issues

DEMETRIOS J. CONSTANTELOS
The Richard Stockton College of New Jersey

This paper provides a comprehensive survey of the role of religion in family life and Greek Orthodox society. In terms of civil and canon law it reviews the nature of the marriage institution in ancient and medieval centuries, and the evolution of marriage as an exclusively sacramental rite.

Whether in Greek antiquity, in Christian Byzantium, or in the post-Byzantine era, marriage has been perceived as hieros, *and ultimately marriage was assimilated to the liturgy of ancient Greek mystery and Christian sacrament. The association of marriage with religion was close in both non-Christian and Christian Greek societies.*

An interrelated topic treated here is the role of the father and the status of women and children in a family. Civil and canon law tried to eliminate or discourage marriages that would dislocate or hurt children. Under the influence of Christianity, the status of both women and children greatly improved during the Byzantine centuries and beyond.

Mixed marriages became thorny problems for the Greek Orthodox throughout their history. The Church inherited from the practice of Judaism and early Christianity a strict tradition about mixed marriages. Historical circumstances have contributed to a reconsideration of, and changes in practice regarding, inter-faith mixed marriages, that is, marriages between Orthodox and non-Orthodox Christians. The Church has not changed its attitude toward inter-

119

religious mixed marriages, that is, those between Orthodox and non-Christians.

The multiracial and multisectarian nature of American society, the rate of divorce and of mixed marriage, the growth of secularism, and the emphasis on the here and now have contributed to the emergence of serious problems in the Greek American Church and society. The Church is presented with a conflict between its doctrinal and ethical teachings on the one hand and contemporary realities in the United States and elsewhere on the other. Notwithstanding the various challenges and temptations that the Greek American family faces, it remains a healthy and steadfast institution.

IN THE HISTORY OF the Greek Orthodox people of the Byzantine era (330–1453) neither civil nor canon law provided a definition of what constitutes an *oikogeneia*, a family. Dispersed but sufficient evidence, however, indicates that "family" meant both space and content, an *oikos* and a *genos*—a house occupied by people, and a *genos*, people who had established a kinship and a relationship through marriage. Family as household served as the basis and the most important nuclear element of Byzantine and post-Byzantine Greek Orthodox society.

The creation of a family presupposed marriage. Marriage was defined in the 14th century by the jurist and canonist Constantine Armenopoulos as "a *synapheia* ['union'] and *synklerosis* ['community'] of a man and a woman for life, a union by divine will and human right" (Constantine Armenopoulos 1971, book 4, title 4.1, p. 226).

For nearly seven centuries in the Byzantine era, marriage followed the prescriptions of Roman law. From as early as A.D. 370, and especially after 505, marriage was perceived as a contract. An official declaration of two heterosexual persons before the government's *ekdikos* (judge) was the only requirement for a couple to be proclaimed officially married. Justinian's legislation in the 6th century indicates that the office of *ekdikos* was open to both clergymen and laymen alike.

Hierologia, a church service for marriage, had been practiced, but it was in the 10th century that Emperor Leo VI legislated that *hierologia* was the only option for a valid marriage. The controversy between a legalistic and a sacramental view of marriage, however, continued down to the early 14th century, when *hierologia* and the sacramental nature of marriage was firmly established and became the only option for a valid marriage for the Orthodox (Constantelos 1975, 49–53). This rule is valid to the present day. As far as canon law is concerned, no marriage performed outside the Church is religiously valid.

The ritualistic and sacramental development of marriage in spirit and in verbal form is closer to the Greek rather than the Roman custom and cultural tradition. Christian Greeks and ancient Greeks held a common cultural and intellectual heritage. It should not surprise us to see parallels between the two, or to see the Greek Orthodox Church using theological terms, ritual usages, symbols, and elements taken from the practices of their ancestors. Thus as in Greek antiquity, where the basic reason for a marriage was religious—that is, to perpetuate family worship in honor of the ancestors and to continue sacrifices, memorials, rituals, customs, and family traditions—likewise in Christian Byzantium marriage assumed a religious character: it was proclaimed one of the Mysteries of the Church. The idea of the *hieros gamos* (holy, or sacred, marriage) that we find in the history of non-Christian Hellenism prevailed in the history and practice of Christian Hellenism.

Marriage as *hieros gamos* and mystery has roots in remote Greek antiquity. First, in Greek mythology the marriage between divinities, such as Zeus and Hera, was called *hieros gamos*. As Greek religious thought evolved, a marriage of a god or goddess with a human person was also called *hieros gamos*. Such was the marriage of Dionysos with the basilisa, or wife of the chief archon, of Athens during the Anthesteria festival, and the marriage of Demeter with Iasion. These marriages became the pattern for a marriage between man and woman (Farnell 1977, 31–35; Guthrie 1955, 53–54, 68–69; Zielinski 1926, 95–96; Nilsson 1964, 33–34, 121–22, 294–95; Hamilton 1992, 53–57).

Later, for Plato and pre-Christian mystery cults, marriage was also sacred—*hieros gamos*. Speaking about marriage, sexual indulgence, and paternity, Plato insists that human beings should honor their *hieros gamos* and have sexual relations only with their wedded spouse. He writes that the state needs to enact laws that would check "free love" and lusts in order to prevent human beings from becoming less than human. "Surely our citizens should at least be better than . . . animals." Sexual indulgence must be attended by a sense of shame because "this feeling will make indulgence infrequent, and the infrequency of the indulgence will moderate the tyranny of the appetite." Fear of God, desire for honorable distinction, and "the development of the passion for a beauty which is spiritual, not physical, would prevent a citizen from touching any but his own wedded wife." Marriage for Plato is *hieros gamos* because it is sanctioned by God (Plato *Laws* 841).

Like other aspects of religious and social life of ancient Hellenism, which were never static but always subject to a constant becoming, the sacredness of marriage as *hieros gamos* evolved to the extent that it became "a communion in worship" in the words of L. R. Farnell (1977, 62), an outstanding authority on the subject. During the Byzantine era, the rite of marriage was elevated into one of the "Mysteries," or sacraments of the Church. The Byzantine Empire was raised on the ruins of Alexander's empire, with its Hellenic and Hellenistic culture, language, and people. Thus both the forms and the spirit of ancient traditions, including mysteries, were preserved, transformed, given new symbolism and new meaning. There are many parallels between non-Christian and Christian Hellenism. In both worlds, marriage evolved into a "communion in worship."

According to the marriage service of the Greek Orthodox Church, it is God who performs the "mystical and undefiled marriage [*o tou mystikou kai achrantou gamou hierourgos*]"; the wedded couple achieve a communion in marriage *(gamou koinonian)*; marriage is *mega mysterion.* St. Paul insists that the spiritual union of Christ with the Church is "a great mystery" and serves as the prototype of a marriage between man and woman. Their union into "one flesh" is a "great mystery."[1] But the same terminology was used to describe the mystery festival and the marriage festivities of the Eleusinian mysteries. In his refutation of heresies, the 3rd century bishop Hippolytos of Rome ridiculed "to mega ... Eleusinion mysterion" and "to mega ... Samothrakon mysterion" (*Elenhos* 5.7.29–30; 5.8.39).

Furthermore, as in Greek antiquity, when marriage was assimilated to the liturgy of the mysteries, such as the Dionysiac and the Pythagorean,[2] likewise, perhaps after the 10th century, a Christian marriage was solemnized during the Eucharistic Mystery (Trempelas 1950, 15–17). On the basis of this evidence, Farnell (1977, 36–37) adds that "the association of marriage with religion was as close in civilized Greece as it is or has been in Christendom." It is in the light of this Greek and Christian background that we should try to understand marriage as a sacred event, and married life as holy in Greek Orthodox society, whether in the Byzantine era or in modern Greek Orthodox communities. There is more continuity in Greek religious culture than discontinuity. Tradition preserves the memory of ancestral experience, an experience lived by ancestors and handed down to their descendants.

One of the major areas where Christianity influenced Byzantine civilization was the status of women and children. Though the father continued to dominate family life, the place of the wife and the future of children greatly improved in the Byzantine era. The legislation of Justinian in particular, but also laws issued by later emperors such as Leo III and Leo VI, protected the rights of wives and children. On the other hand, Church canons of ecumenical synods, such as those of the Council in Trullo, emphasized the sacredness of the family institution (Constantelos 1975, 51–53).

The major functions of women in Byzantine society were having children and looking after the welfare of the household. Legislation provided extra protection for a wife's rights and also the rights of children in both economic and social terms. Motherhood was highly valued and indeed exalted. A woman, however, brought to the marriage not only motherhood, but also a dowry, which often was the center of the family's economic base.

While the wife legally owned her dowry, it was the husband's responsibility to administer it. If a husband mismanaged his wife's property, she could bring him to court to have him forced to restore the losses to her. If the court decided that the husband had been careless or had inadequately handled her property, the court could then give control of the property to the wife. The dowry had several legal constraints that kept it tightly controlled, for the sole purpose of protecting the family and, more important, the future inheritance of the children. It was transferred to the children of the marriage upon the death of the mother. As time passed, the dowry laws allowed dowries to become more usable assets that could be traded, sold, or donated. Dowry laws became more relaxed after the 13th century.

Civil and canon law tried to eliminate or discourage marriages that would confuse and dislocate children. It is for that reason that divorce laws favored keeping the original family intact. The reasons a husband or wife could divorce were very specific. The seeker of the divorce should be able to prove that the other spouse was either a murderer, a sorcerer, a violator of tombs, or an adulterer. There were no "no fault divorces." Divorce for trivial reasons was not tolerated. Furthermore, there were also penalties for the spouse who brought charges that could not be proven. For example, if a wife could not prove her grounds for divorce, she had to give her dowry to her husband; sometimes she was exiled, and would not be permitted to marry another man.

Byzantine legislation was also protective of widows, their economic situation, their status, and their relationships with their children. Widows could undertake the guardianship of their children provided they declared that they would not remarry. If a widow's request to remarry was granted, the man who married her would be obligated to place his own property at the service of the minors, who would also inherit from him.[3]

How large was a Byzantine family? We do not know, but there are indications that because of infant mortality, mothers were expected to give birth to several children. Perhaps the best sources for the study of family size and family life are lives of saints, the textbooks of the common folk. Just a few illustrations: The life of David, Symeon, and George of Mitylene (ca. 900) reveals that they came from a family of eight children. Their biographer has nothing but high praises for the family institution, describing the family of the three saints as a happy one (Van den Gheyn 1899, 211–59).

The life of St. Luke the Younger reveals that he came from a family of seven children. When Luke's mother lost her husband and developed physical problems, Luke "served and tended her as it is fitting a son"—a statement indicating that sons were expected to look after elderly and handicapped parents (Martini 1894, 81–121). Nikon of Lacedaimon was born to a large but wealthy family of Paphlagonia. It included several brothers and an extended family of servants. When Nikon decided to leave the family, his father ran after him begging him tenderly to return back home. He called Nikon "my sweet baby."[4]

Attitudes toward family life and toward parents and siblings were not uniform in the Byzantine Empire. While we read about families with many children, we read of many couples with no children. Euphymianos and his wife, Aglais, were childless, but prayers resulted in the birth of Alexios, an experience shared by others such as Theoklia and her husband, who after persistent prayers became the parents of Kalliopios (Esteves Pereira 1900, 243–53; Latysev 1970, 269–72). Attributing the conception of a child by a barren woman to the intervention of God through prayer became a *topos* in hagiology.

Older brothers usually assumed family responsibilities when both parents died. For example, the parents of St. Euthymios the Younger had one son, Euthymios, and two daughters. Upon the death of both parents, Euthymios assumed the role of a father, guardian, defender, and provider for his sisters (Petit 1903).

Family problems were not always resolved through the court, civil or ecclesiastical. Paulos the Simple (o Haplos) caught his wife with a man in the act of adultery. He tried not to embarrass them. He said to them, "It is okay, it is okay, truly; I am not disturbed [*Kalon, kalon, alethos; ou melesei me*]." He ran away and at the age of 60 he sought to become a monk (Latysev 1970, 252–56). Perhaps there was more tolerance toward an unfaithful spouse than some people may want to admit.

Mixed marriage, both between Christians of different churches and between Christians and non-Christians, was a major problem for the early Christian community, which faced marriages between Christians and Jews, and Christians and pagans. It continued to be a problem for the Byzantine Church, as several of its canons indicate. While some churchmen today see mixed marriages as opportunities to gain new members and enrich the Church, others see them as a threat to the preservation of ethnic and cultural identity and a harmonious family life.[5]

The Christian Church's attitude toward mixed marriage was a direct result of the influence of the Hebraic tradition. While marriage between Christians of different races and cultural backgrounds was allowed from as early as Apostolic times, marriages between Christians and non-Christians, and orthodox Christians and heretics, were discouraged for purely religious reasons.

There are several similarities between Judaism and early Christianity in their attitude toward marriage. Mixed marriages between Jews and Gentiles in the communities of the diaspora were tolerated, provided the Gentile converted to Judaism. These types of marriages were more common in the Greek East than in the Latin West. The Latin historian Tacitus (*Historia* v. 5) relates that the exclusive attitude of the Jews in Rome and endogamy among them were notorious. Roman Jews lived more comfortably among the Greeks. Even in the city of Rome, most of the Jews were Hellenized and spoke Greek rather than Latin. A recent study of 534 Jewish inscriptions in the Jewish cemetery in Rome reveals that 405 (75 percent) are in Greek; of the rest 123 (23 percent) are in Latin, 3 in Hebrew, 1 in Aramaic, 1 bilingual Greek and Latin, and 1 bilingual Aramaic and Greek. "From these figures it is quite apparent that the Roman-Jewish community, which existed from about 100 B.C., was Greek-speaking" (Leon 1959). The case of Paul's disciple Timothy is a good illustration of a mixed marriage between a Jew and a Greek in the East. His mother was Jewish and his father a Greek (Acts 16:1–3).

As in the case of the Jewish attitude toward Gentiles, early Christians were allowed to marry non-Christians on condition that the non-Christian spouse would convert to Christianity. The first letter to the Corinthians indicates that St. Paul discouraged the marriage of a Christian with a pagan. "A wife is bound as long as her husband lives. But if the husband dies, she is free to marry anyone she wishes, but only in the Lord" (1 Cor. 7:39). *En Kyrio* has been interpreted by Greek Fathers and modern scholars to mean a "Christian marriage." Theodoretos of Cyrrhus adds that the key word is *homopisto* (Trempelas 1937, 198 n. 39), that husband and wife should be of the same faith.

In the same letter St. Paul advised that if a Christian was already married to an unbeliever and the latter had no objection to living with a Christian, the unbeliever should not be divorced. In an already mixed marriage, the Christian was advised to remain united to the non-Christian spouse. In such a union, the unbeliever is sanctified *(hagiastai)*, because the physical-sexual relationship has united him or her to the believer, who is consecrated to God in the person of Jesus Christ. By consenting to live with a Christian, the Jewish or pagan spouse accepts a participation in a consecrated life.

In theory, neither St. Paul nor the early Christian community authorized a mixed marriage between a Christian and a non-Christian. Martyrologies and early Christian literature, however, indicate that mixed marriages between Christians and non-Christians were not rare, though they were problematic. People of the same religious faith were considered to have a better chance for a happy married life. Even non-Christian intellectuals such as the Greek biographer and moralist Plutarch (A.D. 46–120) was of the opinion that a marriage cannot be a happy one unless husband and wife are of a similar background (*Peri paidon agoges* 2.19). The Greek tradition had emphasized that marriage should be a source of happiness because "nothing is better or greater than a home where man and wife are living together harmoniously and in love . . . a very great joy to people of good will, and greatest of all to themselves," as we read in Homer's *Odyssey* (trans. Rees 6.180–85).

Early Christian authors also encouraged marriage between believers for the sake of their own happiness. The two believers come under the same discipline, have one hope, and are dedicated to the same service. "The two are brethren, the two are fellow-servants; no difference of spirit or flesh; yes, truly, two in one flesh; where there is one flesh the spirit is one," writes Tertullian (*Ad uxorem* 1.3; 2.8–10[6]).

Our knowledge of Christian marriage and mixed marriages in particular during the first four centuries of the Christian era is limited. With the exception of Clement of Alexandria and Tertullian of Carthage, we have no detailed information either about marriage as one of the Christian sacraments or about the attitude of the Church toward mixed marriage. Even the ecclesiastical historians Eusebios (Eusebius), Socrates, Sozomenos (Sozomen), Philostorgios, and Evagrios (6th century) fail to provide some important pieces of information about our subject.

On the basis of fragmentary evidence we infer that the pre-Constantinian Church condemned mixed marriages not only with Jews and pagans, but also with heretics and even schismatics. Intermarriage, however, between Christians of different races and social positions was allowed, albeit not common. For example, one of the accusations against Callistus, the bishop of Rome in 219, was that he allowed marriages between slaves and freedmen, and even well-born Christian women (Hippolytos *Elenhos* 9:21–40).

Either because of the eschatological nature of early Christianity, or because many of the leading Christian fathers were celibates, very few of them wrote on marriage. Clement of Alexandria was one of the few exceptions. In his *Stromateis* he devoted a brief chapter (2.23) to marriage, and on the basis of certain terms he used, we conclude that he encouraged marriage between fellow believers. He writes that those who enter into marriage must take into account several considerations, such as age, circumstances, and the goal and purpose of marriage. "Every one is not to marry, nor always. But there is a time in which it is suitable, and a person for whom it is suitable, and an age up to which it is suitable." And he adds, "marriage, . . . as a sacred image, must be kept pure from those things which defile it."

Because of the belief that Christians were "a chosen race, a royal priesthood, a holy nation, God's own people . . . called out of darkness into God's marvelous light" (1 Pet. 2:9), the author of First Peter implied that marriage should be between believers (1 Pet. 3:1–17).

With the emergence of the Church from the catacombs and the adoption of Christianity as the state religion of the late Roman or early Byzantine Empire, Church canons were specifically issued condemning mixed marriages. The Arabic list of canons attributed to the Council of Nicaea (325) includes a canon, numbered 53, that specifically orders that "marriages with infidels should be avoided" (in Schaff and Wace 1956, 48). The 10th canon of the Council of Laodicea in 343 forbids members of the Church to marry their children to heretics (ibid., 129). The same council decreed (canon 31) that "it is not lawful to make marriages with all sorts of heretics, nor to give our sons and daughters to them; but rather to take of them, if they promise to become Christians." Marriage with heretics was forbidden because of fear that they would teach the Orthodox their own errors, and lead them to be converted to their beliefs (ibid., 149). The 21st (29th) canon of the Council in Carthage (A.D. 394) decreed that the children of clergymen (deacons, priests, bishops) should not be allowed to marry women who were heretics or pagans.

More than rules of local councils, the canons of ecumenical councils have been more binding. The 14th canon of the Council of Chalcedon condemned marriage "to a heretic, or a Jew, or a pagan, unless the person marrying the Orthodox shall promise to come over to the Orthodox faith" (ibid., 278).

The 72nd canon of the Council in Trullo (692) is equally clear and more elaborate in its condemnation of marriages between Orthodox believers and heretics. If such a marriage has been contracted willingly, the Orthodox spouse is cut off from the body of the Church, and the marriage is declared null. If two unbelievers, however, have contracted lawful marriage between themselves and in the course of time one chooses to become an Orthodox Christian willing to preserve the marriage with an unbelieving spouse, the marriage remains valid. The canon does not advocate separation, on account of St. Paul's teaching that "the unbelieving husband is sanctified by his wife, and the unbelieving wife by her husband" (ibid., 397; 1 Cor. 7:14). This canon indicates that paganism was still alive in the last quarter of the 7th century, and a threat to Christian teachings.

With the subjugation of millions of Orthodox Christians under Islamic rule after the 7th century, mixed marriages between Orthodox Christians and Muslims became an additional problem. Even though Islam, too, advocates endogamous marriage between fellow Muslims, marriage between Christians and Muslims was not an exceptional phenomenon. For example, Theodore Balsamon, Patriarch of Antioch, writes that the Orthodox Georgians were not disturbed that their daughters married Muslims. And John Zonaras, commenting on Photios' Nomocanon, writes: "I myself know that the Iberians [Georgians], who have accepted all from us, give their daughters in marriage to Agarenes [Muslims]. I wonder why the

bishops, who know the Church canons, do not prevent such marriages" (Rhallis and Potles 1852, 271–72).

During the Ottoman period, it was not unusual for one spouse to
convert to Islam and the other to remain faithful to Orthodoxy—
mixed marriages of Muslim men and Orthodox women whether in
Syria, Asia Minor, or Cyprus were not uncommon. Some marriages
were contracted with the permission of ecclesiastical authority. For
example, a document of the 16th century relates that Maria married
Bayram ibn Abdullah with the permission of her father, Papa Toma
of Hagia Yolofi of Lefkosia (Jennings 1993, 29). The marriage of a
Christian man with a Muslim woman, however, was impossible. The
penalty was death.

Mixed marriages between Orthodox Christians and Latin
Catholics became more frequent after the Fourth Crusade. Following that barbarous Western expedition in 1204, several Western
kingdoms and principalities were established in the Byzantine Greek
Orthodox world, such as those of the Franks, Venetians, and
Genoese. Whether for religious reasons or cultural and ethnic considerations, the Church continued to condemn mixed marriages even
though theological opinion was never clear whether the Latins were
heretics or schismatics. Indeed, both churches were inconsistent in
their attitudes toward mixed marriages.

Despite the condemnations, such marriages, especially among
members of the aristocratic and royal families, can be fully documented between the 13th and 18th centuries. There were Orthodox
Christians in the last centuries of Byzantium who believed that
through intermarriage with Western Christians they would be able
to recover Constantinople and the whole Byzantine Empire. Others
however were less sanguine about the Christian West's coming to
their assistance, and were afraid of Roman Catholic domination.

As late as the second half of the 19th century, the Ecumenical
Patriarchate was caustically against mixed marriages. For example,
the Holy Synod of the Patriarchate decreed in 1869 that mixed marriages were not allowed and that the validity of those already contracted was to be denied. Nevertheless, 10 years later, the
Patriarchate, facing an inescapable reality, declared that in order to
avoid painful consequences, the Church would exercise leniency and
forgiveness and would tolerate the blessing of mixed marriages.[7]

To the present day, not only canons, but even civil law in more
homogeneous Orthodox countries like Greece, forbids a mixed marriage between a Greek citizen of any Christian faith, not only Ortho-

dox, and a non-Christian. And a marriage between a Greek Orthodox and a non-Orthodox Christian must be solemnized according to the Greek Orthodox *typikon*.

Notwithstanding official canons condemning mixed marriages, it seems that throughout those centuries in which the Church was a dominant institution, mixed marriages were unavoidable. Whether they were nominal Christians, or because Eros was a more powerful motive than church canons, evidence indicates that Orthodox Christians married non-Christians, as well as heretics and schismatics. Some ecclesiastical jurisdictions, bishops in their dioceses in particular, exercised *oikonomia*, and proved more lenient in granting permission for such marriages than others.

The Greek Orthodox Church in the United States, Canada, South America, and Australia and elsewhere is a daughter of the Ecumenical Patriarchate of Constantinople (present-day Istanbul). It subscribes to the teachings, canons, and rules of the Orthodox Church in history. Furthermore, the Church, ministering to the spiritual needs of people of a common heritage, is conscious of certain linguistic and cultural particularities as well as customs and traditions affecting family and family life. The Greek Orthodox family in the New World maintains its own ethical standards and traditions.

Marriage, family life, religious practices, and even ethnic identity are interrelated topics for the Greek Orthodox communities in America. A failure of marriage is a threat to the well-being of the family; mixed marriage and divorce have been considered destabilizing forces for both church and community.

Writing in 1926, Ioakeim Alexopoulos, bishop of Boston, sounded an alarm and expressed a profound pessimism about the future of the Greek identity in America. He decried the decline of Greek as a spoken language, lamented the growth of mixed marriages, and identified the factors conducive to the breakdown of the family, to assimilation, and to the loss of the Greek Orthodox family.

A few years later Archbishop Athenagoras, too, expressed his alarm over trends, moral and social, affecting the integrity and spiritual well-being of the Greek American family. In several encyclicals he tried to inspire interest and guide the clergy, and also the lay leaders of the communities, to coordinate efforts and work together to save the sanctity of the Greek Orthodox family. In an encyclical issued on November 26, 1934, he appealed to the clergy and ecclesiastical councils to make the security of the Greek Orthodox family their personal concern. "Help," he wrote, "the growth of marriages between our own people and bless them according to Church rules. Convince those married outside the Church to have their marriage consecrated by the Church" (Constantelos 1976, 122–23).

Mixed marriages were viewed as a threat not only to the preservation of Greek ethnic identity but also to the unity and prosperity of the Greek Orthodox family. In several encyclicals Archbishop Athenagoras discouraged mixed marriages and advised priests and all the chapters of the Philoptochos Society to intensify their efforts to help create Greek Orthodox families. In a pastoral encyclical of May 27, 1937, Athenagoras raised the question: "What is going to happen to our children? What can we do to see our daughters happily married? How shall we work to create Greek families blessed in the Church? We don't wish to see our daughters stay single, disappointed and frustrated. What can we do to prevent mixed marriages and to avoid seeing our children flying to foreign nests?" (ibid., 191–92.)

Some 10 years later, in 1948, Archbishop Athenagoras realized that there were many unmarried women and suggested that mixed marriages could be a solution. "Because we have more young women than men there is a need for encouraging mixed marriages between our daughters and non-Orthodox men who are, of course, Christian," he wrote on September 27, 1948 (ibid, 240–41. cf. 236–38).

In the light of Athenagoras' concerns and prevailing realities, some 20 years later Theodore Saloutos (1973, 407), the pioneer in Greek-American studies, observed that "the Greek Orthodox Church faced the inevitable"; the Church finally conceded that it was impossible "to resist the forces of assimilation and preserve the Greek national identity as she once thought."

To this day, neither Bishop Ioakeim's defeatism, nor Saloutos' deduction, has been confirmed. Whether we have to thank John F. Kennedy and his government, which liberalized immigration laws and allowed the arrival of several scores of thousands of Greek immigrants after 1965 (to 1989), or Alex Haley, whose discovery of ethnic roots became contagious and helped many minorities to rediscover their ethnic roots, both the Greek Orthodox Church and the preservation of an ethnic identity have survived and even prosper. In reality both have increased. While many prefer a religious identity, others emphasize the need for an ethnic identity. There are diversity of opinion and diverse trends within the Greek American Church and community.

While Bishop Ioakeim's and Saloutos' views have been challenged,

Archbishop Athenagoras' acknowledgment that mixed marriages were inevitable proved right. His fear, however, that mixed marriages would prove the greatest threat to the retention of an ethnic and cultural identity has not been dissipated. While some see mixed marriages as threats, others perceive them as opportunities. More than 60 percent of the marriages solemnized by the Church between 1990 and 1995 were mixed. Here are some indicative statistics.

Year	Total Marriages	Mixed Marriages	Percent Mixed
1990	5,956	3,769	63.28%
1991	5,711	3,520	61.64%
1992	5,452	3,530	64.75%
1993	5,461	3,429	62.79%
1994	5,231	3,137	59.97%
1995	5,620	3,575	63.61%
Total	33,431	20,960	62.70%

Source: Greek Orthodox Archdiocese, 1998, 103.

Notwithstanding the growth of interfaith marriages and the decline of those of religious and ethnic homogeneity, the Greek Orthodox family remains strong, resisting the forces that have been catalytic for the nation as a whole. It is evident that the stability of the Greek Orthodox family has been influenced by cultural trends in the United States, and that mixed marriages have undermined the cultural identity of the family, but when one sees the Greek family in the context of present-day United States realities, one must conclude that the Greek family is healthier than families of other, different creeds and persuasions. Religious faith, cultural values, concern for the perpetuation of ethnic and cultural identity, family traditions, have contributed to the stability and the unity of the Greek Orthodox family in the United States, Canada, and South America. The divorce rate among the Greek Orthodox is significantly lower than the national average. Let me provide only one indicative illustration: according to the statistical records of the Archdiocese's registry, in 1995 the Archdiocese recorded 5,620 solemnized marriages and 722 divorces (ibid.). The divorce rate is less than 13 percent. But not all divorces among the Greek Orthodox go through archdiocesan courts. Even if we allow another 3–5 percent, we still have no more than 18 percent, far less than the 50 to 52 percent of the national rate.

As already indicated, mixed marriage, both between Christians of different communions and between Christians and non-Christians, has been a major problem for the Church from as early as the Byzantine era, as several Church canons indicate. Attitudes toward mixed marriages today differ. While some see them as a threat to the harmony of Greek Orthodox family life and to the preservation of an ethnic and cultural life, others see mixed marriages as opportunities to gain new members and enrich the Church—an attitude found also in the life of the late centuries of the Byzantine Empire.

The question persists: Is a mixed marriage a threat or a blessing in disguise, especially for Greek communities in the diaspora?

It seems that the more serious question is not whether interfaith marriages are allowed, but what should the Church's attitude be toward intra-religious marriages. Greek Orthodox marriages with Christians of other churches and denominations have been accepted. We no longer live in Justinian's Christian Oecumene, and we no longer identify people as heretics, schismatics, and even atheists. We no longer live in homogeneous societies, and the principle of unity in uniformity died in the first half of the 20th century. The macrocosm of the 19th century has been reduced to a microcosm with the technological developments of the 20th century. The multiethnic, multicultural, multisectarian societies that have emerged in the last 50 years have forced the Church to reconsider its theology and its attitude toward Christian and non-Christian communities and religions.

With more than half of intra-Christian mixed marriages in the United States involving an Orthodox partner, with many mixed inter-religious marriages among Orthodox Christians and Muslims in the Near East, and Orthodox and atheists (for whom the canonical provisions for pagans would apply) in Russia and elsewhere, how can we faithfully apply the canons of Laodicea, Carthage, Chalcedon, and Constantinople, which condemned all forms of mixed marriages?

Canons were measures and rules issued to meet local needs and circumstances, and whether or not they were divinely inspired remains to the present day a controversial question. Even though the Byzantine Church was a unified organization, it is true that there were different attitudes toward canon law, and divergent opinions about it, and the Church was an energetic and evolving organism, never a monolithic and static one—a phenomenon that persists to the present day. The Russian and other Orthodox Churches in Europe and the Near East do not refuse the sacraments to an Orthodox spouse married to a non-Orthodox, even to a non-Christian, as we do in the United States, even though here, too, there is much inconsistency. What should the Universal Orthodox Church do now?

How do we explain so many mixed marriages among the Greek Orthodox Christians in America? Instead of a decline, there is a slow growth of both intra-Christian and inter-religious marriages. Does this phenomenon indicate that the traditional Greek Orthodox family is failing, and its young people are looking elsewhere for spouses? Is the strong, protective, and paternalistic attitude of many Greek Orthodox parents pushing their sons and daughters away from their home? Or is it that our people have little knowledge and less appreciation of the theology of marriage and the teachings of the institutional Church?

College education is a priority for most Greek Orthodox families, but it is exactly among the college-educated people that the Church has lost ground. There is little doubt that the Church has lost many of our intellectuals and professional people through their mixed and exogamous marriages. Most of them now prefer a cultural-ethnic rather than a religious identification. Yet there is no need to lose these people because they have contracted marriage outside the Church. The Church is called upon to exercise more *oikonomia*, and adopt rubrics that would allow many of them to return home. But this is the responsibility of a pan-Orthodox decision and not the individual bishop or priest.

As the Church stands now, no solemnization of a marriage between a Greek Orthodox and a non-Christian is possible. In my view, the Church should act to allow the blessing of a such a marriage, provided the Orthodox member wants it and the non-Christian has no objection to an Orthodox ceremony. The practice of the early Church, which taught that the unbeliever is consecrated through his or her union with the believer, should come back into force.

Mixed marriage is the thorniest and the most troublesome problem for many families, and its solution requires serious and realistic deliberations. It is high time for all Orthodox Churches to study this issue seriously, reflect on the conditions in which we live, and reach mature, humane, and responsible decisions. Deliberations on such a sensitive issue require the participation and wisdom of married priests with many years of pastoral experience—not simply celibate theologians, professors, and bishops. Mixed marriage is a pastoral problem and requires the wisdom of pastoral experience.

Notes

1. Ephesians 6:31–32; all citations of scripture are from the New Revised Standard Version.
2. Farnell 1977, 33; Fustel de Coulanges 1864, unavailable to me but cited in Flacelière 1983, 262–63, 248–249; Burkert 1985, 108–09.
3. Both the *Codex Theodosianus* (1952) and Justinian's *Corpus juris civilis* include many laws protective of women, widows, orphans, and children in general. See especially Justinian's *Pandects*, titles I*f*V, and Justinian's *Novels*.
4. Lampsides 1982, 38: "emon, teknon glykytaton . . . "
5. See the special issue of *The Greek Orthodox Theological Review* 40, nos. 3–4 (1995). What follows is a slightly revised version of an article published in that issue.
6. In *Tertullian: Treatises on marriage and remarriage*, trans. and annotated by William P. Le Saint, 23–36. Ancient Christian Writers, no. 13. New York: Newman Press, 1951.
7. For references and relevant bibliography see Constantelos 1975, 57.

References

Alexopoulos, Ioakeim. 1926. *The dangers facing the Hellenes in America* (in Greek). Boston.
Armenopoulos, Constantine. 1971. *Procheiron nomon e exabiblos*. Ed. K. G. Pitsakis. Athens.
Burkert, Walter. 1985. *Greek religion*. Trans. John Raffan. Cambridge, Mass.: Harvard University Press.
Codex Theodosianus. 1952. Trans. Clyde Pharr. Princeton: Princeton University Press.
Constantelos, Demetrios J. 1975. *Marriage, sexuality, and celibacy: A Greek Orthodox perspective*. Minneapolis.
Constantelos, Demetrios J., ed. 1976. *Encyclicals and Documents . . .* Thessaloniki.
Esteves Pereira, F. M. 1900. In *Analecta Bollandiana* 19:243–53.
Farnell, L. R. 1977. *The higher aspects of Greek religion*. Chicago.
Flacelière, Robert. 1983. *O demosios kai idiotikos vios ton archaion Hellenon*. 4th ed. Trans. into Greek by G. D. Vandorovou. Athens.
Fustel de Coulanges, Numa Denis. 1864. *La Cité antique*. Trans. Willard Smith as *The ancient city*. Reprint Garden City, New York: Doubleday, [1956].
Greek Orthodox Archdiocese. 1998. *Yearbook 1998*. Ed. Rev. Philemon Sevastiades. New York: Delta Printing.
Guthrie, W. K. C. 1955. *The Greeks and their gods*. New York.
Hamilton, Richard. 1992. *Choes and Anthesteria*. Ann Arbor, Michigan.
Homer. *The Odyssey*. Trans. Ennis Rees. New York: Macmillan 1991.
Jennings, Ronald C. 1993. *Christians and Muslims in Ottoman Cyprus and the Mediterranean world, 1571–1640*. New York and London.

Justinian. *Corpus juris civilis.* Trans. S. P. Scott as *The civil law.* 1932.
Lampsides, O. 1982. *O ek pontou osios Nikon o metanoeite.* Athens.
Latysev, V. V., ed. 1970. *Menologri anonymi Byzantini.* Vol. 1. Leipzig.
Leon, Harry J. 1959. The Greek inscriptions of the Jews of Rome. *Greek-Roman and Byzantine Studies* 2, no. 1 (January): 47.
Martini, E. 1894. In *Analecta Bollandiana* 13:81–121.
Nilsson, Martin P. 1964. *A history of Greek religion.* 2nd ed. New York.
Petit, L. 1903. Vie de Saint Euthyme le jeune. *Revue de l'Orient chrétien* 8: 168–205.
Rhallis, G. A., and M. Potles. 1852. *Syntagma ton theiron kai hieron kanonon.* Vol. 1. Athens.
Saloutos, Theodore. 1973. The Greek Orthodox Church in the United States. *The International Migration Review* 7, no. 3: 407.
Schaff, Philip, and H. Wace. 1956. *The seven ecumenical councils.* Series A, Select Library of Nicene and Post-Nicene Fathers, 2nd series, vol. 14. Grand Rapids, Michigan.
Trempelas, P. N. 1937. *Ypomnema eis tas Epistolas tou Pavlou.* Athens.
————. 1950. *Mikron euhologion.* Vol. 1. Athens.
Van den Gheyn, I. 1899. In *Analecta Bollandiana* 18:211–59.
Zielinski, Thaddeus. 1926. *The religion of ancient Greece.* Trans. G. R. Noyes. Oxford.

6. Interethnic marriages and prospects for ethnic group survival: The case of Greek Canadians

PETER D. CHIMBOS

Brescia College, The University of Western Ontario

This paper examines trends in interethnic marriages and how they affect the survival of ethnic culture and identity in a multicultural society, with special reference to Greek Canadians. According to statistical information from the Greek Orthodox Metropolis of Canada, interethnic marriages among Greek Canadians are steadily increasing. Factors contributing to the increase of interethnic marriages among Greek Canadians include the social integration of Greek Canadians into the host society, occupational heterogeneity, liberal philosophies of education, a decline in overt discrimination against ethnic groups, and the philosophy of multiculturalism with emphasis on minority rights. It is suggested that Greek Canadian organizations make the necessary changes to accommodate those new members who join the Greek communities through interethnic marriages.

A HISTORICAL EXAMINATION of the Greek communities in Canada indicates that since the early 1900s Greek Canadians have established organizations such as churches, schools, youth associations, and athletic clubs designed to teach children the Greek heritage and promote ethnic endogamy through social contacts among marriageables in youth conferences, dances, and other cultural events. Such activities would provide opportunities for the young to associate with fellow Greeks with the hope that romantic attachments would develop followed eventually by marriage within the Greek group, thereby perpetuating ethnic cohesion[1] in the host society.

The Greek family has also played an important role in the survival of the Hellenic heritage through the socialization of the young and emphasis on intra-ethnic marital selection. The parents not only teach their children Greek language and culture[2] but also encourage them to participate in Greek organizations and associate with youngsters of the Greek community. When parents fail to perform these tasks, the child's chances of selecting a mate from the same ethnic group decrease considerably. Parents' influence on mate selection is described by Kephart and Jedlicka (1991, 174) as follows:

> Parents' influence on choice of mate begins long before their children mature. Through teaching and through examples, parents impart to their children values, beliefs, norms, and even mate-selection etiquette appropriate for their social class and ethnic group. At maturity this knowledge forms a part of the mental framework that directs love and attraction toward opposite-sex individuals. Through this process, parents transmit the culture and the family heritage from generation to generation.

The efforts of the Greek family and organizations to foster ethnic endogamy, however, have been influenced by structural aspects of the Greek communities (e.g., sex ratio, population size, and heterogeneity), as well as by the cultural and institutional changes that have occurred in Canada over the years. These changes reduce opportunities for ethnic endogamy among Greek Canadians and consequently create barriers to intergenerational transmission of the Hellenic cultural heritage.

The objective of this paper is to examine interethnic marriage and how it affects ethnic culture and identity, with special reference to Greek Canadians. Interethnic marriage, as analyzed here, is a marital union outside one's ethnic group. Another commonly used term for interethnic marriage is *ethnic exogamy*. More specifically I will try to answer three questions: (1) What are the major trends in interethnic marriages among Greek Canadians and what factors contribute to their increase over the years? (2) What are the effects of interethnic marriages on ethnic culture and identity? (3) What can be done to minimize the impact of ethnic intermarriages on Greek culture in Canada?

How common is ethnic exogamy among Greek Canadians? George Vlassis (1953), in his examination of early Greek settlements in Canada before 1900, reports that many pioneer Greek immigrant males took Canadian women for wives simply because Greek women were not available. Because of the increase of Greek female immigrants to Canada after 1905, the ratio of the sexes became more balanced; consequently, endogamous marriages increased. Throughout the decades, ethnic endogamy among Greek Canadians remained relatively strong. According to the 1931 and 1951 editions of *Statistics Canada*, Greek Canadians had much greater endogamy than other ethnic groups. With the influx of post-World War II Greek immigrants to Canada in the 1960s and 1970s, the percentage of Greek endogamous marriages also increased. According to Ram (1990, 217), in 1981 at least 92 percent of Greek-born wives were married to husbands of the same ethnic origin. This compares with 83 percent of the Greek-born husbands married to wives of the same ethnic origin. The rest of the Greek-born had married spouses who were Canadian (non-Greek) or came from a different country (see Table 1). The higher percentage of ethnic exogamy among Greek-born males suggests that males had more opportunities to associate with non-Greek females in the place of work and other social activities. Greek immigrant women, on the other hand, were less exposed to persons from other ethnic origins because they had fewer opportunities for occupational integration into the host society. Ram (1990, 226) also argues that "foreign born women are unable to find suitable partners from other origins who can provide them with a better social status than they are able to attain by marrying a person from their own group."

Table 1

ETHNIC ORIGIN OF SPOUSES MARRIED TO
GREEK-BORN CANADIANS (1981)

Gender	Canada	Spouse's Ethnic Origin Different Country	Greece
Males (husbands)	10.9%	6.5%	82.6%
Females (wives)	3.1%	4.8%	92.1%

Source: *Statistics Canada*, 1981.

Note: The data do not distinguish marriages between members of two different countries of birth (e.g., husband born in Greece and wife of Greek parentage born in Egypt) that may not strictly be interethnic marriages.

Since the mid-1980s, the Greek Canadian minority is becoming increasingly more exogamous. According to the Greek Orthodox Metropolis of Canada, 53.3 percent of the weddings performed by

Greek Orthodox churches in Canada during a five-year period (1989–93) were interethnic (mixed) marriages (see Table 2). The percentage of interethnic marriages is probably higher, since marriages between Greek Orthodox Christians and other Eastern Orthodox Christians (e.g., Serbs, Russians, etc.) are not recorded as "mixed" by the Greek Orthodox Metropolis of Canada. Furthermore, interethnic civil marriages (registered or common-law) and marriages of Greek Canadians in non-Greek Orthodox churches or synagogues are not included in the Greek Orthodox Metropolis' official statistics. Although there is no statistical information of the place of birth of exogamous individuals, impressionistic evidence suggests that second- and third-generation Greek Canadians[3] are more likely than immigrants to have chosen a spouse outside their ethno-religious group.

The rapid increase of interethnic marriages among second- and third-generation Greek Canadians has created much anxiety and confusion among parents as well as among leaders of the Church and other Greek Canadian organizations. Interethnic marriages, many parents and community leaders argue, will diminish the Greek family's role in maintaining the vitality of Greek language and culture in the host society. As Herberg (1989, 205) indicates:

Ethnic culture becomes a family affair, of collective practice and celebration of cultural heritage. And, if endogamy is a powerful cohesion influence, then ethnic-group fertility can be seen as the progenitor of the ethnic group itself, a *sine qua non* of ethnic-group cultural maintenance.

Table 2
GREEK CHURCH WEDDINGS IN CANADA
(January 1, 1989, to December 31, 1993)

Year	Greek Orthodox Marriages		Mixed Marriages	
	No.	Percent	No.	Percent
1989	443	44.7	548	55.3
1990*	—	—	—	—
1991	559	52.0	516	48.0
1992	481	46.7	550	53.3
1993	501	47.4	556	52.6
Total	1,984	47.76	2,170	52.24

Source: Greek Orthodox Metropolis of Canada, Toronto, Ontario

*Statistics for 1990 have not been processed by the Metropolis.

The Greek Canadian trend of ethnic exogamy reflects the overall increase in Greek Orthodox exogamous marriages in North and South America. According to statistical data of the Greek Orthodox Archdiocese in New York, during the 1980s and 1990s there has been a steady increase of mixed marriages in the United States, Canada, and South America combined. For example, in 1976, 47 percent of Greek Orthodox Church weddings were mixed (outside the Eastern Orthodox group). In 1992, the percentage increased to nearly 66 percent (see Table 3). The average of mixed marriages in the United States, Canada, and South America combined (1976–92) was 60 percent. More research is needed, however, to examine other variables related to ethnic exogamy. For example, is the propensity to intermarry higher among second-generation males than females? What is the religious affiliation of the non-Greek spouse? Which of the parents (father or mother) is most likely to be responsible for inculcating and retaining Hellenic principles and practices? Do the children of exogamous marriages trace their cultural heritage through the father or mother? Are interethnic marriages associated with upward social mobility, especially with positions of political power? Are interethnic marriages more likely to end in divorce than ethnically endogamous marriages?

Table 3

GREEK CHURCH WEDDINGS IN THE UNITED STATES AND CANADA
(January 1 to December 31, 1992)

Type of Marriage	U.S.A.		Canada		Total	
	No.	Pct.	No.	Pct.	No.	Pct.
Between Greek Orthodox	1,424	32.6	481	46.65	1,905	35.28
Mixed	2,945	67.4	550	53.35	3,495	64.72
Total	4,369	100	1,031	100	5,400	100

Source: Statistics of Greek Orthodox Archdiocese of North and South America, New York, 1992.

What factors contribute to the increase of ethnic exogamy among Greek Canadians? Sociological analysis suggests that there are at least four interrelated factors which contribute to the increase of interethnic marriages in a multicultural society:

1. *Social integration of ethnic group members.* According to Gordon (1964), interethnic marriage is the inevitable by-product of social integration (structural assimilation), the entrance of ethnic group members into the socioeconomic matrix of the host society. For example, the entrance of young Greek Canadians into colleges, universities, and social clubs, and the occupational structure of the host society, facilitate social interaction with non-Greeks and therefore increase the chances for interethnic dating and marriage. This argument is supported by research indicating that we tend to marry those with whom we associate at work, school, or other places that involve social interaction with out-group members of the opposite sex.

2. *Occupational heterogeneity is another important predictor of interethnic marriage.* Ram (1990, 226) suggests that the heterogeneous nature of certain ethnic groups exposes people to differential opportunity for intergroup contact and therefore to a differential propensity to intermarry. Thus, the more occupationally diverse the Greek minority becomes, the higher the chances of its members' seeking non-Greek marriage partners. Ram (1990, 221) writes:

> A group's greater occupational heterogeneity implies a greater diversification of its members in terms of socioeconomic background. Greater heterogeneity in a group encourages its members to establish contact with members of other groups and therefore provides more opportunity for them to marry outside the group. It also reduces their chances of marrying within their own group.

According to available data, children of Greek immigrants in Canada have attained more years of schooling and higher occupational status than their parents. In one Canadian study (Chimbos 1993, 21–33), over 50 percent of the children of Greek immigrants had received degrees in accounting, law, economics, engineering, computer science, teaching, and social science—all indicating occupational diversity and social integration into the host society.

3. *Decline in overt discrimination against ethnic groups in Canada because of political and legal measures taken by Canadian governments to fight inequality and racism.* The Canadian Charter of Human Rights and Human Rights Commissions at the provincial level are examples of such legal measures. Sociologists argue that discrimination against an ethnic group increases ethnic group cohesion (participation and interaction within the ethnic group) and consequently facilitates ethnic endogamy. Thus, the higher the degree of

discrimination against an ethnic group by the host society, the higher the degree of ethnic ingroup interaction and therefore the higher the chances for ethnic endogamy.

4. *Liberal education, which breaks up traditional ethnic barriers.* As a result of such educational experiences, ethnic group members, as well as middle-class Canadians, acquire more cosmopolitan attitudes and values, and they are more inclined to date and marry outside the ethnic group. It is expected, then, that interethnic marriages are more likely to occur in modern heterogeneous societies characterized by upward social mobility, the philosophy of multiculturalism and minority rights, liberal education, and individual freedom. Gordon (1964, 152) in his earlier analysis of assimilation in American life argued

> In a society of advanced industrialization, mass communications, a high degree of urbanization, heterogeneous contacts, and virtually unlimited mobility, many interests and influences besides those of an ethnic culture will play upon the individual.

Although social and demographic variables are important in explaining rates of interethnic marriages, personal reasons for choosing a mate outside the ethno-religious group cannot be ignored. There are at least three personal reasons why ethnic group members choose and will continue to choose outsiders as marital partners:

1. Individuals may see that ethnic endogamy does not necessarily guarantee marital happiness. Marital survival rates tend to be influenced more by age at marriage and social class rather than by ethnic or religious affiliation.

2. Some individuals consider personality traits and personal resources more important for marital adjustment than ethnic or religious background. Such personal attributes may include self-confidence, nurturance, capacity for love and affection, social skills, academic training, and adaptability to change.

3. Love, and especially romantic love, which fulfills certain psychological needs of individuals, is an important factor in determining marital selection in Western societies. In fact people are socialized to believe that love and romance must precede marriage. Thus, social class and ethnic and religious background are often diminished as criteria of mate selection by interethnic couples in love.

What are the effects of ethnic intermarriages on ethnic culture and identity? Krotki and Reid (1994, 21) have argued that ethnic exogamy is the route to assimilation in the sense that it is through intermarriage that assimilation is both begun and completed. The study of Goldstein and Seigel (1985) in Winnipeg, Manitoba, showed that ethnic exogamy is highly associated with lower levels of ethnic identity and loyalty. Reitz (1980, 114), in his Toronto study, also found that to some extent ethnic exogamy leads to dilution of ethnic culture and creates obstacles to intergenerational ethnic cultural transmission. Not surprisingly the propensity for ethnic exogamy is much greater for the children of mixed marriages. The disappearance of the mother tongue and ethnic values is also higher among children of mixed marriages than among children of endogamous marriages. Ethnic endogamy then becomes an essential institutional practice for the perpetuation of the ethnic group's cultural cohesion. As Herberg (1989, 184) puts it:

> The degree to which endogamous marriage exists within an ethnic group reflects the potential power of the ethnic heritage to hold sway and of the ability of the mutually-reinforcing influences of this and other cohesion forces to create the next generation of the ethnic community. . . . With low endogamy the future of the group's cultural cohesion becomes bleak. Ethnic endogamy can thus be likened to the glue binding the other cohesion factors together in one of the major arenas in which ethnic community cohesion is sustained.

Although an ethnic subculture in a pluralistic society is adversely affected by interethnic marriages, that does not necessarily imply eventual disappearance (total assimilation), especially when immigration from the homeland continues to flow. As Newman (1978, 40) suggests, ethnic subcultures change and adapt to new social and economic conditions without disappearing. It can be argued, however, that a steady increase of interethnic marriages, along with limited or nil immigration from Greece in the next ten years, will adversely affect the social cohesion and political strength (lobby) of the Greek minority in Canada.

The proponents of ethnic endogamy often ask "What can be done to prevent interethnic marriages?" In modern multicultural societies like Canada, where ethnocultural groups experience social integration, occupational heterogeneity, and a decline in overt discrimination, and the young are exposed to liberal education and the values of individualism, interethnic marriages are unavoidable. Parents, knowingly, or unknowingly, may also push the child away from ethnic cultural sources and consequently facilitate interethnic marriages. They may reward the child for activities which lead him or her away from the ethnic group (Elkin 1983, 156). The child, for example, may be rewarded for achievements in public schools or participation in holiday activities and sports of the host society—situations that increase interaction with out-group members.

Perhaps the only "effective" way to prevent ethnic exogamy is to segregate the ethnic group from the larger society (e.g., establishing ethnocultural communities similar to those of the Hutterites and Mennonites). But Greek Canadians prefer social integration rather than social segregation, and as indicated earlier, social integration increases the chances for interethnic marriages. It is unrealistic, then, for Greek Canadians to demand both social integration and ethnic endogamy. These two processes contradict each other.

Since interethnic marriages are difficult to prevent, what can be done to minimize their impact on ethnic group culture? The acceptance of interethnic marriages after the deed is done may be a beneficial alternative for the ethnic community. For example, some sociologists argue that interethnic marriages can be viewed as a means of recruitment for the ethnic group. The Greek community may gain members if the newlywed non-Greek (1) acquires the Greek language and culture, (2) converts to Greek Orthodoxy, and (3) actively participates in the Greek community's institutions and cultural affairs. Impressionistic evidence suggests that some of the newcomers participate in ethnic institutions and contribute to their economic and social growth.

To encourage this process the Church, as well as other Greek Canadian organizations, could make adaptations by encouraging newcomers to involve themselves in Greek community organizations. This would also encourage parents of mixed marriages to send their children to Greek schools, where they can learn Greek language and values and become members of Greek youth organizations. The need for ethnic institutions to adapt to social changes and maintain their social cohesion and culture has been described by Herberg (1989, 87) who writes:

> Since it is suggested that the particular ways in which a group adapts and changes over time [influence] its degree of ethnocultural cohesion, then what we are inspecting when we study cultural cohesion and the

nature of ethnic social organization in a group is the result of all forces to date which influence people to remain members of a particular ethnicity.

Should the Greek Orthodox Church in Canada go to the extreme of shifting from Greek language to English and promote the idea of Pan Orthodox congregations (i.e., putting all Eastern Orthodox churches under the jurisdiction of one archdiocese),[4] its effectiveness in promoting Hellenism and ethnic cohesion will diminish considerably. For example, a multiethnic and English-speaking Eastern Orthodox parish structure will facilitate social interaction among various ethnic groups (e.g., Greeks, Serbs, Bulgarians, Romanians, Russians, Syrians, Albanians) and consequently increase the chances for interethnic marriages significantly. In other words, the Greek Orthodox Church, as a blended religious institution, will cease to function as an intergenerational carrier of Greek language and culture in the host society.

In conclusion, then, the increase of interethnic marriages among Greek Canadians over the years is the inevitable result of social integration and other social and demographic factors which influence the social interaction and values of the marriageable Greek Canadians. Although interethnic marriage adversely affects the ethnic group's cultural cohesion, its impact can be reduced by accommodating the newcomers within the Greek community. Thus, the Greek Orthodox Church, as well as Greek Canadian secular organizations, ought to reevaluate their means for achieving social cohesion and cultural survival and make the necessary adaptations to ongoing social and demographic changes that occur within the Greek Canadian community and the larger society.

FACTORS CONTRIBUTING TO ETHNIC EXOGAMY
AMONG GREEK CANADIANS

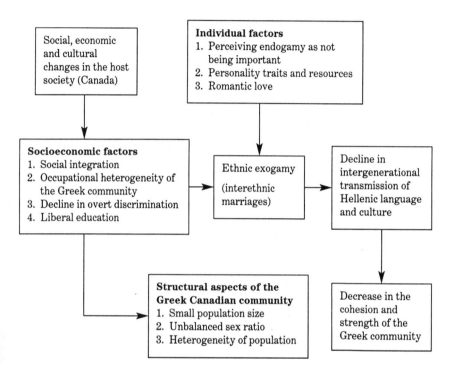

Notes

1. *Ethnic cohesion* refers to membership, involvement, and participation in ethnic organizations and ethnic group life by persons of common ethnic ancestry (Reitz 1980, 109).
2. *Ethnic culture* refers to the total system of ways by which a group of people with a common ethnic ancestry think, feel, and act. The folkways, customs, art, value systems, patterns of recreation, and language of ethnic group members are somewhat dissimilar to those of other groups in a society.
3. Second-generation Greek Canadians are the children of immigrants. The term "third generation" refers to the children of the second-generation Greek Canadians.
4. In a conference at the Antiochian Village in Ligonier, Pennsylvania, U.S.A. (November 30–December 2, 1994), leaders of 11 Orthodox Christian churches with 6 million members in North America came together for the first time to establish an administratively united church with one voice on social, religious, and political issues. The bishops stated that their task in North America is not limited to serving the immigrant and ethnic communities, but has at its very heart the missionary task of making disciples in Canada and the United States.

References

Canadian Government. 1981. *Statistics Canada: Ethnic groups*. Ottawa.

Chimbos, Peter D. 1971. Immigrants' attitudes toward their children's interethnic marriages in a Canadian community. *International Migration Review* 5: 5–16.

_____. 1993. A comparative study of intergenerational mobility: Children of immigrants in Canada and children of the same age cohort in a Greek village of origin. *International Journal of Family and Marriage* 1, 1:21–33.

Elkin, Frederick. 1983. Family socialization and ethnicity. In *The Canadian family*, by K. Ishwaran. Toronto: Gage.

Goldstein, J., and A. Segall. 1985. Ethnic intermarriage and ethnic identity. *Canadian Ethnic Studies* 17 (3):60–90.

Gordon, Milton. 1964. *Assimilation in American life*. New York: Oxford University Press.

Herberg, Edward. 1989. *Ethnic groups in Canada: Adaptation and transition*. Toronto: Nelson, Canada.

Krotki, Karol, and Colin Reid. 1994. Demography of Canadian population by ethnic group. In *Ethnicity and culture in Canada*, by Berry and Laponte. Toronto: University of Toronto Press.

Kephart, William, and Davor Jedlicka. 1991. *The family, society, and the individual*. Toronto: Harper Collins Publishers.

Newman, William. 1978. Theoretical perspectives for the analysis of social pluralism. In *The Canadian ethnic mosaic*, by Leo Driedger. Toronto:

McClelland Stewart.

Ram, Bali. 1990. Intermarriage among ethnic groups. In *Ethnic demography*, by Shiva S. Halli *et al.* Ottawa: Carleton University Press.

Reitz, Jeffrey. 1980. *The survival of ethnic groups*. Toronto: McGraw-Hill Ryerson Ltd.

Vlassis, George. 1953. *The Greeks in Canada*. Ottawa: Leclerc Printers Ltd.

7. "I don't have to worry about money anymore, and I can live like a lady": Greek immigrant women and assimilation

ANNA KARPATHAKIS

Assimilation theory and research have been based on the assumption that as immigrants assimilate into American society, they acquire wealth, power, freedom, and rights in all social spheres; assimilation for women in turn has entailed the expectation that women will acquire these resources in the family and in particular in relation to the husband. Neither theory nor research asks the question what it is precisely that immigrants assimilated into. An examination of Greek immigrant women's capacity to manage their families' financial affairs reveals a very different reality for working-class women who achieve upward mobility through their family's purchase of a small family business. Economic assimilation for the immigrant family enables immigrant women to leave the informal labor market and focus their full-time energies on being housewives and mothers. Part of the changes in the family relations resulting from this is the man's taking responsibility for managing the family's financial affairs. For the women, this is a welcome change, a change which symbolizes their now being able to live like "ladies." This is an American image and ideology of a "lady," in which the women and the children are taken care of and protected by the man. The paper is based on 80 in-depth interviews with Greek immigrant women who arrived in New York between the ages of 12 and 40.

GIVEN THE POLITICAL history and nature of the concept of "assimilation" (i.e., entry into and identification with host society institu-

151

tions), the term is laden with ideological issues and values (see Bash 1979; Fernandez Kelly and Schaufler 1996). The assimilation "formula" in both popular and social-scientific thought has until recently been as follows: as immigrants "assimilate" into American society, they achieve upward mobility and acquire greater individual freedoms, power, and rights in all spheres of life. For women, the expectation follows, assimilation entails the acquisition of rights, freedoms, power, and privileges in the home and in relation to the husband. Assimilation is assumed to free the woman from Old World patriarchy and enable her to enter into more gender-equal relations. These assumptions underlie much of our examination of immigrant women's experiences in the United States and seem to be especially prevalent in studies of Greek Americans and Greek immigrant women.

Patriarchy, a dynamic and changing nexus of structures, is not a quantifiable institution that exists in more-or-less forms; patriarchy rather takes a variety of historically specific forms (see, for example, French 1985; Gordon 1990; Nielsen 1990). Given the existing class and gender structurations of the host-society institutions, as immigrants assimilate they interweave themselves into a different set of preexisting patriarchal ideologies and relations unique to American society (see, for example, Hondagneu-Sotelo 1992; Scourby 1989).

While assimilation is a long-term process and in this sense acquires a life and dynamic of its own (see, for example, Gordon 1964 for a macrostructural view of assimilation), it also entails the immigrants' own short-term decisions, choices, and selective behavior (see, for example, Kim and Hurh 1993). On the micro level, this process of assimilation or "Americanization" entails the creation of a new self within particular matrices of gender, class, and ethnic relations (see, for example, Hooks 1994; Ng 1987; Kimmel 1995; Muszynski 1989 for discussions on how race/ethnicity, class, and gender are essential elements of all identities). Becoming "American" by definition entails the immigrants' creation of a new self based on the interconnections of ethnic, gender, and class realities unique to American society.

The overwhelming majority of Greek immigrants to the United States have been from the rural and urban working classes in Greece (INS 1990). Whether at the beginning or in the second half of the 20th century, these immigrants have, like other immigrants, upon their arrival entered primarily the secondary and tertiary labor markets, often working for coethnics in diverse industries (see, for example,

Burgess 1913; Saloutos 1964; Lovell-Troy 1990; Bailey and Waldinger 1991; Marshall 1987; Sassen-Koob 1987; Sassen 1991). Like other immigrants, Greek immigrant men and women also enter the segmented labor markets of the host society (see Piore and Doeringer 1971; Bonacich 1973 for labor market segmentation by race, gender, or age of workers). While the men enter the restaurant, florist, and construction industries, women are found in the garment, restaurant, florist, and hotel industries.

Although not recognized for their economic roles, Greek immigrant women have historically contributed to their families' income through a variety of means. Depending on the region of the country the immigrants settled in, immigrant women at the turn of the century contributed to their families' income by running boardinghouses for fellow immigrant men, doing piecework (in the garment industry), and working in the family business (see, for example, Kiriazis 1989; Papanikolas 1987; Patterson 1989). The recent immigrant women have taken full-time jobs in the growing service industries and often supplement this income by taking in additional piecework, sharing the superintendent work for apartment buildings with their husbands, baby-sitting, and occasionally working as domestics (Karpathakis 1993).

The working-class Greek immigrant woman is the least understood among all Greek immigrants to the United States. While some describe her as a loving and passive figure under the iron fist of the husband-father figure (see, for example, Callinicos 1990; Scourby 1984; Demos 1994), others describe her as a powerful figure, taking active roles in her family's affairs; Kourvetaris (1981), for example, describes the Greek immigrant woman as being the wife, mother, public relations person, and economic advisor of her family. Similarly, the Greek immigrant woman takes on the responsibility of creating and maintaining important community institutions and groups (Karpathakis 1996).

Anthropologists studying peasant and urban working-class women in Greece similarly paint complex and often contradictory pictures (see, for example, Dubisch's 1986 volume on Greek women). In the meantime, anthropological research points to the diversity of Greek family structures and gender relations in Greece throughout the 19th and 20th centuries (Campbell 1964; Loizos and Papataxiarchis 1991; Sutton 1986). Sutton (in this volume) argues that there is no one Greek family structure; rather, there is a diversity of family structures and relations, depending on a number of factors, including region of origin and family migration histories. Although Greece is a patriarchal society, there is no one unique form or set of patriarchal relations characterizing the Greek family. There is thus little in the literature that will help us create a background standard with which we can compare the Greek immigrant women's assimilation into American society.

While it is difficult to reconstruct the overall patriarchal relations in the immigrant family and trace their transitions to a new nexus of relations, it is nevertheless possible to choose one dimension in and through which power is exercised in the family and trace this to women whose families have achieved economic assimilation, i.e., upward mobility. It is only this way that we can begin to understand, for example, how economic assimilation (upward mobility) for Greek immigrant women entails their entry and incorporation into a different set of patriarchal relations.

Greek immigrants in the United States have traditionally achieved upward mobility through the purchase of a small family business in a limited number of business sectors. Earlier immigrants purchased or begun the family business in the restaurant, candy, and florist industries; the more recent immigrants have (as a result of changing economic structures in the host society) entered the restaurant and construction sectors (see, for example, Moskos 1979 and Katsas 1992).

Upward mobility through the purchase of a small family business brings a new economic ease and social status for the family, to which status the woman contributes by leaving her low-paying job in the secondary labor market and dedicating her full-time energies to raising and caring for the children and husband. In the process, she "gives up" some of her previous responsibilities, including the management of the family's daily finances and her position as *noikokyra*. This process of upward mobility or economic assimilation and its concomitant changes in the family is accompanied by the women's creation of an ideology whose core is the concept of a "lady." With the help of the American mass media, intent on presenting America as a class-free society (Mantsios 1995), the women create an ideal image of a gendered "American" that guides them in their assimilation. This class and gendered American image is that of a "lady," and the immigrant women work towards living up to and living through this ideal image. Contrasted to the American image of a "lady" is the Greek working-class image of a *noikokyra* (house-mistress), which the women's working-class mothers and other working-class women uphold as their parallel ideal. While a "lady" is protected and financially taken care of by her husband, the *noikokyra* is the mistress (i.e., female version of a master) of her household and family. While the "lady" dwells within the domestic sphere, the *noikokyra* is found in the various social spheres to which her responsibilities to her family may take her. As the working-class women thus maintain their position as the mistresses of their households, the upwardly mobile (often younger) women willingly hurry into their new roles and positions as "ladies."

The transition from a *noikokyra* to a "lady" can be seen through the family's changing financial management patterns and the ways in which the women explain and justify these changes. Three management patterns are found among the immigrants, independent of length of stay in the United States. This paper will focus on immigrant women from the working class and those whose families of procreation achieved upward mobility through the purchase of a small family business (primarily in the restaurant, construction, or florist industries). This latter group are the women who experienced a radical transformation in their roles and responsibilities as their families' financial managers.

Description of methods, sample, and site

This paper is based on ethnographic research carried out with Greek immigrants in Astoria, Flushing, and Bayside, New York, between February 1990 and October 1996. The analysis for this paper is based on 80 unstructured in-depth interviews carried out with immigrant women. Participant observation was also carried out in a variety of public and private sites, including community organizations and agencies, women's coffee gatherings in their homes, and also during several family gatherings.

The women appearing in the sample ranged in age from 24 to 68, all having arrived in the United States after the age of 12. The women in the sample came from diverse rural and urban regions in Greece, from both the mainland and the islands; and all but 5 of the 80 women came from working-class families. The average level of formal education among the women was 9.3 years. Of the women in the sample, 38 were at the time of the interviews members of the working class, and 42 had entered the lower middle class through the purchase of a small family business. To the extent that the aim of the project was to understand assimilation as it relates to class and gender rather than to gauge the statistical extent of the process, the sample was constructed so as to have as equal a number of working- and lower-middle-class women as possible; as such, the paper does not claim to be representative of the community's class structures. The term *lower middle class* refers to those who own and run a small family business, while *working class* refers to those who engage in manual labor; members of the working class lack a college education and do not own a business.

Thirty of the interviews were tape-recorded and later transcribed, but the remaining 50 interviewees refused to be tape-recorded. For these, extensive notes were taken during the interviews and then recorded immediately after the interview sessions. The direct quotes appearing in the text are portions of only the recorded and transcribed interviews.

Managing the money

Immigrants described three different patterns of managing their family's daily financial affairs. The first, "she [the woman] knows best," is one in which the woman is the *noikokyra;* the second is a comanagement pattern in which both the husband and wife are responsible for managing the family's finances and both the men and the women are respected in their abilities to be *noikokyreoi* (house-masters and house-mistresses); the third is a managerial pattern in which "he [the man] knows best," and it is the management style in which the man is the *noikokyris* (house-master).

"She knows best"—The *noikokyra*. In this management pattern, the working-class husband brings home the paycheck, signs it, and gives it to the wife, trusting that she knows best. All wages (husband's, wife's, nonmarried Greek-born working children's) go into a "common pot," and the woman apportions the money among the various weekly and monthly expenses. She balances the checkbook (where available), pays the bills, does the shopping, and finally allots various family members enough for their weekly expenses. While the husband and working children receive a set (negotiated) amount for their personal expenses, the woman's and non-working children's personal expenses are taken care of from the household's running account; all who receive a weekly amount are expected to eventually return the unused portion to the common pot (in the form of a gift or shopping for the household) or deposit it in the savings account.

While the woman takes care to inform her husband of the daily financial matters, it is still she who nevertheless is more intimately aware of these issues. Maria, a part-time office maintenance worker married to a grillman, says:

> The bankbooks are in the drawer. If he [her husband] asks, I point him to the books. . . . I guess he checks once or twice a year—no, not even that much. If I have problems I'll go to him, but otherwise he doesn't get involved. Who are we kidding? The man doesn't even know how much the mortgage is. When my brother asked him, he didn't know. His response was, "ask the accountant"—meaning me.

The woman in this type of management pattern similarly manages the nonmarried working children's earnings. That having been said and recognized, however, differences emerge in the mother's role in the management of the children's earnings depending on the children's place of birth. Immigrant women who may rule (at times with an iron fist) over the husbands' and the Greek-born children's earnings have less managerial control over their American-born working children's earnings. Susan for example, a 19-year-old college student, holds a part-time job at a neighborhood grocery shop. When describing how "she manages" her money, Susan said,

> I save for my trips to Greece in the summer and pay for my books. I save $40 a week. . . . I went to Greece [and] wanted to go again, and when I told my mother she told me they—my parents—didn't have the money for me to go two summers in a row. So I said I could save, and she said she would help. . . . She gives me $500 and I pay for the rest. . . . The thing I like about my mother is that she never asked me for any of my money. Once in a while she'll comment about my spending too much and not saving enough, but she never took any of my money. Like Eleni, the girl that works here in the evenings and weekends, she has to give her mother her money each week. My mother never did that with me. My father doesn't say anything either.

Immigrant children's earnings are more tightly managed by the mother. She will negotiate with the children the amounts to be apportioned to their personal expenses, the household account, and their savings. Eleni, the young woman that Susan referred to, is 17 and has been contributing to her family's income for two years. Eleni arrived in New York with her parents and older brothers in the early 1980s. Eleni described a very different process from Susan's for managing her weekly wages of $100.

> I usually keep 30 or 40 and give the rest to my mother. It depends. She saves 30 or $40 for me and uses the rest for the house. . . . She'll use maybe 20 or $30 for the house. She does the same for my brother. . . . My father? No. My father never said a word to me about money. My father likes to spoil me. My mother is the cheap one. . . . I'm not sure what I'll use the money for. I thought for a car, but my mother told me to forget about throwing my money away. . . . It was the same for my brother. . . . We want to buy a house. I saved over $2,000 in two years.

The following case is indicative of how the woman manages her family's daily finances. Michael came home and as usual left the envelope with his pay (a combination of cash and a check) on the dining room table for his wife, Maria. Maria walked over, examined the money, and followed Michael into the other room. When she returned, Maria described the weekly ritual as follows:

> When he comes home he leaves the money on the table. Before he goes out he'll take what he'll need for the week. . . . I tell him what we need, what we have to do. Some weeks he can take more, others less. This week is my birthday. He needs more because he wants to buy me a gift. There is a dress I saw and want and he and the kids will get it for me. . . . They'll give me the money in the card and I'll pick it up. . . . I know the expenses in the house because I pay the bills, do the banking. . . . I know the details of our finances more than he does. . . . He doesn't even know how to write a check. What am I going to do? Fight with him? It's my job anyway. Do I do his job? No. Why should I expect him to do mine?

Women point to the strict gender division of labor in the family and make the argument that their responsibilities as their families' daily financial managers are simply part of their responsibilities as *noikokyres*, as "wives," as "mothers"; the reason for this is that the woman, who knows the family's affairs more intimately than the man, is better equipped to budget the money, do the banking, and pay the bills. The men, for example, said Katina, do not understand "cooking and feeding the family. They don't know where a glass is in the kitchen. How are they going to know where the milk is in the super-market? How would they know how much a gallon of milk costs? How many gallons you need a week? No. I'm the *noikokyra*. Doing these things—doing the shopping, paying the bills—is my responsibility."

That women explain their role as their family's financial manager as part of their traditional gender-defined responsibilities is seen when women who at times see themselves as overburdened with work and responsibilities fear being defined as "whiners" and "complainers." One woman, for example, added, "I am not complaining. After all, it's my job to do these things. What kind of a mother would I be if I didn't take care of my family's needs? What kind of a *noikokyrio* ['household'] would I be running if I didn't do these things?"

Often enough, a husband whose wife is the family's financial manager will joke about his wife's being the "accountant" or the "boss," and at times even refer to her as "Scrooge." During a nameday celebration, Nikolas was asked by his nephew if he wanted to try a new accountant; Nikolas pointed to his wife, Maria, sitting a few feet away, and said in a loud voice for all to hear, "Ask the boss. I lost that position when I got married." While such responses are treated as jokes and provoke short bursts of laughter from the men gathered, the women will respond with a wave of the hand and return to their conversation. Indeed, after a few laughs from the men and smiles from the women sitting at the other end of the room, Maria's nephew directed the question to her and she responded, "If he's a friend of yours and he's good, we'll try him. And don't listen to your uncle. He jokes in the most childish ways."

Katina, a 43-year-old mother of two married to a waiter added: "I don't know why you men complain. Why are we bosses? Because we do the things we are supposed to do for our families?"

These frequent jokes among working-class family gatherings are rooted in a patriarchal society in which the man is formally (although often not in reality) the head of the family and ideally responsible for the family's financial matters. While the men may joke (and complain) about their wives' being the "bosses" or "accountants" or both, the women remind them (and one another) that this right has tradition-ally been part of their responsibilities as *noikokyres* to their families.

Comanagers—The *noikokyreoi*. In this pattern, the husband and wife are comanagers of the family's daily finances, and both spouses are referred to as *noikokyreoi* (house-masters and -mistresses).

Financial discussions are often informal, taking the form of consultations and information exchange. Again, the weekly earnings are a "common pot," and both mentally apportion the available resources to the numerous bills. To the extent that the woman does the daily housekeeping, however, she is more familiar with daily expenses and so she explains or defines more than the husband the precise apportioning of the funds. Finally, each spouse discusses his or her personal expenses for the coming days, and more often than not these are negotiated; again, the man takes or is given a set amount for the week, while the woman's expenses are part of the daily running account. While it is the woman who more often does the banking, the husband may also do so, depending on the spouses' working schedules.

This management pattern is exemplified by George and Maria, a working-class couple. George is a painter, and Maria works part-time by sewing for friends and neighbors. Maria described her family's financial management in the following terms:

> I remember when he brought home his first paycheck, put it on the table, and said, "Come, we have to talk." We sat, figured out the expenses—the rent, electricity, phone, food, everything. . . . I was only 18. I didn't have the chance to learn these things from my mother. But he saw how his parents did it and he taught me how to budget. . . . Sometimes I do it, other times he does it, depending on what's going on with the kids. You know, all these years he never said no to me about anything I wanted. But I am not wasteful. . . . Ah, once in a while I have to say no to him. He likes going out to nightclubs. When I say no he listens. He always asks, "Maria, can we go out this week?" or "Maria, can I go out this week?" I tell him the truth, and he the same, and things go well. We fought for money twice, years ago. He wanted to treat his friends to dinner, and I told him we couldn't afford it. Instead we had parties here. The women cooked and we had a wonderful time. We're not rich. When one goes astray the other has to pull him back.

The children's earnings in the comanager pattern are also managed primarily by the mother. The mother negotiates with the children how much they will need for their weekly expenses, how much will be contributed to the household account, and how much will be saved in the children's accounts. One man explained his family's reasons for his wife's managing the children's money:

In the family both the wife and the husband have their own important work. It's important for the two to work together. When one goes astray or makes a mistake the other corrects things. It's important for both the man and the woman to have a good head and be reasonable. But it's different when the mother does these things. The children know that the mother will never take one penny from them to do something else with it. The mother is closer with the children; they trust her more. It's important that your children feel they are treated fairly. I'm the father. . . . A father may have a short temper and say things he may regret, but a mother's relationship with her children is different.

This comanagement pattern is found both in working-class marriages, regardless of the woman's employment history, and in lower-middle-class families in which the wife is gainfully employed in or outside of the family business. Not one lower-middle-class couple in which only the husband was gainfully employed exhibited this form of financial management.

"He knows best"—The *noikokyris*. This third management style was found in 67 percent of lower-middle-class marriages in which the woman was not employed and also in 71 percent of the seven working-class families in which the woman arrived as an immigrant bride or had lived in New York for a considerably shorter time than the husband before the marriage.

In this third financial management style, the husband's position as the actual head of the family is publicly acknowledged. He knows the family's finances in detail, since he manages the money, pays the bills, does the banking, and gives his wife a weekly allowance for household and personal expenses. Lower-middle-class women's weekly allowances tend to be, as is often described by the women themselves, "overgenerous." Kathy's family's financial management is typical of this pattern. Married to a successful small-business owner, Kathy is a housewife and mother of two; she is given a weekly allowance of $200 and an additional $200 at the end of each month (i.e., a total of $1,000 every month). With this money, Kathy pays for the weekly shopping and the children's less expensive recreation needs (e.g., movies, small gifts for classmates' and friends' birthdays). Her husband pays the mortgage, utilities, insurance, and doctors' bills, and gives Kathy additional money for holiday or other clothes shopping for the family. Kathy said:

The money I get is more than enough. I go to the supermarket, do some small shopping for the children . . . birthday gifts for their friends and things like that. He does the savings, pays all the bills. Whatever I want is mine. All I have to do is ask. . . . Things for the house like decorations I charge. It's not part of the daily expenses I keep. He's very generous. Next month there is a wedding we are invited to. He will give me the money for the dress and shoes, and he will give the money in the envelope [gift card]. . . . He has taken out health and life insurance; the children and I will never be in need no matter what.

Working-class women who described their husbands as being the family's financial managers, on the other hand, often complained of the insufficient amounts allotted to the running account for food and other small-item expenses. Katerina, who says that her husband's wages reach the mid-30s, complained that "he's too tight with money sometimes. He's obsessed with saving. . . . He doesn't really understand how to run a household, and we end up fighting."

Because of the mechanics of bill paying, lower-middle-class women whose husbands pay the bills from the office were at the time of the interviews the least likely to know the family's weekly income in detail, the costs of running bills (such as telephone and other utilities), and the balance in the checking account. As one 29-year-old mother of two said, "I don't know these things. [My husband] takes care of all the bills. The bills come; sometimes I open them, sometimes I don't"; again, "Why would I know? He does all these things at the store." Only seven of the 32 nonemployed lower-middle-class women could tell for certain the running balance in the checking account and if and how much had been deposited in the savings account in the previous two weeks.

In attempting to answer the question, "Without revealing the exact amount, do you know your husband's weekly or monthly earnings?" some women tried to "figure out" the husband's earnings indirectly from the expenses paid (information that, as was mentioned above, was not certain). As one 39-year-old woman married to a small-restaurant owner said,

I know how much he gives me, and I could probably guess with the bills, but I couldn't say. It varies depending on the week. Two or three thousand a week, maybe 15 hundred. I don't know. It varies. . . . I know that a few months ago he opened up an account for the little one and there is already three or four thousand in it. Then we gave 80,000 for

the house and another 20 to fix it up. Money we saved in four years, so
he's making good money. Fifteen or 18 hundred a week. Maybe a little
more or less, but not much.

Working-class women whose husbands managed their families'
finances, on the other hand, did know, often in great detail, the family's finances. When asked about the mechanics of the weekly budgeting, all but one of these women described the following process: the
husband will sit at the kitchen table with the weekly or monthly bills,
and the woman, who is busy with other activities, will occasionally
approach and "take a look at what he's doing." The women take the
opportunity to ask questions and, when necessary, intercede, make
suggestions, and negotiate on particular items. In short, even in cases
where the husband is formally the family's financial manager, the
working-class woman is knowledgeable about details and influences
the managing process in ways that the lower-middle-class woman
cannot because of the separation of home and the place from which
the bills are paid. (More on this later.)

While working-class women whose husbands are the financial
managers for the family take an active role in the management of
their children's earnings, their lower-middle- and middle-class coun-
terparts do not. Instead, the children's earnings are more often managed by the father or by the children themselves. Mary is married to
an accountant who (along with his brother) owns three donut shops.
As Mary said regarding her children's earnings from their part-time
jobs in their father's business:

> Their money is theirs to do with as they like. They make 60 or $70 a
> week. Their father has taken care of their college funds. This is their
> spending money. My husband deals with money, so he knows best. My
> father was not good with money, so my mother would do everything.
> She can't understand how I can't manage money. I took after my father.
> It's one of the things I can't do. I can't teach my sons to do something
> I can't do. Their father takes care of these things. I mean he . . . has a
> college degree in accounting. I went to college for two semesters and
> studied linguistics. What do I understand about money? [Laughing]
> Besides spending it, that is.

Transformations of management patterns

Families' financial management arrangements do change over time. While in two cases the spouse responsible for managing the family's daily finances experienced a long illness and the other spouse took on this responsibility, all other transformations in the family's financial management patterns accompanied a major change in the family's finances; for the majority of the women, this meant that the husband or the family bought or began a small business. Upward mobility— i.e., economic assimilation—emerged as the factor most closely related to changes in financial management patterns.

The women described three changes in the ways in which their families' finances were managed. The first two changes, from "she knows best" or "he knows best" to "comanagement," were described by women who gave an intergenerational perspective, comparing their parents' management style with the management style they developed with their husbands. Only three women in the sample described an intragenerational change (in their own marriage) that resulted in their acquiring more of the management responsibilities; in one case, the change resulted after the couple, who had been living with the man's parents, moved into their own apartment. In the second case, the man lost the small family business. And in the third case, after 20 years of marriage, the husband (a successful business owner) agreed to invest in a small but successful restaurant business for his wife.

The third and most frequent change that women discussed was the shift from "she knows best" or "comanagement" to "he knows best," and this was found first among nonemployed women who entered the lower middle classes. The majority of immigrant women whose families' financial management processes underwent changes, in other words, described processes through which they lost some or most of their managing capacity. We will in this section focus on the third and most frequently discussed change, namely, the transformation from "she knows best" or "comanagement" to "he knows best."

The purchase of the small family business reduces the woman's purview over the family's finances because the small business removes the management process out of the home and takes it into the office or the small business—i.e., the realm that the man inhabits and commands. First, since restaurants and florist shops (two of the three sectors in which Greek immigrant business owners are found) are cash-based businesses, the income tends to be received in the form of cash. The fluidity and variations in the amount of cash make it difficult for the woman to monitor and manage unless she works the cash register or keeps the books for the business. The woman who does not work in the family business lacks the opportunities to monitor the business's cash flow and thereby the family income. This is a special problem for women whose husbands are in business partnerships, because this removes the money pool even one step further from the women's reach and monitoring.

Second, since small-business owners receive their income in the form of cash, it is often unwise to bring the cash home late at night after work; to safeguard against possible robberies, the men do the banking near the place of work and bring smaller amounts of money home. Seventy-three percent of the lower-middle-class families in the sample did their major banking at an institution located near the business. While an additional 9 percent lived in the same neighborhood as the family business, the women said that their husbands did the banking throughout the week as the need arose.

As one 32-year-old woman said:

> It was dangerous for him to come home with cash. If anybody sees this, it's dangerous. He would come home on the train at 10 or 11 at night. It's dangerous. So we opened up an account at a bank near the store. It made sense that he would do these things—you know, do the banking and pay the bills from there. At the beginning I would go and help in the store and do these things, but when my little one came I couldn't. . . . So he started doing all these things.

Eight of the 32 lower-middle-class couples in which the woman is not gainfully employed have maintained a checking or savings account at a bank near the home, where the woman will do the "local banking." These tend to be accounts for the smaller household bills and special-project accounts—in one case it was a savings account to finance the family's upcoming trip to Greece, in another case it was a savings account for the daughter planning to buy a car.

Short of special-project savings accounts and the checking account for the smaller household bills, which some of the women insist on maintaining after the purchase of the business, the man takes on the responsibility for the actual budgeting of the money, doing the major banking (savings, insurance, IRAs) and the major bill paying (e.g. mortgage, credit cards, and in some cases utilities). It is in this way that the man acquires greater control over major assets and greater opportunities to monitor the family's financial affairs as well as the woman's own expenses.

As the following case illustrates, the husband, writing monthly checks for credit cards that the wife uses, has greater opportunity to monitor even her movements—an opportunity the wife lacks. Lena, a 28-year-old mother of one, described the changes in how the family's daily financial decisions were made after her husband opened up a business with his brother.

> We kept the checking and savings account we had at Astoria Federal, but he opened up another account at Citibank near the store. He brings home a check or cash and I do the shopping, pay some of the small bills. ... He pays the mortgage from the other account and the credit cards ... the bigger bills. They're my credit cards, but he pays for them from the store. . . . The poor man doesn't use his cards; he doesn't get the chance to go anywhere. He works from morning till night. Before we got the store he would go the coffeehouse, but now he doesn't even do that. Many things changed since we bought the business. I would sit for hours trying to balance the stupid checkbook: rent, electricity, phone, credit cards. Write out a thousand checks a month. Now I don't have to worry about it.

As immigrant women and their families achieve upward mobility, the women withdraw from the labor force—a luxury their working-class mothers or they themselves could not have afforded just a few years earlier. In the meantime, the families will most likely follow and reinvent the tradition of buying a house in the suburbs and leaving the immigrant neighborhood. Hicksville and Blue Point on Long Island, Whitestone and Bayside in Queens, are just some of the towns that these upwardly mobile Greek immigrants move to, another step in their entry and incorporation into American mainstream institutions. There, the women will be even further removed from the family business; i.e., one step further removed from their family's source of livelihood.

"Living like a lady"

The small family-owned business is for the immigrants the achievement of their immigrant goals; both the men and the women spend years "dreaming" of the day they will own a small business and live in comfort. This new economic ease means that the family can now earn respectability and enjoy their newly acquired social status; more than this, the woman contributes to the family's social status by leaving the labor force. For the women, this new economic ease means that they, unlike their working-class mothers and sisters, have the opportunity to leave their low-paying and menial jobs in the sweatshops, piecework in the garment industry, and minimum-wage jobs as cashiers and salesgirls in the neighborhood shops—jobs they held while helping their husbands begin and secure the business. The women can finally dedicate their time to being full-time mothers and wives; they can finally be "ladies"; they and their families can finally receive the respect of their friends and neighbors.

The women speak passionately about their experiences growing up in the working class. Whether they grew up in the urban or the rural areas in Greece, those women who immigrated as adults speak bitterly about leaving school at an early age to begin working. While the women in the rural areas talk about entering the fields immediately after elementary school, the women from the urban areas talk about their childhood experiences of being taught a trade (usually sewing). Those women who immigrated in their early or middle teens talk about the after-school jobs they held, helping their parents to meet the bills. All of the women talk about the *steriseis* (lack of necessities) they experienced growing up.

Litsa arrived in New York in 1971 at the age of 12. While the extremity and intensity of her experiences were similar to those of only three other women in the sample, the poignancy of her account bears mention. Litsa's father held two jobs as a kitchen aide, and her mother worked as a seamstress in a local sweatshop and supplemented the family's income by taking in additional piecework. Her father died in the late 1970s, and her older brother dropped out of his last year of high school to take a full-time job. As Litsa is sipping her coffee, her voice wavers and her eyes are red and moist.

The winter of '78 came, when we had the big storm, and I didn't have a coat, boots, a scarf. I went to work that week in a light jacket and secretary pumps. I waited for the bus after work. . . . I was so cold I was feeling faint. I looked up and prayed such a deep prayer, such a hard prayer, it frightened me. I was so desperate, cold, frightened. I said, "God, you owe me. You owe my family. You did enough harm to us, now you have to give us something good. I am cold. I need a coat, God, I need boots. You don't have to give me a scarf, but at least a coat and boots." [Laughing as she wipes the tears from her eyes] I was bargaining with God. He didn't have to give me everything, just some things to make life easier.

Given the often difficult experiences of these women's early years, the family business is a reprieve. While the women take an active role in the early stages of the family business, they stop working and contributing to it once the business acquires economic stability. This is especially the case for women whose family businesses are in the restaurant sector, because the work is difficult and seen as demeaning to women. When asked why they stopped working in the restaurant or coffee shop, the women would emphatically point out that "restaurant work is not for a woman." As Mary, a 32-year-old mother of three, said, "If he needs me I'll go in and stay at the register, but I won't work there like I used to. Waiting on tables, lifting trays of food and dirty dishes, is no work for a woman." Grace, a 41-year-old mother of two and wife of the owner of a small but successful restaurant, is sitting across from her mother at the kitchen table of her newly purchased home; smiling, Grace says:

> I chose to stop working. I chose not to have to worry about bills. I could have continued to work in the restaurant, my mother could have stayed with the kids. But I wanted to be a full-time mother. I wanted to pick up my children from school. . . . I wanted to be home if my kids got sick. I wanted a clear head, not worrying about money and bills all the time. All my life we worried about money. I started working when I was 15. . . . Worked immediately after high school with two jobs. I deserve to live like a lady. My mother deserves to live like a lady. She couldn't. Ten years after we got married, I finally can. Listen, isn't this why we left home anyway? To be able to live this way? In comfort?

The women's descriptions and definitions of a "lady" are a mixture of elements from American popular culture and imagery (especially as these images are presented in the mass media), a negation of the women's working-class and Greek backgrounds, and a uniquely ethnic community standard of involvement in the Greek Orthodox Church (the most Americanized of all immigrant institutions—see for example Jusdanis 1991, on this last point).

The term "lady" is an American one and the concept too is American, as is shown by the fact that bilingual women interviewed in both languages would alternate between the two languages and use the term "lady" rather than the term's Greek demotic counterpart, *kyra*. Grace, quoted above, for example, spoke in Greek until she began searching for the appropriate term; she then said "lady" and even made the argument that although she could have used the term *kyra*, it would have been inaccurate; it was then that she went on to describe and define the term "lady" by rapidly switching between Greek and English. The strictly Greek-speaking women (i.e., women who have not yet had the opportunity to internalize and re-create American gender imagery), when asked to define *kyra*, argued that the term *kyra* implies a "strong," "powerful," "intelligent" woman in "command of her family." Bilingual women were hesitant to use the term *kyra* as equivalent to the term "lady" and pointed out that it is not the same term.

Despite the frequent humor of the women's descriptions (and their own poking fun at the image they are describing), the women are describing an image and reality they have only recently begun to explore. Being or becoming a "lady" is a conscious and deliberate choice that the women make as they look around them in popular American magazines and television shows for guidance on new definitions of propriety and etiquette. Some of the women's descriptions of a "lady" are humorous stereotypes of wealthy women presented on television programs. As one 38-year-old woman said,

I would see all those women on TV and think, they are ladies. Will I ever be this way? . . . You know, the women don't work, they're always dressed beautifully, their makeup is perfect. Do you know who my favorite character was when I was growing up? Krystle on *Dynasty*. I wanted to be like her.

A "lady" lives in material comfort, does not work, and need not worry about financial matters. A "lady" is always "dressed pretty," wears "perfect makeup," "can shop at the best stores"—and always "with her husband's money." Marina, 26, who prides herself on having "the best humor around," said that if she

could paint a picture of a lady it would look like this: Her hair is perfectly done, her makeup real but natural, her lips outlined lightly. She is beautiful, of course, standing on the porch of her huge, expensive home—tall, slim; long legs; soft, powdered skin; expensive outfit (my preferred colors are the natural colors, of course); of course has lots of money. Oh yes, her new car is just on the side of the house there, parked in this big driveway. You know, she is the woman we all want to be. She is classy. That's what I want to be. Classy.

"Ladies" work only if they have a college education and a well-paying career; as Marina said, "She's a high-powered lawyer or executive or something. Certainly doesn't work in sewing like I did for years."

A "lady" is a much-sought-after reality, in contradistinction to the women's own working-class and Greek backgrounds. Being a "lady" is on one level a rejection of being Greek, and it entails and announces the woman's "Americanization." With further probing, the women add even more characteristics to the list of a "lady's" persona: "she doesn't yell like Greeks do," "she has table manners," "she is not a loudmouth like Greeks are," "she knows how to dress in style," "she is not a *horiatissa* [Greek woman from a village]." Often enough, when extended families living on both sides of the ocean come together for holidays, lower-middle-class immigrant women will refer to their relatives from Greece as "villagers," "hicks," and "crude." As one woman said of her newly married cousin who visited her family in New York with her husband, "She should take classes on table manners. On how ladies behave." Regarding another relative visiting from Greece, one woman said, "I'm embarrassed to introduce her to my friends. She's a *horiatissa* ['villager']."

A "lady" is active in the ethnic community, but only in groups that are defined as appropriate for a "lady." A Greek American "lady," for example, is active in the P.T.A. and other groups related to the Greek Orthodox Church; women active in the Philoptochos (Friends of the Poor) chapter of their church, the most prestigious of all the women's Church-related groups, are often described as "ladies." To the extent that only the women who are not gainfully employed have the opportunity to be active members of these groups, the Church-related groups have always been composed of the more financially successful immigrant women (see for example Coumantaros 1982 for the nature and demands of this volunteer group). Marina, cited above, says that, "when I have my kids I will be active in all sorts of things. I will go into that Philoptochos with my Fendi bag and Gucci jacket and all the women will say, 'This is Mrs. . . . . .' And they will treat me like a lady, the way they treat one another."

Grace, cited above, describes a "lady" as "someone who doesn't have to worry about money. She . . . lets the man be a man. I don't have to fight with my husband about money the way my mother fought with my father. He can finally do it all on his own, and I can enjoy things." That the women "let the man be a man," as Grace described the process, is important given the women's own histories of being *noikokyres* (house-mistresses). The newly acquired economic ease means that the women can now leave this role as *noikokyres* and enter the new one of "ladies."

Being a "lady" of course necessitates a "gentleman" who allows and enables the "lady" to live free of stress and worry; since he is a financially successful man, he is responsible for meeting the family's needs, including finances. The man is an abundant provider who never "allows his family to lack for anything"; while the house is always "filled with food and everything for the children and guests," at the same time the man provides for the family's long-term financial needs—there is no longer the need for tight budgeting; he no longer must choose between the present and the morrow, because he can provide for both.

At the same time, the man must be a "gentleman." This image is again in contradistinction to a "Greek man," who is "loud," "crude," "rude," and lacking in "finesse." It is important that the women enable the men to fulfill this new role, and if need be the women are willing to work hard to create these new men for themselves and their families. The women often talk, again in humorous ways, of the "small lessons" they had to give their husbands in their attempts to create them or turn them into "gentlemen." One woman said, "I had to teach him to open the car door. He would keep forgetting and I would have to keep reminding him." Said another woman, "I taught him to help me with my coat. He got frustrated a few times and yelled, but I persevered."

Often enough, the women bring the children to join in their crusades to create "gentlemen" out of their husbands. One woman recounted a story in which her 10-year-old daughter was giving her father lessons in how to be a "gentleman." Again, one woman told the story of her daughter's telling her father, "Daddy, gentlemen bring ladies flowers for their birthday. Where are mommy's flowers?"

One woman, who said that she had "given up all attempts to reform her husband" and has since returned to work in the family business on a part-time basis, recounted a birthday dinner she and her daughters prepared for her husband. Mariana explains,

> my little one [her eight-year-old daughter] said to him, "Daddy, did you

know that gentlemen are supposed to hold the chair for the lady to sit?" The poor man looked so confused and so hurt; he yelled out, "I am not a gentleman. I am not an Englishman. I come from the mountains of Greece, and your mother is not a cripple. She can get her own chair." That's when I realized how funny this whole thing was—trying to become something I wasn't, trying to make my husband and my family into something we weren't. I can always rely on my husband to remind me "apo pou krataei i skoufia mou [literal translation: nature/origins of my hat]."

Mariana and her husband were one of the four lower-middle-class married couples in the sample who insisted that it was important for them to maintain their understanding of their own class and ethnic origins; it was this way, explained Mariana, that she hoped to raise her daughters, with the hope that they would "become good people, successful in whatever they do, and be good *noikokyres*."

As the majority of the women described the process, however, the men were only too willing to take on their new roles as gentlemen. Indeed, the successful small-business owners take pride in their new-found ability to afford a new home, fine (or at least better) clothing, and furnishings and decorative items for their homes and families. They are proud of the fact that their wives can now spend hours in the shops the way their neighbors, or at least other Americans, seem to be doing. Michael, a 45-year-old restaurant owner, smiles proudly as his wife shows off the pearl necklace he gave her for Christmas. Later in the evening, Michael's 27-year-old sister-in-law says: "You know all these years they worked like dogs. I never thought he would feel so much pride at his being able to afford this $400 necklace. What is a man? Just small things to make him happy. My sister is finally a lady."

Conclusion

Assimilation theory and research on assimilation have till now assumed that entering American institutions was a positive and progressive event for those immigrants who succeed in it—progressive both in the sense that it happened in stages and in the sense that it improved their lot. But we have failed to ask what it is that immigrants are assimilating into and, in particular, what assimilation entails for women.

This paper has asked the question how upward mobility—i.e., economic assimilation—has affected Greek immigrant women's position and role as their families' financial managers; the focus was on working-class immigrant women who achieved upward mobility through the purchase of a small family business. It was discovered that this particular group of women lose and often willingly give up their roles as their families' financial managers as this position and responsibility are taken over by the husbands.

The newly acquired small family business is for these immigrant women the fulfillment of their original reasons for and intent in leaving home and immigrating to a strange land. The new business is the reality of their immigrant success story and provides the women (and their families) with an economic ease that they had till now only aspired to. This economic ease also means that the women can now leave behind the low-paying jobs in the informal labor market and devote their energies to being full-time mothers and housewives; in short, it enables the women to enter and live out the American ideology of the woman as a "lady."

References

Bailey, Thomas, and Roger Waldinger. 1991. The changing ethnic/racial division of labor. In *Dual city: Restructuring New York*, ed. John H. Mollenkopf and Manuel Castells. New York: Russel Sage Foundation.

Bash, Harry H. 1979. *Sociology, race, and ethnicity: A critique of American ideological intrusions upon sociological theory*. New York: Gordon and Breach.

Bonacich, Edna. 1973. A theory of middleman minorities. *American Sociological Review* 38 (October): 583–94.

Burgess, Thomas. 1913. *Greeks in America*. Boston: Sherman, French & Co.

Callinicos, Constance. 1990. *American Aphrodite*. New York. Pella.

———. 1991. Arranged marriage in Greek America: The modern picture bride. In *New directions in Greek American studies*, ed. Dan Georgakas and Charles C. Moskos, 161–79. New York: Pella.

Campbell, John K. 1964. *Honour, family, and patronage: A study of institutions and moral values in a Greek mountain village*. Oxford: Oxford University Press.

Coumantaros, Stella. 1982. The Greek Orthodox ladies Philoptochos Society and the Greek American community. In *The Greek American community in transition*, ed. Harry Psomiades and Alice Scourby, 191–96. New York: Pella.

Demos, Vassiliki. 1994. Marital choice, gender, and the reproduction of Greek ethnicity. In *Ethnic women: A multiple status reality*, ed. Vassiliki Demos and Marcia Texler Segal. Dix Hills, N.Y.: General Hall Inc. Publishers.

Dubisch, Jill. 1986. *Gender and power in rural Greece*. Princeton: Princeton University Press.

Fernandez Kelly, Patricia M., and Richard Schaufler. 1996. Divided fates: Immigrant children and the new assimilation. In *The new second generation*, ed. Alejandro Portes, 114–45. New York: Russel Sage Foundation.

French, Marilyn. 1985. *Beyond power: On women, men, and morals*. New York: Summit Books.

Gordon, Linda. 1990. The new feminist scholarship on the welfare state. In *Women, the state, and welfare*, ed. Linda Gordon. Madison: University of Wisconsin Press.

Gordon, Milton M. 1964. *Assimilation in American life: The role of race, religion, and national origins*. New York: Oxford University Press.

Hondagneu-Sotelo, Pierette. 1992. Overcoming patriarchal constraints: The reconstruction of gender relations among Mexican immigrant men and women. *Gender & Society* 6: 393–415.

Hooks, Bell. 1994. *Outlaw culture: Resisting representations*. New York: Routledge.

Jusdanis, Gregory. 1991. Greek Americans and the diaspora. *Diaspora* 1, no. 2: 209–22.

Karpathakis, Anna. 1993. Sojourners and settlers: Greek immigrants of Astoria, New York. Ph.D. diss., Columbia University, New York.

————. 1998. Managing and producing ethnic and religious identities: Greek immigrant men and women Church volunteers. In *The power of gender in religion*, ed. Georgie Ann Weatherby and Susan A. Farrell. New York: McGraw Hill.

Katsas, Gregory. 1992. Differential self-employment among the foreign-born and the native-born: The case of Greeks in New York. Ph.D. diss., Fordham University, New York City.

Kim, Kwang Chung, and Moo Won Hurh. 1993. Beyond assimilation and pluralism: Syncretic sociocultural adaptation of Korean immigrants in the U.S. *Racial and Ethnic Studies* 16: 696–713.

Kimmel, Michael S. 1995. Judaism, masculinity, and feminism. In *Through the prism of gender: Readings on sex and gender*, ed. Maxine Baca Zinn, Pierette Hondagneu-Sotelo, and Michael A. Messner. Needham Heights, Mass.: Allyn and Bacon.

Kiriazis, James W. 1989. *Children of the Colossus: The Rhodian Greek immigrants in the United States*. New York: AMS Press Inc.

Kourvetaris, George. 1981. The Greek American family. In *Ethnic families in America: Patterns and variations*, ed. Charles H. Mindel and Robert W. Habenstein. New York: Elsevier.

Lovell-Troy, Lawrence Allen. 1990. *The social basis of ethnic enterprise: Greeks in the pizza business*. New York: Garland Publishing.

Loizos, Peter, and Evthymios Papataxiarchis, ed. 1991. *Contested identities: Gender and kinship in modern Greece*. Princeton: Princeton University Press.

Mantsios, Gregory. 1995. Media magic: Making class invisible. In *Race, class, and gender in the United States: An integrated study*, ed. Paula S. Rothenberg. New York: St. Martin's Press.

Marshall, Adrianna. 1987. New Immigrants in New York's economy. In *New immigrants in New York*, ed. Nancy Foner. New York: Columbia University Press.

Moskos, Charles. 1979. *Greek Americans: Struggle and success.* New Brunswick, N.J.: Transaction Books.

Muszynski, Alicja. 1989. What is patriarchy? In *Race, class, and gender: Bonds and barriers*, ed. Jesse Vorst et al., 65–86. Winnipeg: Society for Socialist Studies.

Nielsen, Joyce McCar. 1990. *Sex and gender in society: Perspectives on stratification..*Prospect Heights, Ill.: Waveland Press.

Ng, Roxana. 1987. Immigrant women in the labor force: An overview of present knowledge and research gaps. *Resources for Feminist Research* 16, 1.

Papanikolas, Helen. 1987. *Aimilia Georgios. Emily George.* Salt Lake City: University of Utah Press.

Patterson, George J. 1989. *The unassimilated Greeks of Denver.* New York: AMS Press.

Piore, Michael J., and Peter B. Doeringer. 1971. *Internal labor markets and manpower analysis.* Lexington, Mass.: Heath.

Saloutos, Theodore. 1964. *The Greeks in the United States.* Cambridge: Harvard University Press.

Sassen, Saskia. 1991. The informal economy. In *Dual city: Restructuring New York*, ed. John H. Mollenkopf and Manuel Castells. New York: Russel Sage Foundation.

Sassen-Koob, Saskia. 1987. Growth and informalization at the core: A preliminary report on New York City. In *The capitalist city*, ed. Michael Peter Smith and Joe R. Feagin. Oxford: Blackwell Publishers.

Scourby, Alice. 1984. *The Greek Americans.* Boston: Twayne Publishers.

————. 1989. The interweave of gender and ethnicity: The case of Greek Americans. In *The ethnic enigma: The salience of ethnicity of European-origin groups*, ed. Peter Kivisto. Philadelphia: The Balch Institute Press.

Sutton, Susan Buck. 1986. Family and work: New patterns for village women in Athens. *Journal of Modern Greek Studies* 4: 33–49.

U.S. Immigration and Naturalization Service. 1990. *Immigration and Naturalization Service statistical yearbook.* Washington, D.C.

8. On being gay and Greek American: A Heraclean labor to fuse identities

PERRY N. HALKITIS

New York University

Tolerance of the gay lifestyle remains an elusive reality within Greek American society. The powerful forces of family and Church have created an existence for gay Greek Americans in which it is often impossible to fuse sexual and ethnic identity into one's life, because of the prescribed roles of men in Greek American society. The struggle to have these identities coexist within the society is so overwhelming that many Greek American gay men abandon their ethnic roots in order to fulfill a life that is true to their sexuality. This reality is examined through the words of five such men.

> In the case of a society dominated by men who sequester their wives and daughters, denigrate the female role in reproduction, erect monuments to male genitalia, have sex with sons of their peers . . . it is not inappropriate to refer to a reign of the phallus. Classical Athens was such a society.
> —Eva C. Keuls, *The Reign of the Phallus*

DURING MY LAST TRIP to Greece, I thought often of my father. As a young man, he left Kos, a small island off the coast of Turkey, to join his brother in New York City. The poverty that had overtaken Greece after World War II necessitated this move for him and thousands of others like him. To date in the United States, approximately 3 million individuals trace their ancestry to Greece (Dabilis 1990).

By all accounts, my father was a success in *Ameriki*, as Greek

177

Americans call the United States. He married within his culture (a girl from his hometown), ran a successful business, owned a home, and provided his two sons with a parochial school education where they learned about his culture, his language, his religion, and his values.

I, the older of the two sons and the first-born of his generation, was the proclaimed prince. In my youth, I was surrounded by thousands of other Greek Americans in Astoria, Queens, New York, where I was entrenched in the working of our culture. My closest friends, my neighbors, teachers, and role models were all Greek Americans. For the greater part of my childhood, other ethnic groups were an abstraction safely confined to the workings of our television or to novels we were asked to read by the non-Greek American teachers at our school.

My path was clear—identify a Greek American woman, engage her, complete my education, marry my bride, and continue the lineage of which we are so proud. I followed that path for years. This existence is typical of many who are either first- or second-generation Greek Americans (Callinicos 1990).

As I sit at a café on the harbor of Kos, I wonder how my father, who died in 1992, would assess me now. His first-born, as others would indicate, was the fulfillment of his father's expectations. The laborer had raised a scholar for a son—a son, who as my father often noted, would not have to "work with his hands" and come home with [the] smell of feta and kasseri and olive oil all over his skin. All was right except for one thing: the son was gay.

In the pages that follow, I hope to provide a critical view of the reality of the gay Greek Americans. If we are to accept the 10 percent population figure assigned to gays and lesbians in the United States (Michaels 1996), then perhaps upwards of 300,000 gay men and women of Greek heritage reside in our country. Their existence is not an easy one as one grapples with the expectations and the requisites of a culture deeply immersed in family and religion.

Throughout this essay and discussions to follow, I caution the readers to not use the terms *Greek* and *Greek American* synonymously. These are two very distinct beings. Embedded and secure within their culture, those who live in Greece are confident in their ethnic identity. For Greek Americans, the struggle is greater as they seek to perpetuate their culture, their language, their values, and their religion in an environment where the lines of ethnic and cultural identity are often blurred. And it is this very struggle to maintain and perpetuate the Greek culture within the mosaic of the United States that has led to views that are often conservative and unaccepting of difference and that have created a complicated reality for the gay sons like me:

> The attitude of Greeks towards homosexuality in America is more conservative and more negative than that of the Greeks of Greece, because the Greek Americans are closer to the Church and stay more attached to the old traditions as a way of defense and resistance against integration into American society.

Finally, the quotation that opens this essay (Keuls, 1985) needs always to be remembered as we proceed through this discussion, for the world of the ancient Athenians and the existence of "modern" Greek Americans represent two polar opposites. The world of fun-loving gods, where homosexual acts were incorporated into the society, has given way to a culture where religion and family have branded homosexuality as the ultimate taboo. In our strides forward, our "modern" Greek world has taken many steps back, and our task of fusing our sexual and ethnic identities into a rational whole represents a task as enormous as any that the demigod Herakles undertook. Further, this fusion must occur in an environment in which the essence of existence is already heavily burdened by complications of the AIDS epidemic (Halkitis 1998).

My ultimate goal is to move beyond the stereotypical, limp-wristed impression of gays in our society, and rather to demonstrate the individuality that each person brings to his own life as he grapples with a sexual orientation that is often in great conflict with the Greek American culture. I have intentionally chosen to write solely about Greek American gay men, feeling inadequate in my preparation to write of lesbians. For those interested in a companion to this essay, I direct you to a piece written by Leah Fygetakis (1997).

The Approach

To drive this discussion, I draw upon the experiences and words of four who have shared their thoughts about these matters with me in a variety of ways. I also draw upon my own experience as a gay Greek American man.

Four of the men identify themselves as gay and Greek American. One is not gay-identified in that he labels himself a heterosexual man, lives his business and personal life as such, and occasionally has sex with other men. From a behavioral perspective, he is a heterosexually identified MSM (a man who has sex with men but who considers himself heterosexual).

It is here that a distinction should made. Gay identity refers to a sensibility of one's self as a gay man, an immersion of one's self into a community of others like one. These men practice same-sex behavior, and exist in a realm that supports and normalizes this behavior. There are others, like the man described above, who also practice this sexual behavior but who do not possess a gay identity. Gay identity, in turn, is a psychological and communal reality that includes but also transcends the constitutive, emotional, and sexual attractions to others of the same sex (Sullivan 1995). Those who possess this identity label themselves as queer, gay, or homosexual. It is this identification that creates a struggle for Greek American men.

The men to whom I refer throughout the essay shall have their confidentiality protected for the purposes of this discussion, and thus will never be referred to by name. This cohort consists of men who range in age from 28 to 40 and reside in the metropolitan areas of the eastern United Sates. The group is intentionally diverse: three were born of Greek parents who immigrated to the United States; one was born to a Greek father and non-Greek mother; and one immigrated to the United Sates from Greece. Three of the men identify themselves as single, one is in a partnership relationship with another man, and as indicated above, one is married with children. Professionally, these five men are also very different from one other. Two possess advanced degrees, one works as a printing manager, one is a financial officer of a university, and the last is an investment counselor. All but one speak Greek and were raised within the Greek Orthodox Church, and one is HIV seropositive.

Because these data are anecdotal, the number of experiences described is small, and there is therefore no attempt to label this work as research or to draw broad generalizations about all Greek American men. The realities described must be viewed in this light as those of only a small subset of all gay Greek American men in the United States. Nonetheless, I will let the words and ideas of these men guide the discussion.

Sources of conflict: The church and the family

At the center of the struggle for gay Greek Americans exists a powerful and often overwhelming culture—a system of values, rites, and traditions that a set of individuals share and that bonds them. To understand the Greek American culture means to understand the importance of the religion and the family, for it is these two central institutions that drive Greek American culture as we know it.

Yet one may argue that church and family are the sources of conflict for any gay man attempting to establish his sexual identity regardless of ethnicity or race. To this, I would argue that these elements in the Greek American culture cannot be viewed as the same as those of other European ethnicities. As Fygetakis notes (1997), there is a tendency for researchers in the United States to treat the white race as a monolithic ethnic culture, a conglomeration of all Europeans that assumes a commonality among all, regardless of ethnic origins. This tendency lends one to make generalizations about all, regardless of their ancestry, and assumes that the experiences of those from Sweden or Switzerland are identical to those from Portugal, Romania, or Greece. I raise this point because I believe it to be an important one in the discussion. While one may argue that church and family are certainly sources of conflict for many who struggle with their gay identity, these institutions and their manifestations are uniquely different, and yield a differential impact depending upon one's ethnic origins. In this view, the structure of the church and family among the Greek Americans needs to be examined as entities that are unique to those whose ancestral roots can be traced to Greece.

Ekklisia, the Church, and *oikoyenia*, the family, are the solid foundations upon which the Greek American culture exists. They are the cement and the water that bond together to create the basis of the cultural structure. And for Greek Americans, they create the foundation and wall of protection in the American society, where both these entities are certainly in jeopardy as we approach the 21st century.

More than 95 percent of all Greek Americans identify their religious affiliation as Greek Orthodox (Clogg 1992). Within the doctrines of this religion exists a very negative and pessimistic view of homosexuality. Yet for new Greek American immigrants, the Church was the centerpiece of the *koinotis* (community) as they struggled to maintain the values, language, and religion of the "old country" (Bonnage 1997). Today, numerous Greek Orthodox churches exist in all of the metropolitan areas of the United States. The greatest of these is the community of St. Demetrios in Astoria, New York, which because of its size was granted cathedral status by the Archdiocese of North and South America. Often these *koinotites* also established schools affiliated with the churches in which to educate the future generations in the Greek and Christian traditions.

Thus, for many of us, the Church was an inescapable reality. When we were young boys, religion was a centerpiece of our existence. We attended church services, received religious training, and were immersed in an environment of mysticism and fear that only the most secure of individuals could comprehend. As the scents of incense and burning candles filled our senses, and as we witnessed the sacraments of baptism and marriage, one could not help but wonder how our gay identities would fuse with a religion that often appeared intolerant of change. And in fact, the inability of the Greek Orthodox Church to move forward is best typified by its elders, who to this day sport wardrobes which are throwbacks to the Byzantine Empire. One of the men describes this aspect of his life when he says, "I was very religious during my teenage years until I realized that the same religion made me unhappy." Similarly, another notes,

> I wanted so desperately to love the Church. It is what I knew. On weekends, I would go to church with my *yaya*, who placed her handkerchief on the floor for me to kneel on when it was time to pray. As an adult, this memory still lives in my mind. . . . I also remember my mother telling me that she could not receive communion because she was menstruating, and the priest who told me he should slap me when, at age 13, I told him during confession that I had looked at porno magazines. This stuff all confused me. . . . I was pretty sure the Church would not be happy with me being gay.

Yet unlike the vociferous Catholic Church and its loud and clear intolerance of homosexuality, the Greek Orthodox Church is more silent (yet just as intolerant) on such matters. The voices of the patriarch and archbishops rarely sound as loudly as those of the pope and cardinals on these matters. Yet in this silence there exists an equally clear and equally intolerant doctrine towards homosexuality (The Orthodox View 1993). In this view, homosexuality is an enormous sin and an attack on the sanctity of the family. Homosexuality is not to be tolerated, and homosexuals are sanctioned to treatment to cure them of their sexual ailments.

In response to such intolerance and in hopes of opening a discussion about their religion, gay, lesbian, and bisexual Eastern Orthodox Christians (including Greeks, Russians, and others) have founded chapters of AXIOS throughout the United Sates. (A similar organization among gay Catholics, Dignity, also exists.) The organization first emerged in 1980 in Los Angeles and has since founded chapters in over ten cities, including New York; Washington, D.C.; San Francisco; and Las Vegas (AXIOS 1997, 3–4). AXIOS, whose name means truly worthy and deserving, was founded to address the issues of human sexuality within Eastern Christianity and "in order to affirm that gay men and women can live an active life of prayer and witness" (AXIOS 1997, 1).

Yet the impact of religion on the existence of a young man beginning to grapple with his sexuality is inescapable, and the intolerance perpetuated by the Church is also intimately tied to the dynamics of the Greek American family, which is guided by and immersed in the religious doctrine. One of the men reflects on this matter as follows:

> The Church is very stringent regarding its views on sexuality (and just about everything else), so there really is no room within Greek Orthodoxy for the gay lifestyle. Since family and the Church are so intertwined, especially in the U.S., where the Church is the link back to the homeland, coming out to one's family or looking to one's family for support or guidance becomes almost impossible, and a young gay man would have to look elsewhere. This is unfortunate, because it produces the potential for a young gay man to be driven "underground," only experiencing the sexual aspects of the gay culture without experiencing the many positive benefits of it.

It is the same doctrine that condemns gay men that also exalts marriage and procreation, which then become revered as the ultimate accomplishment for Greek American youth. One need solely attend a Greek American wedding with all its pageantry to realize this phenomenon:

> I remember the wedding of my cousin Tony, in which I served as an usher. As is customary, we greeted the guests as they left the church, only to be heralded by the typical comment "Kai sta thika sou," suggesting that the family looked forward to the day on which you too would achieve this great goal of marriage. As I stood there wondering why my partner had not accompanied me to this event, I remained

dumbfounded, unable to provide a response to all the well-wishers.

Similarly, another describes the inescapable role of Greek American men in regard to marriage as follows:

> They [Greek American men] do what they're supposed to do for the culture. They find a woman and get married. It's what they're taught to care about. This is what they're accustomed to. This is a comfort zone for them. So something like being gay, is something that they keep separate or can't deal with. I think it's a cultural thing, a fear through ignorance.

Thus, for the Greek American who is struggling with gay identity formation, the obstacles in surmounting the cultural rules established so strongly by the family and the Church are enormous. For us, there must be an ability to see beyond the confines established, to reassess and reconsider what we have been taught is the norm, and to take a leap of faith that allows us to realize our own sexual identities while attempting to remain intact, as a whole.

But the workings of the culture make no room for such decision-making, since the family and the Church work in synchronicity to assure that one day every one of us would find a nice Greek American woman and perpetuate the tradition: "Due primarily to the pressures placed on all men to marry, have children, and carry on the family name, it becomes very difficult to openly live out the gay lifestyle."

In fact, the Church works diligently to assure this reality, and most Greek Orthodox churches in the United Sates provide ample opportunities for this hope to be realized. The Greek Orthodox Youth of America (GOYA) provides such an opportunity where young Greek American adolescents gather to socialize with their peers within the confines of the Church and with the loving support of the family. Here, in a type of Church-sanctioned dating service, young men and women have the opportunity to identify their future partners. "All but one of my girlfriends during adolescence was met in this manner."

Religion and family for Greek Americans are perhaps best typified during the religious holidays when families gather in celebration of their culture and of their god. The greatest of these in the Orthodox tradition is Easter, when Greek Americans gather for Midnight Mass with their families, with lit candles of holy light, and return home to brand their doors with crosses made by the holy light and to celebrate with lamb, and eggs dyed red, and soups made with the internal organs of the beast. Even for the one of the men who was raised Roman Catholic, such events were typical of his upbringing: "We celebrated Greek Easter with the red eggs and Midnight Mass and all." So too, discussions at these family gatherings often revolve around marriage and procreation. One of the men recalls several holiday dinners when he was asked why he wasn't married, and one in particular:

> At Christmas dinner in 1994, I was asked why I wasn't married. I tried to answer in many different ways, when my mother asked me in a kidding manner if I was gay. And I answered in a very serious way, "Yes."

Thus to understand the struggles that gay Greek American men face, one must look directly to the intimately tied workings of the Church and the family. It is here that the perpetuation of intolerance and bigotry finds it roots, and it is from within this structure that the gay Greek American male must hope to emerge in search of an existence that allows him to both accept and fulfill his sexuality while not losing the heritage in which he was raised. As Fygetakis notes (1997), it is the intolerance perpetuated by the Church that in turn drives the family, and thus makes establishing a cohesive identity so difficult for gay and lesbian Greek Americans.

I raise one other point about the Church and the family to drive this point home. Intolerance, albeit greater towards gay Greek American men and women, is also experienced by heterosexual Greek American men and women should they act in a manner other than has been prescribed for them. (I have often refereed to this set of rules as the Greek American Handbook of Proper Behavior.) Consider the young Greek American man who chooses to marry a Puerto Rican, a person outside his faith and his culture, without requiring her to convert to Greek Orthodoxy, or the Greek American woman who at age 30 has made a conscious decision not to have children, or my dearest friend, a successful businessman who at age 35 lives with his 25-year-old Venezuelan girlfriend whom at the present he does not intend to marry. These too are deviations from the norm which often receive negative reactions. In the words of the father of my friend, "How can you possibly be happy?" It is as if any deviation from the prescription must necessitate an existence that is miserable and unfulfilled, simply because it is different.

The emergence of the gay self within
the Greek American culture

It is against this powerful backdrop of culture that gay Greek Americans grapple to realize their sexual orientation. Numerous theorists (McDonald 1982; Troiden 1979) have considered the emergence of gay identity and have described a linear progression through a stage-like model that incorporates self-realization, disclosure, and integration of one's gay identity into other aspects of one's life. Troiden (1979) describes the difficulty of this phenomenon, suggesting that gay men grow up with heterosexual scripts that specify heterosexually appropriate choices of sexual partners and behaviors. Thus, gay men are forced to reevaluate the cultural and societal scripts and establish a new script that fits their existence. One of the cohort describes this reassessment as follows:

> This was in Athens in 1974. I met a 26-year-old guy in a subway station. I went with him to his place and we had sex. We continued our relationship for three years. He was very nice and mature and helped me to accept and love myself for being gay. I would say he educated me. He taught me that being gay is not only sex, but is a totally different way of living, thinking, and acting that straight people . . . that we are different.

It may be argued that in emerging as a gay man, the Greek American travels through an emotional self-realization, followed by disclosure of one's identity to others, and ultimately to integration of gay identity into one's being. The processes of self-realization, disclosure, and integration are complicated ones regardless of one's ethnic identity, as society never has endorsed sexual expressions other than the heterosexual one. Rather all aspects of society, including the family, the church, business, and the military, have long championed heterosexual dispositions, as if orientation were a matter of choice and heterosexuality is the only correct one (Vargo 1998). And certainly within the realm of the Greek American culture this is a tenet that is upheld. Young men who grapple with their sexual identity struggle to determine whether their feelings are solely those of a "passing phase." In a culture where gay role models are nowhere to be found, the struggle becomes an intense one. For those of us raised in such an environment, passing through the required stages of heterosexual courtship was all we knew, and we thus undertook the steps that had been ordained for us.

Like others, our only source of information about our initial gay feelings were books, movies, or other materials. In the United States, some 15 percent of gay men realize that they are gay in this manner (Dank 1971):

> I remember being 17 years old. The movie *Making Love* had just been released and I asked my girlfriend at the time to go see it. I remember the audience screaming in disgust as the two men went to bed. But I was aroused.

The inability to identify role models, coupled with the power of the family and of the religion, make this self-realization or self-disclosure extremely difficult for gay Greek Americans. For some there is no choice, as is the case for one of the men, who is married and heterosexually identified but who has sex with men when the opportunity exists. In some ways, one might argue that he has made the easier choice, at least on the surface, of fulfilling the clearly delineated expectation of the Greek American culture. Yet in this apparently "normal" existence, he sneaks away to bathhouses to have sex with anonymous men when his wife is occupied, while all the time concerned that he will be seen. But perhaps this existence is the one that has been prescribed for us by our tradition. No one thought twice of the ancient Athenian man who sought sexual and intellectual stimulation from another man as an escape from the antagonism of the heterosexual relationship (Keuls 1985). One point needs to be repeated: gay identity and homosexual sex are two distinct constructs. The MSM, in some cases, has no gay identity at all.

For those who chose to realize our gay identity, the struggle is more complex, as we attempt to assert our own existence, which because of its very essence is viewed as an attack on the foundation of Greek American culture. One of the men describes this difficulty in reevaluating and assimilating his identity, and describes his ability to do this only after his father had died:

> I waited until my parents died. It was easier then to be gay and to become active in the gay community. Before then, I struggled with it a great deal.

These words describe the struggle encountered by gay Greek American men as they seek to live their lives as gay men while at the

same time maintaining their ethnic identity. This is, however, a difficult balancing act, as one determines the steps that are essential to
live a complete life. At the heart of this struggle for these men as well
as for other gay men is the issue of sexual identity-disclosure commonly referred to as "coming out." The act of coming out to one's
friends and family is viewed by theorists as an element of the developmental track to self-actualization of the gay man. Troiden (1979)
describes this process as identity-assumption which begins with the
internal self-realization and the desire to express the self as a gay
man and ultimately reaches the comfort level of labeling one's self as
gay.

It is here that gay Greek American men encounter the greatest
obstacle to their identity formation, fearing the response of family
and the potential rejection that may ensue. As a result some choose
to keep their identities hidden for fear of secretly made comments
such as, "He is smart, he is handsome, he has a good career, but . . .
[he is gay]." Referring to disclosure to his mother, one man says "I
don't tell her, because she is old and there is no need for this discussion. It will just get her too upset," and another comments, "Disclosure to family is difficult when addressing family members born in
Greece, as the traditional values (and the need to preserve the traditional values in the Americas) almost preclude acceptance."

It is as if the reaction of family and friends, who are driven by the
tenets of the Greek American culture, is sufficiently powerful to keep
these men "in the closet" albeit at their own emotional expense. To
help relieve this burden and to allow for the formation of his identity,
another of the men described his disclosure to his mother as follows:

> I told her on her deathbed. I think she always probably knew. But I
> needed to do this. I had to get on with my own life, which meant being
> honest with my mother before she died . . . so that she would know that
> I was gay.

For some, the process of disclosing to one's family and friends can
become an overwhelming experience. If, for example, reactions are
hostile or rejecting, then the individual's coming-out process may suffer a serious setback (Vargo 1998). Ultimately, the need for explicit
acceptance and acknowledgment of their gay identity becomes a matter of crucial importance to gay men in their emotional development
(Stein and Cabaj 1996):

I told my father when I was 18. I was away at college and had returned home for a few days and felt the need to tell him. It was too much for me and I needed someone in my family to know. So I told him. He asked me if this choice made me happy and I said that I didn't know yet. His final words in that conversation were, "Tell your mother."

For the gay Greek American, this element is surely the one to present the greatest difficulty. Self-realization of sexuality is a necessary step in the development trajectory, but one that is separate and isolated from the relations of others. Disclosing to one's family, who may be immersed in the tradition and conservative workings of the Greek American culture, is something else. Here, gay men are subject to the harm and potential hostility and rejection that may follow. For those of us who are fortunate enough to have parents who are accepting of all the elements of our being, the process is less traumatic. But this is certainly not the norm:

A friend of mine told me a story about his business associate, a handsome Greek American guy who was gay. For years, he didn't tell his parents. Last year, he met another Greek American guy and they have been in a relationship every since. So he decided to tell his parents. The reaction wasn't good. He still talks to and sees his parents, but he can never visit them with his lover. The parents blame the lover for making the son gay and for "ruining their lives."

Even when the acceptance of the parents does manifest itself after gay identity disclosure, the Greek American man is still left to confront the reactions of an extended family that may not be as understanding. Because of the importance of this family structure within the culture, these reactions cannot be overlooked, as *thies* (aunts), *thios* (uncles), and *exadhelfia* (cousins) are sure to have their own unique reactions. For the gay Greek American man who has been raised surrounded by these family members, the reactions can be equally painful:

So my aunt called and invited me to my cousin's graduation party. She knew that I was in a relationship, and asked if I could come to the party alone. Apparently my *thios* had decided that he could not allow me and my lover to be in his home. I spoke to my mother about this and she was sympathetic, but said, "Every one is entitled to their opinion," to which I responded, "Intolerance and bigotry should never be allowed." I didn't go to the party.

In the end, we are left with a struggle to be one's self openly within a culture that makes no room for differences and certainly views our existence as inimical to the fulfillment of marriage, procreation, and ultimately the perpetuation of the culture. Yet this phenomenon is also one that transcends gender and cultural lines, although it is manifested in different ways. Fygetakis (1997) suggests that the sexuality of Greek lesbians is viewed by some as a threat to the social order, as an unnatural element that desecrates the cleanliness of the home and is thus intolerable. So too among African Americans, homosexuality is viewed as the act of a traitor to family and to the race, because it does not lead to procreation (Adams and Kimmel 1997).

The ultimate goal: Integration of identities

Unfortunately, the intolerance of the Greek American culture towards homosexuality is so strong, that many of us seek to abandon the roots of our ethnic identity in order to exist or to have two mutually exclusive identities as these two men suggest. Said one:

> It is very simple. The Greek American attitude towards homosexuality is so negative. . . . And since I don't live in a pure Greek environment, I don't have to be part of the Greek community in order to survive . . . to function. I chose the easy way out.

Another describes it this way:

> It entails a functional separation, being "Greek American" and having one identity at family functions, in church, at holidays, and having another identity within the gay community. From the standpoint of the gay community, these are not mutually exclusive, but are for all intents and purposes exclusive from the Greek viewpoint. The difficulty lies not particularly in being both, but deciding how much conflict one is willing to undergo or endure in order to assert one's sexuality within the context of a very rigid social structure—for instance, how much effort is it worth in terms of arguments, conflicts, etc., in order to bring one's lover to Christmas dinner? The extent of this will of course vary from family to family, but given the high hurdle that is involved in most situations, would lead most people to decide that it's just not worth trying, that it's better to just lead the "double life," being open to one's friends and (possibly) within the workplace, but

hiding it from one's family in order to just keep the peace.

As the title of this section implies, the integration of one's gay and Greek American identity is an overwhelming task, perhaps equal in emotional stature to the labors of Herakles. But Herakles was a demigod, a fictitious image that always succeeded in achieving his goals. We as gay Greek American men are perhaps less well equipped to handle the obstacles that we encounter as we seek to integrate our gay identities with our culture. And ultimately we seek to do so in a society in which gay men and lesbians seek to live their lives free of the persecution, stigma, and prejudice that often surround them (Haddock and Zanna 1998).

Yet many of us are left alone, separate from the security of the culture that nurtured us, to establish our identities and to assert our equal protection under the law. As an ethnic group, Greek Americans have by all accounts succeeded in the United States, holding major posts in government and universities and large corporations. But in succeeding, we have remained quiet, kept to ourselves, gathering in our *koinotites*, living safely within a few blocks of where we were raised, and socializing with others who seek to perpetuate the Greek American dream.

This is not an option for the gay Greek American. The *koinotis* makes no room for his difference, has no desire to accept him and integrate him into the cloth of the community. So as gay Greek American men we seek to establish our identities elsewhere, perhaps in the gay community which encompasses all, or among friends and families whose assimilation into American society furnishes them with a tolerance that our own families lack. Fygetakis (1997), in fact, notes that it is this lack of assimilation into American society that breeds the intolerance of the Greek American community.

As I conclude my thoughts on this matter, I am reminded of my encounters with other gay Greek American men and the joy that I experienced in realizing that I was not the only one who had these thoughts—that others like me, who loved their families, their language, and their culture, felt isolated and separated from being immersed in the workings of the Greek American culture as openly gay men. Some months ago, I became aware of a group of gay Greek Americans that meets monthly at the Gay and Lesbian Community Center of New York City. While the voices of other gay men, including African Americans, Latinos, and Asian Americans always seemed proud and organized to me, the voice of gay Greek Americans remained unheard by me, perhaps as a response to the culture that asked us not to reveal who we truly are. It is perhaps best viewed as a type of "Don't ask, don't tell." One can only hope that this group of out and gay Greek Americans can find their voice and develop a momentum so that others like them can find the courage to realize their whole selves.

In the end, I must admit that many of the ideas shared throughout these pages reflect the often negative aspects of the Greek American culture. This, fortunately, is not always the reality. For some like me, there exists a loving family who are able to maintain pride in their culture and heritage, and share it with me regardless of the fact that I am gay. Perhaps in time, this too can be the norm as we struggle to realize that we are both gay and Greek American and that this duality can exist comfortably and peacefully within one person.

References

Adams, C. L., Jr., and D. C. Kimmel. 1997. Exploring the lives of older African American gay men. In *Ethnic and cultural diversity among lesbians and gay men*, ed. B. Greene, 132–51. Thousand Oaks, Ca.: Sage.

AXIOS. 1997. What is AXIOS. May 26. Available from www.axios.faq.ios.com

Bonnage, J. A. 1997. The doors!! The doors!! *Axios newsletter* (New York chapter, January): 1–4.

Callinicos, C. 1991. Arranged marriage in Greek America: The modern picture bride. In *New directions in Greek American studies*, ed. D. Georgakas and C. Moskos, 161–79. New York: Pella.

Clogg, R. 1992. *A concise history of Greece*. Cambridge: Cambridge University Press.

Dabilis, A. 1990. A tale of two countries: Greek Americans call the U.S. home. *Boston Globe* (July 28): 1, 6.

Dank, B. 1971. Coming out in the gay world. *Psychiatry* 34: 38–44.

Fygetakis, L. H. 1997. Greek American lesbians: Identity odysseys of honorable good girls. In *Ethnic and cultural diversity among lesbians and gay men*, ed. B. Greene, 152–190. Thousand Oaks, Ca.: Sage.

Haddock, G., and M. P. Zanna. 1998. Authoritarianism, values, and the favorability and structure of antigay attitudes. In *Stigma and sexual orientation: Understanding prejudice against lesbians, gay men, and bisexuals*, ed. G. M. Hereck, 82–107. Thousand Oaks, Ca.: Sage.

Halkitis, P. N. 1998. Advances in the treatment of HIV disease: Complexities of adherence and complications for prevention. *The Health Psychologist* 20, no. 1: 1, 7, 14–15.

Keuls, E. C. 1985. *The reign of the phallus: Sexual politics in ancient Athens*. Berkeley, Ca.: University of California Press.

McDonald, G. 1982. Individual differences in the coming out process for gay men: Implications for theoretical models. *Journal of Homosexuality* 8, no. 1: 47–60.

Michaels, S. 1996. The prevalence of homosexuality in the United States. In *Textbook of homosexuality and mental health*, ed. R. P. Cabaj and T. S. Stein, 43–64. Washington, D.C.: American Psychiatric Press.

Orthodox View, The. 1993. Guidelines on homosexuality. *Orthodox Observer* (August): 7.

Stein, T. S., and R. P. Cabaj. 1996. Psychotherapy with gay men. In *Textbook of homosexuality and mental health*, ed. R. P. Cabaj and T. S. Stein, 413–32. Washington, D.C.: American Psychiatric Press.

Sullivan, A. 1995. *Virtually normal: An argument about homosexuality.* New York: Alfred A. Knopf, Inc.

Troiden, R. 1979. Becoming homosexual: A model of gay identity acquisition. *Psychiatry* 42: 362–73.

Vargo, M. E. 1998. *Acts of disclosure: The coming out process of contemporary gay men.* Binghamton, N.Y.: Harrington Park Press.

Transformations: Clinical issues

9. Greek American families: Immigration, acculturation, and psychological well-being

SAM J. TSEMBERIS

*Clinical Assistant Professor, Department of
Psychiatry, New York University Medical Center*

*This chapter examines the processes of acculturation of first- and
second-generation Greek families in the United States and discusses
the psychological challenges encountered by both generations. It
presents a brief history of recent Greek immigration to the United
States and a description of the Greek American communities created
by that immigration. The main focus of the chapter is a comparison
of the major value differences between Greek and American cultures
and the psychological consequences of these disparities for Greek
American families. A family systems perspective is used to examine
the tensions that emerge from the differences in which husbands,
wives, parents, and children adapt to American culture. Clinical
interventions to address family problems resulting from acculturation are also presented.*

GREEK FAMILIES, like those of other ethnic groups, encounter enormous physical and psychological upheavals upon immigration to the
United States. Immigrants leave their homes, villages, islands, relatives, friends, language, customs, and all other familiar connections,
and must settle quickly and be productive in a completely unfamiliar
place—a foreign land with alien customs. The distress created by this
dramatic separation from the homeland often manifests in feelings of
alienation, disorientation, and anxiety. In their routine encounters
with Americans, new immigrants to the United States are always
reminded that they are different in language, customs, and beliefs.

197

While many families undertaking this journey adapt effectively, the process nonetheless entails permanent changes for the family members' intrapsychic and interpersonal worlds. Immigrants are fundamentally altered by the process of assimilation. They constantly struggle to define their evolving individual ethnic identity in relation to the mainstream culture. As part of a family, immigrants are challenged to maintain familial cohesion while simultaneously coming to terms with the significant differences in the ways in which the first- and second-generation members adapt to American culture.

A brief history of immigration to the United States

Georgakas cogently presents the history of Greek immigration to the United States and the continuity of the Greek American community (Georgakas 1999). A brief synopsis is offered here to provide a context for the issues discussed in this chapter.

Greek immigration to the United States is broadly divided into "old immigrants," who arrived at the turn of the century (1890–1920), and two waves of "new immigrants." The First Wave of new immigrants, approximately 150,000 in number—half of them illegal—arrived between 1947 and 1965. The Second Wave, totaling 160,000, arrived after the Immigration Act of 1965 (Georgakas 1999). This chapter pertains to the two waves of new immigrants.

The First Wave, the cohort that arrived from the end of World War II to the mid-1960s, consisted overwhelmingly of permanent settlers (Gavaki 1991). This group, leaving Greece after the destruction and poverty resulting from World War II and the years of devastating civil war that followed, was composed of families, sailors who jumped ship, and "import" brides and bridegrooms. This group arrived with scarce financial resources, little education, and few skills (Moskos 1989).

The Second (post-1965) Wave of new immigrants, better educated and more skilled than the First, comprised mainly entire families (ibid.). Like their predecessors, they dreamed of earning significant wealth and returning to Greece to become proprietors of businesses. They hoped, as well, that their children would graduate from the best American universities and enter professional life in Greece.

The new immigrants settled primarily in the northeastern United States. Many major cities in this region include a Greek community replete with churches, after-school programs, civic organizations, and Greek businesses. One such neighborhood, Astoria, New York, serves as an example of the immigration trends of the past three decades. Astoria is a working-class community that has attracted large numbers of Greek immigrants since the 1960s. By the mid-1980s, approximately 150,000 Greek immigrants were living in Astoria, making it the largest Greek community outside of Greece (Drucker 1993). Today, it is still a lively immigrant enclave with plazas, coffeehouses *(kafenia)*, restaurants, churches, hometown and region-based organizations *(topika somatia)*, and sports clubs. With immigration of Greeks to the United States at a standstill, however, the Greek presence in Astoria has changed dramatically in the past 10 years. Indeed, the 1990 census showed a decline of more than 10 percent in Astoria's residents who claimed Greek ancestry. Greek Americans continue to occupy the shops, but not the apartments; many have moved to more affluent communities in Flushing, Bayside, and towns in Long Island (Onishi 1998).

Sociologists believe immigrant communities, such as Astoria, facilitate the resettlement of newly arriving immigrants and that when immigration ceases the residents assimilate into the mainstream. The first generation's members struggle to keep their traditions, while their children are expected to integrate successfully into the United States. As their children and grandchildren become more American, significant numbers of this first generation may return to Greece, usually for retirement. An index of the strength of the ties between first-generation new immigrants and the home country is found in an analysis of New York City death records; in 1996, 16 percent of first-generation Greeks were sent home for burial (Sontag and Dugger 1998).

With Greek immigration ending and the departure of many from the first generation, members of the second generation face the challenge of sustaining their ethnic identity without the support of the previous generation. Will subsequent generations of Greek Americans conform to the pattern of assimilation established by other European immigrants and blend into the masses of the American mainstream, or will they retain some discernible elements of Greek culture and identity?

Cross-cultural value differences:
Individualism and collectivism

One of the major dimensions affecting the facility of assimilation is the degree to which the immigrants' cultural values are similar to those of the host culture (Lambert 1987; Rosenthal et al. 1989). Indeed, the psychological problems experienced by Greek immigrants relate primarily to their adjustment to the manifestations of cultural differences, whether they are external (place, language, customs, etc.) or internal (personal beliefs, attitudes, sense of self, relationship to the community, etc.).

Some cultural characteristics significantly facilitate a group's ability to assimilate into another country, while others impede the process. Social scientists have described several differences in customs and values between Greek and Anglo culture which affect the success of Greek assimilation.

Individualism and collectivism are key cultural dimensions in Greek American studies. Generally described as two end points of a cultural dichotomy, this construct characterizes *individualists* as those giving priority to personal goals, and *collectivists* as those either making no distinction between personal and collective goals or subordinating personal goals to those of the collective (Triandis 1989). The individual, or Western, self is described as egocentric, while the holistic, or Eastern, self is referred to as sociocentric (Shweder and Bourne 1984). These orientations influence many aspects of social relations within a society. Rosenthal et al. (1989) examined individualism across several ethnic groups and found, as expected, that Greeks—long known for their strong family orientation—scored lower on individualism than did Anglos, but were more individualistic than members of Asian cultures. This study supports what writers, poets, and historians have discussed for years: the unique position held by Greece, perched as it is between West and East geographically, socially, and culturally.

Collectivism is at the core of Greek culture and is deeply ingrained in every social interaction. It is reflected in innumerable examples: the close extended family kinship systems, the manner in which family resources are shared, the fluid boundaries between parents and children, the traditional "group" dances, the comfort of physical contact among friends, the tolerance of close personal distance among strangers in public spaces, the acceptability of looking at strangers, the sense of responsibility and loyalty, the *parea* ("company," a momentary family), and myriad other examples. As in the Arab countries, there are no Greek words for "privacy." When translating from English to Greek, words meaning "secret" or "confidential" are used. In a similar vein, the lack of clear physical boundaries is reflected in the fact that there is no word for "rape" in Greek or Arab cultures. There are approximations, such as *abduction* or *violation*, but nothing approaching the American meaning that is expressed in that one word.

Storace (1996), a keen observer of Greek people and customs, offers a historical perspective on the influence of the Byzantine era, which had a collectivist rather than an individualist orientation, on Greek culture. In her book *Dinner with Persephone*, Storace notes how Greece remained largely unaffected by the Renaissance, which profoundly encouraged the development of individualism in the rest of Europe. She provides several illustrative examples of collectivist behavior in Greek life today. One is the taverna evening, during which the diners share food from a few central dishes (in the same manner that Byzantine paintings depicted the Last Supper). The individual place setting, a development of the Renaissance period, remains absent from today's Greek tavernas—a fact that serves to sustain and reinforce collective cultural practices.

Though a strong case has been made for using dichotomies, such as individualism and collectivism, to describe cultural values as either Western or non-Western, these conceptualizations are ultimately overly simplistic. Many theorists argue that broad cultural values, like individualism and collectivism, are not polar opposites of the same construct, but are distinct values ordered in a particular sequence that reflects the primary, secondary, or tertiary orientation of the person, family, or culture (Hermans and Kempen 1996; Kluckhohn and Strodtbeck 1961). Similarly, Wolf (1982) contends that using such dichotomies turns a dynamic phenomenon into static entities. Thus, values seen as dichotomies provide false models because they use a classification system that endows nations, societies, and cultures with one internally homogeneous quality, as if such values are externally distinct objects (Hermans and Kempen 1996).

It follows that Greeks and Americans are not simply collectivistic or individualistic. The relationship between individualism and collectivism is complex, as demonstrated by the long Greek tradition that celebrates individual accomplishment: collectivism provides the context in which individualism is expressed. In the collectivism of Greek culture, the family is the primary social unit, and—in contrast to American culture—the needs of its individual members are secondary. Every member is expected to defer to or sacrifice for the greater needs of the family. In return for this loyalty, the family emphasizes support for *individual members* striving to succeed, and reciprocally, the family's status is enriched by the accomplishments of any of its members. The importance of *individual* accomplishment for Greek immigrants motivates them toward greater personal and, by extension, collective achievement—a motivation that has served them well in adapting to the United States.

Immigration and psychological well-being

A direct relationship exists between immigration and psychological well-being. Immigration is almost always a stressful emotional experience. Immigrants suffer from disruptions in attachment of person and place, and often feel a sense of loss and nostalgia that renders them psychologically vulnerable, since a sense of belonging is essential for psychological well-being (Fullilove 1996). Stressors contributing to the development of psychological symptoms include the move itself, family members' different responses to relocation, adapting to a new culture, and learning a new language. The family unit may suffer severe disruption, especially if social or emotional supports are not available upon arrival. Culture shock assaults an individual's psychological and physiological systems, and can result in altered sleep patterns, depression, marital problems, anxiety, identity problems, and an inability to concentrate (Fowler and Silberstein 1989). If any or all of these symptoms affect even one family member, the entire family system is disrupted and must marshal resources to overcome these difficulties.

Children are especially vulnerable during the immigration experience because they lack adequate coping skills to handle its significant demands. These youngsters must contend with feelings of loss, fears of the unknown, and lessened parental attention—all of which may result in psychological distress (Simpson and Fowler 1994). Even children born in the United States who experience a disruption of community through unscheduled school transfers report poorer academic performance and social difficulties, such as impaired peer relations and diminished self-esteem (Jason et al. 1993).

Acculturation and mental health: Empirical evidence. The larger social and political forces operating in American society at the particular time an immigrant group arrives have enormous consequences for its adjustment. Greek immigrants arriving after World War II and in the early 1950s found an America that was politically conservative. It was considered a criminal act to be a Communist, and there was little tolerance for political, social, or ethnic diversity. Early empirical studies of Greek immigrants in Anglo cultures that examined the relationship between immigration, acculturation, and mental health reported greater psychological distress accompanying higher levels of acculturation (Abel and Hsu 1949; DeVos 1955; Hallowell 1950), while later studies indicated that the relationship between acculturation and mental health is more often positive and considerably more complex.

The Second Wave of new immigrants, arriving during the mid-1960s, was welcomed by a different cultural context. The 1960s marked the heyday of the love generation, soon followed by Alex Haley's *Roots*, which created the Black (and every other color or ethnicity) Is Beautiful movement. Cultural diversity was accepted and celebrated. As a point of illustration, consider the names used by members of these two waves of immigrants. Members of the post–World War II group experienced tremendous pressure to "fit into" American society and hide their Greek identity. Understandably, they exchanged their own Greek names for American-sounding equivalents (e.g. *Dimitri* became *Jimmy, Yanni* became *John*). By contrast, members of the Second Wave, who arrived in the America of the 1960's, felt free to keep their Greek names and, to a much greater extent, their Greek customs.

Madianos (1984) examined the relationship between acculturation and mental health in recent Greek immigrants (those residing in the United States less than six years) and old immigrants (those living in the United States more than six years). For recent immigrants, he reported a negative correlation between acculturation and mental health, a finding that is consistent with the earlier studies. For old immigrants, however, he reported that higher levels of acculturation are associated with fewer psychiatric symptoms. These findings suggest that there is a developmental component to the process of immigration and acculturation such that after the initial problems of adjustment to a foreign culture, individuals develop the resources required for effective adaptation, thereby restoring their psychological well-being.

In their study of mental health and culture change, Papajohn and Spiegel (1971) examined the psychological well-being of Greek

Americans as a direct function of their value orientation. The results suggested that there may be gender and social-class differences in their sample's responses to acculturation: among lower-class females the internalization of American core values was associated with psychological health, while among lower-class males the internalization of American core values was associated with greater psychological distress. Similar gender differences were observed in a more recent study of Greek Cypriot immigrants in South London (Mavreas and Bebbington 1990). The authors found that lower levels of acculturation were associated with pathology for females, but higher levels of acculturation were associated with pathology for males.

Nicolaides (1989) studied a sample of Greek immigrants living in New York City and found that respondents' self-esteem was related to their degree of involvement in the Greek community; individuals who were actively involved in the Greek community and in transmitting traditions to the next generation were less acculturated and had lower self esteem.

Similarly, Papajohn's later study (1979) of cultural adaptation in Greek families in Boston indicates that the relative acculturation of the first generation may have serious consequences for the adaptive responses of the second generation. Papajohn observed that the parents of children with psychotic symptoms, even after 40 years of residence in the United States, still adhered remarkably closely to traditional Greek value orientations, while the parents of children with normal psychological profiles generally showed movement toward adaptation to American values.

Similar results were obtained in an English study that examined the acculturation patterns of individuals with severe psychiatric problems. In their study of Greek Cypriot patients in North London, Adamopoulous and his colleagues (1990) reported that acculturation is related to health in that the least acculturated were the least healthy and suffered higher levels of psychological disturbance.

In a recent study of Greek immigrants in New York City, Tsemberis, Orfanos and Eisenberg (forthcoming) found that given the same number of years in the United States, those respondents who immigrated as children and adolescents showed higher levels of acculturation (use of English language, adoption of American customs, etc.) than those who immigrated as adults. These findings, consistent with other recent studies, reported that psychological well-being was positively associated with higher educational achievement and adoption of American values. In a notable exception to the general pattern, greater well-being was also associated with *maintaining* more traditional Greek *sex-role* attitudes. These authors conclude that psychological well-being is dependent on successful acculturation through adoption of most American cultural values, but—especially for the second-generation—it can also be a matter of selecting which American values to adopt and which Greek values to maintain. A similar pattern of maintaining traditional sex-role attitudes was found in Karpathakis' study of Greek American women (Karpathakis 1999).

Tsemberis and colleagues (forthcoming) also examined gender differences in factors predicting psychological well-being. As expected, women reported significantly more progressive (American) sex-role attitudes than men. In addition, for Greek men, higher education, more siblings, having children, and higher levels of acculturation were the only variables significantly related to psychological well-being, while for women, only progressive values and acculturation were significantly related to well-being. These differences in the manner in which Greek American men and women achieve well-being challenge the popular stereotype that women are dependent on their families for emotional stability. In fact, it was the men who relied on their families to maintain their psychological well-being, while the women fared better by embracing American customs and adopting progressive values.

In summary, evidence from these studies supports the concept that acculturation is a dynamic process that affects members of the same immigrant culture in different ways and is generally related to greater psychological well-being. The First Wave of new immigrants experienced greater psychological problems than the Second Wave—and did not fare as well as longtime American residents—but they also experienced greater upheaval and isolation and were required to make more adjustments in a host country where they were often unwelcome. As the first generation begat the second, studies document a consistent pattern of increased adaptation as demonstrated by proficiency in the English language and American customs. Psychological functioning improved with each successive generation and, conversely, there was an increased risk of psychological distress for immigrants who failed or refused to adopt at least some host-culture customs and, instead, rigidly retained Greek values and customs.

Sources of distress within the Greek American family

The family life cycle and immigration. The family's stage in its life cycle is one factor that determines which psychological problems may emerge for that family. Family-systems theorists postulate that there is a normative course of development consisting of a series of stages that occur sequentially throughout the life cycle of most nuclear families. These stages, usually defined as major life events, have their own set of developmental challenges for all members of the family. Opinions vary regarding the exact number and nature of these stages, but a consensus exists about the following six: (1) early marriage; (2) the birth and raising of young children; (3) the children's early school years; (4) the children's adolescence; (5) adult children leaving home; and (6) later life, including the birth of grandchildren and retirement. Naturally, many events can disrupt this sequence, including separation, divorce, illness, death, remarriage, catastrophe, and massive dislocation. For most families, stress is highest at the transition points from one stage to the next. The degree and manner of distress resulting from immigration within a particular family are related to the life stage of the family during immigration.

The structure of Greek American families. Some problems en--countered by Greek American families result not only from immigration, but also from the endemic, traditional patterns of organization and other norms and customs that regulate family life. First-generation Greek Americans uphold family traditions that are more conservative than those of second-generation Greek families. The first generation lives a marginal existence between two worlds: the Greek culture that they endorse but left behind no longer exists, and the American culture they live in is not one they will ever fully join.

The general structure of traditional Greek families is based on a patriarchal system of governance that includes deeply binding lateral kinships—including those with godparents *(koumbari)*, in-laws *(sympetheri)*, and other affines *(synyenis;* Sant Cassia and Bada 1992). Men, women, and children are socialized to observe hierarchical social rules that offer people respect due to their gender and generational status. For example, children must show respect for their parents' peers by addressing them as uncle or aunt *(theio* or *theia).* This extended kinship system, which creates a cohesive family structure and extended family to offer emotional and economic support, serves immigrant families well.

In the United States and Canada the rate of intermarriage for second-generation Greek immigrants is estimated at between 60 and 70 percent (see Chimbos 1999; Constantelos 1999). Intermarriage has traditionally been perceived as a flagrant breach of family and community cohesion. (When one second-generation son informed his first-generation mother of his wish to date a girl from another culture, her response was, "I know you wouldn't hurt your mother.") Still not acceptable among the first generation, intermarriage is widely practiced by the second.

The marital subsystem. The present-day structure of Greek American marriages has roots dating back to the Byzantine Empire (see Kazhdan 1999). A major source of marital difficulties is embedded in the cultural norms that regard marriage as a property exchange between families—including dowries—and afford few socially sanctioned opportunities for legitimate courting. Arranged marriages were common for first-generation immigrants; indeed, it was not until 1983 that the dowry *(proika)* was declared illegal in Greece. It was also until fairly recently that unmarried people were expected to live with their parents. In the contemporary Greek Orthodox wedding ceremony, the bride and groom make no pledges. This practice may reflect the tradition of arranged marriages, since the absence of such a ritual evades the question of the bride's and groom's consent (Storace 1996).

It is noteworthy that no Greek word exists for "dating"; the most commonly used expression is borrowed from the French, *rendezvous*, which is defined as a meeting or an appointment. With few opportunities for prospective husbands and wives to meet individually—outside of group gatherings—they cannot develop meaningful communication or intimacy prior to marriage. Once married, the social roles of husbands and wives remain narrowly defined—a situation that continues to hamper their chances for the open, emotionally expressive discourse that can lead to intimacy and understanding.

Bringing these traditional customs across the Atlantic, some first-generation Greek men and women in America sought prospective spouses through relatives or close friends who arranged marriages. In later years, young men traveled to Greece during summers to seek eligible brides whom they married after only a brief courtship. In both cases, these couples found themselves in marriages that were preceded by little or no courtship and few opportunities to develop effective communication. The husbands were generally older than the wives, thereby creating a generation gap in the couple. In addition, it was customary for the young brides to live with their husbands' families for the first few years after immigration and marriage. Left without the support of their own families, such immigrant women frequently felt lonely and isolated.

It is perhaps fortunate, therefore, that Greek men and women have unusually meager expectations for fulfillment in a marriage. In a survey that examined differences between American and Greek couples' responses concerning their love for each other, Vassiliou and Vassiliou (1973) reported that Americans understood marital love to concern a set of behaviors that include being intimate, sharing feelings openly, and doing things together. Greek couples, on the other hand, believed marital love concerned such behaviors as the husband's being a good provider and the wife's being faithful and obedient to him and a good mother to her children.

When the couple transitions to parenthood, the mother is entrusted with the care of the children and the maintenance of the Greek language, customs, and values. The father is typically uninvolved in domestic matters and concerns himself primarily with responsibility for the family's economic stability. In exchange for her husband's financial support, the wife is expected to offer affection and make few demands. The inevitable interpersonal conflicts that arise between husband and wife are expected to be resolved through the wife's silent submission to her husband's wishes.

At home, where most family issues are decided, the mother and children are often in alliance to influence the father. Thus, even though the Greek father is formally defined as the head of the family, the Greek mother is acknowledged as being "the neck which makes the head move." The marital power relationship resembles a chess game: the king, who has the *symbolic* power, is highly restricted in his ability to move across the board, while the queen, though of lower status, moves about the board with decidedly greater freedom of movement and, thus, ultimately has more *actual* power than her mate.

The couple generally behave differently in public or social situations from the way they do in private. In social situations, where interpersonal exchanges often serve as symbolic representations of their actual interactions, the wife (and children) will defer to the husband as head of the house. Any departure from expected social norms—for example, public display of superiority by the wife—puts her at risk of severe reproach or in extreme cases physical abuse by her mate (Koos et al. 1994). Even though women, whether as wives, daughters, or sisters, are not supposed to compete with, correct, or grow impatient with men, whether they are husbands, sons, or brothers, men are permitted to openly scold, quarrel with, or reprimand women (Vassiliou 1969).

The rigid sex-role socialization that is characteristic of Greek culture is potentially destructive for both sexes. Certainly it restricts men's emotional development and limits the extent to which they can participate in the benefits of familial intimacy, attachment, and nurturance. When social roles do not provide a man with acceptable modes of expressing such feelings as tenderness, sadness, or fear, his experience of these emotions can make him feel anxious and vulnerable. To alleviate his discomfort, he may automatically resort to the more acceptable "manly" display of verbal or physical violence.

Acculturation is often a profound stressor on the traditional marriages of the first generation because the generally younger wives acculturate more rapidly than their older husbands and adapt more of the egalitarian American norms governing women's choices. At the same time, their husbands lose their patriarchal status in the more democratic American culture. When a Greek American family seeks therapy, however, the husband and wife seldom present such marital issues; instead, they cite their child as being the problem. After a brief discussion of the underlying issues that create the child's problems, the therapist will lead the parents to explore the possibility that their marital dysfunction may, in fact, be the critical issue.

The two worlds of Greek American childhood. Greek American children live, simultaneously, in two cultures. To adapt successfully to each culture, they must master the language, social rules, and role expectations of both. They must further learn the translation of social roles from one culture to the other and know when to demonstrate behaviors appropriate to each cultural context, such as which behaviors will obtain the approval of their Greek parents and which will generate acceptance from their American peers. The bicultural existence of immigrant children affects every major area of their interpersonal world, including their personal identity and their relations with family, peers, and teachers.

Within their families, these children are placed in an awkward and burdensome position of over-responsibility for their parents—a circumstance that cuts short their childhood years. For example, because they master American customs and the English language more rapidly than their parents, Greek immigrant children often take on the roles of cultural liaison and language translator for the family. Parents may depend on children's assistance, as well, with shopping, attending medical appointments, and other decidedly adult responsibilities. Through these and other role-reversal situations, children repeatedly experience acute anxiety as they see their parents feeling helpless and inadequate to handling routine life tasks (Alvarez 1995).

In the area of peer relations, children who attend Greek parochial afternoon schools encounter additional challenges. These children yearn to be accepted by their American teachers and peers in the American school, as well as by their peers in the Greek parochial school. Displaying social skills that are considered "cool" or that demonstrate social competence and improve a child's popularity with his or her American peers, however, may be regarded as inept by the child's Greek friends. The pressure to switch between these mutually exclusive cultural norms can be confusing and distressing for Greek youngsters (Rotheram-Borus and Tsemberis 1989).

Greek immigrant children may experience painful mockery or rejection by their American schoolmates because they and their immigrant parents (and other relatives) are different from the American mainstream. Longing to be accepted by their peers, the children frequently develop a secret wish that they and their family were not different. This wish to be more mainstream is the beginning of a psychological schism in the child's ethnic identity that may never fully heal, and it begins the process that ultimately erodes attachment to family and Greek community, as becomes evident with the second generation.

Achievement and acculturation. Greeks highly value achievement and success. For Greeks, achievement motivation is composed of a complex set of beliefs that include external attributions about fate and God—"if God wishes it" *(an theli o Theos)*—and internal attributions regarding the efficacy of work, family honor, and community norms (Marinou-Mohring 1986). Education and achievement are strongly emphasized, and from a very early age children are expected to do well in school. One of the paradoxical outcomes of the high value placed on achievement is that it is at odds with the value of family closeness, because if the children are to succeed in American schools, they must embrace more American ways.

Parents pressure their sons far more than their daughters to succeed. The Greek mother is nurturing and extremely ambitious for her son. In an early paper on immigrant families, Hines (1973) reported that when boys demonstrated motivation and were high achievers, their mothers showed great warmth and had high levels of aspiration for their sons. Firestone's (1972) Marxist interpretation of Freud's beliefs about family relations construes the strong alliance between a mother and her male child as the mother's effort to offset her disadvantaged position vis-à-vis her husband and possibly improve her situation in the family and community when her son is older and has more power. Not surprisingly, with such support, sons in Greek families, like Oedipus, are not expected to *follow* their father but to *surpass* him. This inherently competitive relationship between father and son stems from the rigid gender-role socialization of Greek men, where competition is emphasized over empathy.

Restrictive gender roles for females—girls and women, daughters and wives—are pervasive in Greek culture. Daughters in immigrant families are raised to emulate the mother's role, including subordinating their needs to those of their father or brothers. Their career goals are often considered secondary to those of their brothers. When young Greek women seek family support in pursuing professional careers, it is not uncommon for first-generation parents, under the guise of protection, to discourage such action and pressure them to marry and remain close to their families. Thus, daughters may be overlooked educationally and left on their own without parental pressure in this regard. Ironically, the resulting freedom may account for the fact that Greek American females generally do better academically than their overly regarded brothers.

Family therapy for Greek American families

Most Greeks consider participation in psychotherapy stigmatizing. To seek therapy, they must be in crisis or mandated by an authority. A family therapy approach is well suited to Greek American families because their primary social unit is the family and because they have an intuitive understanding of systems theory through their experience in extended kinships. The clinical observations summarized here are drawn from the experience of the author in working as a family therapist with Greek American families for the past 20 years. The majority of the families were treated at a counseling center in

Astoria, New York, during the 1980s and since then, in private practice (see Tsemberis and Orfanos 1996 for earlier version). Approximately two thirds of the families who sought counseling at the center
were nuclear families directed by the school guidance counselor to
seek services for their child, who manifested a school-related behavior problem in such areas as academic performance, discipline, atten-
dance, motivation, or peer relations. Invariably, it was the mother
who made the initial telephone call to request counseling. During the
information-gathering process, it was usually evident that she understood the presenting problem from the perspective of each of her
family members—husband and children—even though they might
not understand each other. There were also several court-mandated
cases, usually involving allegations or findings of physical child
abuse, and a small number of cases involving sexual child abuse. In
summary, most families did not seek counseling voluntarily or
because they had insight into a problem that required professional
assistance.

The myriad stressful life events that constitute the immigration
experience require mental health practitioners to be especially sensitive to the context of the immigrant family's and individual's life circumstances when considering the meaning of their presenting
problems (Rigamer 1985). Common presenting problems for families
who seek therapy often relate to difficulties experienced by the members in their unsuccessful shift from one developmental stage to the
next. Such difficulties are frequently the result of a family's having
developed a rigid emotional pattern that does not promote change
when experiencing stress. Haley (1973) posits that pathological
behaviors tend to surface at points in the family life cycle when the
process of disengagement of one generation from another is prevented or delayed.

Parent-child–related presenting problems. The most frequently
presented problems concern the themes of parental control and
family separation. Children acculturate more rapidly than their parents and, as a result, are more conversant with the language and customs of American culture. This creates anxiety for parents who feel
that they are losing control and influence over their children. As children continue to acculturate to American culture, they abandon
Greek norms and customs; and parents become anxious that their
children are separating from their family and the Greek American
community.

These issues are manifested in a variety of forms including discipline and school-related problems. Discipline issues for Greek American families are often rooted in the family's concern over the impending separation that must inevitably occur between parents and children. For immigrant children, this normative developmental step toward individuation occurs simultaneously with an increase in their acculturation, i.e., embracing American norms and values while rejecting Greek ones. Immigrant parents fear that their children are separating not only from the family, but also from their history and culture and, consequently, they react by imposing restrictions in a desperate effort to sustain the family unit. Such responses are experienced as repressive by the children who rebel further against their parents' wishes.

The separation of female adolescents from parents can be especially problematic for Greek American families (Hibbs 1999). Traditional Greek immigrant fathers often impose early curfews, forbid their daughters to date, and encourage close contact with the Church. Mothers may secretly support their daughter's independence, but cannot persuade their husbands to relax controls. Such families must negotiate a compromise between traditional and modern attitudes in order to successfully meet the daughter's need for increased independence and the father's desire to protect her.

Children and adolescents acculturate more quickly than their parents, which exacerbates the parents' loss of control or influence over their children. To deal with this problem, Greek parents may use a number of culturally sanctioned child-rearing methods in an effort to reinforce family cohesion. Some parents use such phrases as "shame on you *[dropi]*" and "what will people say *[ti tha ley o cosmos]*?" to emphasize the importance of a person's standing in the Greek community and impart to the child the importance of family loyalty and honor *(philotimo)*.

Court-mandated treatment. Some Greek immigrant parents believe that Americans spoil their children by "sparing the rod." Physical abuse—corporal punishment of children—has been culturally sanctioned in Greece for centuries. Greek American families that still use such practices may be reported to child-protective services and mandated to participate in therapy because the court has ruled that they were guilty of physical abuse. These are among the most difficult families to treat. The parent, usually the father who is charged with abuse, is often outraged that a social worker from an

American agency—a "foreigner"—has mandated family counseling because of his harsh discipline. The therapist in such cases must make it clear to the father that the U.S. legal system does not consider corporal punishment a private matter. Thus, the therapist can translate American cultural norms to the family and encourage the father to adopt better forms of discipline.

In order to create a therapeutic alliance with the parents, it is important for the therapist to discuss the feelings of outrage and humiliation that they usually experience during the court hearings. Significant misunderstandings can occur among the parents, judge, and counsel at many levels. Parents who see themselves as loving and as good providers are often treated as inadequate caretakers by the judge and the attorneys for the child protective services agency. A father's impassioned denial of physical abuse and exasperation at not having his actions understood as common disciplinary practices can create the impression for judge and legal guardians that he has little insight into his problems. The American courtroom judge, who expects defendants to be remorseful for their actions and act respectfully towards the courts by being soft-spoken and contrite, will unfavorably regard the father's explanations of his behavior and his indignation at the suggestion that he is an unfit parent.

Single-parent families. Divorce is still seen by the Greek American community as a selfish abdication of family responsibilities. Because of this stigma, single parents are alienated within their own community. The second largest group of Greek families seeking services at the Astoria counseling center was comprised of divorced, working mothers and their young children. For the most part, the women received little or no financial or emotional support from their ex-husbands. The women and their children usually lived alone or in their mothers' homes. Their mothers' attitudes towards them were paradoxically supportive in some respects, yet sharply critical in others. (For instance, mothers said they wanted their daughters to remarry, but discouraged them from dating.) With divorce still imposing a strong stigma within the Greek American community, these single mothers' prospects for remarriage within the community were discouraging.

The single mothers also experienced value conflicts arising from the clash between American and Greek cultures. In Greek culture, fulfillment comes by serving others—family in particular—whereas in American culture, fulfillment comes from individual accomplishment—obtaining a good education, building a career, and being true to oneself. These opposing values created a psychological split that left the women feeling ashamed and guilty because they had not fulfilled their mothers' expectations, yet angry and frustrated because they had not pursued their own goals. One of the most helpful therapeutic interventions for these women was the formation of a support group consisting of several other women in the same predicament. The support group reduced members' sense of isolation and stigma and served to validate their feelings and perceptions regarding their common problems.

The role of the therapist

The first task of the therapist who counsels a Greek American family is to ensure that each member of the family feels understood. During the first session, the therapist must ensure that he or she develops sufficient rapport with the parents and gains their respect so that they will return. The goal of each session should be to make sufficient progress in working through the presenting problems to encourage the family to attend the next session. The therapist's key diagnostic challenge in the early stages is to determine whether the family's dysfunction results from the family's inadequate adjustment to its present life stage, from the stress of immigration, or from a particular family member's psychological problems.

The therapist must display culturally sensitive behaviors that reassure the family that they are not sitting with a complete outsider (*xenos;* Stagoll 1981). In this regard, the therapist must be respectful and serious. Therapists should not greet a Greek family with a smile. In the Greek vocabulary of nonverbal expression, smiling does not convey a nuance of welcome as it does in the United States. Indeed, Greeks may regard smiling as a kind of placation, a sign of submission. It is important for the therapist to convey, both verbally and nonverbally, the message that therapy is serious work.

In the early stages of counseling, the therapist should respect the lineal relationships of the traditional hierarchical family organization (Primpas-Welts 1982). The therapist can be sensitive to these traditional roles, yet prescribe behavioral changes. At the same time, the therapist must indicate to any adolescents in the family (who are usually more acculturated than their parents) that their issues are also heard and understood.

If the therapist is uncertain about Greek customs and culture, the session can begin by conducting an interview in which the family members are treated as experts. The inquiries can begin with cultural customs and lead to questions regarding the family's patterns. The therapist should also be sensitive to the English-language fluency of each member and select one person to translate when there are wide disparities in comprehension among members. In cases where the therapist speaks Greek, she or he should note any power struggles surrounding which language will be spoken in the session and at what point family members will switch from one language to another. The therapist should pay attention to the family members' physical relations to each other (such as where people sit during the session) and other forms of nonverbal communication because they also offer clues to alliances, boundaries, and conflicts.

To reduce any stigma related to the presenting problem, the therapist can reframe psychological or psychiatric symptoms as health-related or stress-related problems (Stagoll 1981). It is useful to proceed with interventions or prescriptions designed to effect measurable or observable behavior changes. Small, consistent successes inspire the family to trust the therapist and believe that counseling can be beneficial. To allay the family's fears of getting "stuck" in therapy, the therapist can emphasize that therapy is short-term. Indeed, a finite number of sessions may even be suggested to the family.

During initial sessions, the therapist often encounters a clinical paradox. The wife is expected to be a medium through which the husband speaks, but she often disagrees with him. Goldner (1985) and Hare-Mustin (1978) initially observed this phenomenon when they pointed out that family therapists erroneously conceptualize the parental subsystem as two equals, whereas in reality, men and women in the same family rarely have equal power. This is especially relevant in Greek families, where wives are not expected to disagree with their husbands in public, particularly in the presence of an outsider.

The wife thus finds herself in a difficult situation. For example, it may be clear to both her and the therapist that the child's raucous behavior in school is a response to the father's overly strict discipline and beatings at home, but she may have difficulty expressing this belief during therapy. Feeling helpless to change the father's behavior, the mother resorts to protecting her child as best she can. Her protection, an act of disagreement with her husband, angers the father, who increases his efforts to maintain control by becoming more intolerant of the child's playful or reckless behavior. The therapist must develop interventions to expand the conflicted and narrow roles of each parent in order to reduce marital discord and create greater tolerance for the child's behavior. For example, the therapist might begin with a proposal designed to increase the mother's role as disciplinarian and soften the father's harsh role by suggesting he spend time in play and recreation with his child.

Conducting a full assessment early in treatment can be a useful way to build an alliance with a family. A full assessment includes inquiring about each family member's understanding of the presenting problem and drawing a genogram—a map that provides a graphic picture of a family structure and its emotional process over time—to determine the family's life stage and level of acculturation (Bowen 1978). One must keep in mind that though family members may have lived in the United States for the same period of time, they can be at distinctly different stages of acculturation or feel differently about the acculturation process.

Because gender roles are rigidly defined in Greek culture, the gender of the therapist will be a powerful determinant in the interactions among the family members. Male therapists are likely to be perceived as having more power. Assuming a formal, conservative manner will help therapists—male or female—to enhance their perceived authority.

The therapist must acknowledge the importance of the family's cultural continuity while introducing the positive aspects of acculturation. Unless this process is handled in a sensitive manner, the husbands may experience any request for change as a demand that they relinquish power and acculturate. Cooperation by each member is increased if they understand what is to be gained, e.g., increased familial intimacy. Wives will usually expect the support and validation that has long been missing in their relationships with their husbands. Wives should be encouraged to express themselves directly, and the therapist must assist the couple in constructing a safe environment that reduces the wife's fear of reprimand or reprisal, especially when discussing difficult topics. The most challenging aspect of working with the Greek marital dyad is assisting the couple to participate in a dialogue that is emotionally open and direct and that leads to increased collaboration and intimacy.

In the best of outcomes, the therapeutic process with first-generation Greek immigrant families can serve as a powerful, capsulized acculturation experience that is rewarding for every member of the family. The therapist, who is usually more acculturated than the parents, can provide valuable guidance. The children must be able to express their concerns, knowing that the therapist understands the demands of both the Greek *and* the American worlds. Wives must feel supported and encouraged to develop their newly felt independence, whereas their husbands must trust that the therapist's urging them to become more emotionally expressive will lead to their desired increased closeness with their families. If such a therapeutic milieu is created, the therapist can serve as an effective cultural broker and assist the family to successfully meet the difficult challenges of bridging the transition from one culture to another.

Conclusion

Greek families are among the more successful European immigrant groups in the United States. The core Greek values of individual achievement are highly compatible with American culture, and Greek Americans are rapidly assimilating into the mainstream. Today, in the face of diminishing Greek immigration to the United States, the challenge facing Greek American families is whether their acculturation will allow them to sustain any of their personal or cultural Greek identity. The major conflicts faced by families are primarily between the members of first- and second-generation immigrants, but the tension and anxiety surrounding the key issues of familial separation (privacy, independence, intermarriage) are likely to lessen with successive generations.

The issues of separation, assimilation, and Greek identity are still very much alive for the first generation. A personal anecdote illustrates this point. I was invited to participate in a panel discussion entitled "The Future of Hellenism in North America" at the 1998 annual meeting of the Pan-Laconian Federation. As both a Laconian and a psychologist, I was very glad to accept the invitation. The meeting was attended by approximately 300 first-generation Laconians, primarily men over the age of 65. This group is active in encouraging the continuity of Greek language and religion, enhancing the place of Greek culture in the United States, and discouraging intermarriage between those of Greek and non-Greek heritage. The group is also involved in community-improvement projects in Greece, such as building schools in the villages of Laconia.

This group of first-generation Laconians was very successful:

They worked hard, earned money, shared generously with family and community, and educated their children. Yet in spite of all these accomplishments there was a tone of lament *(kiamos)* to the conference proceedings. This was not a group celebrating their considerable successes. Why?

The first generation had fought and won a very difficult battle: They had built a bridge from Greece to America, established vibrant communities, and raised children for whom they had high hopes and aspirations. With the support of these bridge builders, their children quickly acculturated, obtained an education, and held good jobs. Many have intermarried and are no longer active in the Greek community. The bridge builders are thus faced with the paradoxical outcome of their labors: On the one hand, they proudly watch their children achieve material success and social status in the new country; on the other hand, they must cope with the unanticipated outcome that their deeply treasured Greek culture is dissolving into the morass of American culture.

References

Abel, T. M., and F. L. Hsu. 1949. Some aspects of personality of Chinese as revealed by the Rorschach test. *Rorschach Research Exchange and Journal of Projective Techniques* 13: 285–301.

Adamopoulous, A., G. Garyfallos, N. Bournas, and G. Kouloumas. 1990. Mental health and primary care in ethnic groups—Greek Cypriots in London: A preliminary investigation. *The International Journal of Social Psychiatry* 36: 244–51.

Alvarez, L. 1995. Interpreting new worlds for parents. *New York Times*, October 1, sec. B, pp. 29, 36.

Bilanakis, N., M. Madianos, and A. Liakos. 1995. Demoralization and mental health. *European Journal of Psychiatry* 9, no. 1: 47–57.

Bowen, M. 1978. *Family therapy in clinical practice.* New York: Jason Aronson.

Chimbos, P. 1999. Interethnic marriages and prospects for ethnic group survival: The case of the Greek Canadians. In *Greek American families: Traditions and transformations*, ed. S. J. Tsemberis, A. Karpathakis, and H. Psomiades. New York: Pella Press.

Constantelos, D. 1999. Church and family in Greek Orthodox society from the Byzantine era to the present-day United States: Problems and issues. In *Greek American families: Traditions and transformations*, ed. S. J. Tsemberis, A. Karpathakis, and H. Psomiades. New York: Pella Press.

De Vos, G. 1955. A quantitative Rorschach assessment of maladjustment and rigidity in acculturating Japanese Americans. *Genetic Psychology Monographs* 52: 51–57.

Drucker, S. 1993. Immigration, media development and public space: The transformation of social life from Greece to a Greek community in New York. *Hofstra Horizons* (spring): 12–16.

Firestone, S. 1972. *The dialectic of sex*. New York: Bantam Books.

Fowler, S. M., and F. Silberstein. 1989. Intercultural adjustment of families living abroad. In *Crossing cultures in mental health*, ed. D. R. Koslow and E. P. Salett. Washington, D.C: International Society for Education, Training, and Research.

Fullilove, M. 1996. Psychiatric implications of displacement: Contributions from the psychology of place. *American Journal of Psychiatry* 153: 1516–23.

Gavaki, E. 1991. Greek immigration to Quebec: The process and the settlement. *Journal of the Hellenic Diaspora* 17, no. 1: 69–89.

Georgakas, D. 1999. The America beyond Ellis island. In *Greek American families: Traditions and transformations*, ed. S. J. Tsemberis, A. Karpathakis, and H. Psomiades. New York: Pella Press.

Goldner, V. 1985. Feminism and family therapy. *Family Process* 24: 31–48.

Haley, J. 1973. *Uncommon therapy*. New York: W. W. Norton & Co.

Hallowell, A. I. 1950. Values, acculturation and mental health. *American Journal of Orthopsychiatry* 20: 732–43.

Hare-Mustin, R. R. T. 1978. A feminist approach to family therapy. *Family Process* 17: 181–94.

Hermans, J. M., and H. J. G. Kempen, 1996. Moving cultures. *American Psychologist:* 53, 1111–20.

Hibbs, E. 1999. Separation-individuation issues in the Greek American mother-daughter dyad. In *Greek American families: Traditions and transformations*, ed. S. J. Tsemberis, A. Karpathakis, and H. Psomiades. New York: Pella.

Hines, G. H. 1973. The persistence of Greek achievement motivation across time and culture. *International Journal of Psychology* 8: 285–88.

Jason, L. A., et al. 1993. A one-year follow-up of a preventive program for high-risk transfer children. *Journal of Emotional and Behavioral Disorders* 1, no. 4: 215–21.

Karpathakis, A. 1999. "I don't have to worry about money anymore, and I can live like a lady": Greek immigrant women and assimilation. In *Greek American families: Traditions and transformations*, ed. S. J. Tsemberis, A. Karpathakis, and H. Psomiades. New York: Pella Press.

Kazhdan, A. 1999. The Greek family in the Byzantine Empire. In *Greek American families: Traditions and transformations*, ed. S. J. Tsemberis, A. Karpathakis, and H. Psomiades. New York: Pella.

Kluckhohn, F. R., and F. L. Strodtbeck. 1961. *Variations in value orientation*. New York: Harper and Row.

Koos, M. P., L. A. Goodman, A. Browne, L. F. Fitzgerald, G. Keita, and N. Russo. 1994. *No safe haven: Male violence against women at home, at work, and in the community*. Washington, D.C.: American Psychological Association.

Lambert, W. E. 1987. The fate of old country values in a new land: A cross-national study of child rearing. *Canadian Psychology* 28: 9–20.

Madianos, M. 1984. Acculturation and mental health of Greek immigrants in

USA. In *Social psychiatry*, ed. V. Hudolin. New York: Plenum.

Marinou-Mohring, P. 1986. Life, my daughter, is not the way you have it in your books: Why Greek immigrants did well in the United States. Paper presented at the meeting of the Greek American Behavioral Sciences Institute, September, New York City.

Mavreas, V., and P. Bebbington. 1990. Acculturation and psychiatric disorder: A study of Greek Cypriot immigrants. *Psychological Medicine* 20: 941–51.

Moskos, C. C. 1989. *Greek Americans: Struggle and success*, 2nd ed. Englewood Cliffs, N.J.: Prentice Hall.

Nicolaides, M. G. 1989. Aspects of Greek-American ethnic identity: An intergenerational study of Greek-Americans. Unpublished doctoral dissertation, Teachers College, Columbia University, New York City.

Onishi, N. 1998. Old rift heals in a modern crisis: As population dwindles, Astoria's Greeks repair a schism. *New York Times*, January 12, sec. B, pp. 1 and 4.

Orfanos, S. D., and S. Tsemberis. 1987. A needs assessment of Greek American schools in New York City. In *Education and Greek Americans: Process and prospects*, ed. S. D. Orfanos, H. J. Psomiades, and J. Spiridakis. New York: Pella.

Papajohn, J. 1979. Intergenerational value orientation and psychopathology in Greek-American families. *International Journal of Family Therapy* 1: 107–32.

Papajohn, J., and J. Spiegel. 1971. The relationship of culture value orientation change and Rorschach indices of psychological development. *Journal of Cross-Cultural Psychology* 2 (3): 257–72.

Primpas-Welts, E. 1982. Greek families. In *Ethnicity and family therapy*, ed. M. McGoldrick, J. K. Pearce, and J. Giordano. 1st ed. New York: Guilford.

Rigamer, E. F. 1985. Stresses of families abroad. *Travel Medicine International* 3, no. 3: 137–40.

Rosenthal, D. A., R. Bell, A. Demetrious, and A. Efklides. 1989. From collectivism to individualism? The acculturation of Greek immigrants in Australia. *International Journal of Psychology* 24: 57–71.

Rotheram-Borus, M. J., and S. Tsemberis. 1989. Social competency training programs in ethnically diverse communities. In *Primary prevention and promotion in the schools*, ed. L. A. Bond and B. E. Compass. Newbury Park, Calif.: Sage.

Sant Cassia, P., and C. Bada. 1992. *The making of the modern Greek family*. Cambridge, England: Cambridge University Press.

Shweder, R. A., and E. J. Bourne. 1984. Does the concept of the person vary cross-culturally? In *Culture theory*, ed. R. A. LeVine. Cambridge, England: Cambridge University Press.

Simpson, G. A., and M. G. Fowler. 1994. Emotional adjustment to geographic mobility. *Pediatrics* 93, no. 2: 303–9.

Sontag, D., and C. W. Dugger. 1998. The new immigrant tide: A shuttle between worlds. *New York Times*, July 19, sec. A, p. 1; sec. B, pp. 28, 29, 30.

Stagoll, B. 1981. Therapy with Greek families living in Australia. *International Journal of Family Therapy* 3: 167–79.

Storace, P. 1996. *Dinner with Persephone*. New York: Vintage Books.
Triandis, H. 1989. The self and social behavior in differing cultural contexts. *Psychological Review*.
Tsemberis, S., and S. D. Orfanos. 1996. Greek families. In *Ethnicity and family therapy*, ed. M. McGoldrick, J. Giordano, and J. K. Pearce. 2nd ed. New York: Guilford Publications.

10. Separation-individuation issues in the Greek American mother-daughter dyad

Euthymia D. Hibbs

This chapter first reviews the historical roots that may have influenced the handling of the separation-individuation stages in Greek mothers, then discusses the existing theoretical framework, and presents case histories of individuals who sought psychotherapy to resolve these issues. This chapter is based solely on a developmental theory of psychopathology, on clinical observations, and on many years of working with Greek families, not on research data.

THROUGHOUT THE YEARS, I have been fascinated by the way Greek parents deal with their growing children and by their ability to facilitate or impede the stages of separation-individuation or encourage independence. Although Greek families, like any others, may present with different types of problems rooted in various etiologies (Tsemberis and Orfanos 1996), this chapter will discuss material and case examples the psychopathological etiology of which is mainly related to separation-individuation issues. In addition, it is important to note that the material presented in this chapter is based on a sub-sample of a patient population and cannot be generalized to all Greek mothers or families.

Historical perspectives

Historically, before the Second World War, Greece was a poor country whose main income derived from agriculture and maritime business. As is the case in most developing countries, children—in addition to being appreciated as members of an integral family unit—

satisfied various practical needs by assuming different roles in the family. Male children were particularly appreciated because on the one hand they would preserve the family's name, and on the other hand they could work in the fields, do other types of work, and help the family financially. It became an unwritten agreement that sons would financially support their families of origin, even after they were married. Not long ago, Greek men who immigrated to the United States considered it their duty to send money back home to support their families. Daughters, on the other hand, were socialized to stay home, and encouraged to remain close to the family and marry someone from the same geographical area, with the objective of physically caring for the parents when they grew old. Even to this day the conviction persists that daughters are responsible for the physical care of parents.

Greek families who immigrated in the early part of the century brought with them the values from their home country that determine how a family should function. By firmly holding to these values and by maintaining and respecting the preassigned roles of the various family members, they helped protect themselves from the unknown, frightening new culture. Being strangers in a country that embraces different lifestyles and family values forced them to become strict and somewhat inflexible, because by maintaining the status quo and the cultural values they felt more secure. Parents became fearful that their children's, especially their daughters', moral values might be spoiled by the foreign, liberal society's influence. To this day one may hear mothers say, "We are not Americans," when their American-born, American-educated, professional daughters find jobs in cities other than where the parents live, or when they date non-Greek men.

One such (imported) moral value concerns the daughter's "honor" —that is, virginity. In Greece the honor of the daughter had to be protected. Parents stressed its importance to the daughter, and the men of the family made sure that she behaved accordingly in order to safeguard the family's good name. A virgin daughter could marry someone of "good standing"; that is, someone who has a good job, who earns good money, who is a good provider, and who accepts the responsibility for, in due time, assuming the care of his in-laws when they are old.

Protecting the honor of the daughter meant for the men (father and brothers) of the family that they delegated the task to the mother as chief executor while they maintained a supervisory role. That is, they placed the mother in charge to make sure that all the rules were enforced. Male family members intervened only if the rules were broken by the daughter and they had to punish her. For example, if the daughter was in love—even an amorous platonic relationship—with a young man, the brothers and father might press the young man to clarify his intentions. One must note that most of the pre-World War II marriages were matchmade and had to be approved by the parents regardless of the daughter's age. To say the least, daughters were not encouraged to flirt or even fall in love, especially with a man who had the reputation of not being a good provider—judged by the way he cared about his parents—or was from another village and presented a threat of her moving away. A daughter was considered amoral if she dared to be emotionally involved with a young man. Daughters were usually socialized to be good *noikokyres* (housekeepers), good wives, dedicated mothers, and eventually caretakers of the parents. It is also of interest to note that mothers, in Greek households, are blamed if the children misbehave or do not perform well academically; but fathers are credited for their children's successes.

Mothers, in general, had great power and free rein to determine which of the children's behaviors could be accepted. They decided which behaviors and developmental tasks to encourage and which to suppress. Independence (meaning not following prescribed rules), including independence of thought, was looked upon as bad morals. The worst stigma for a young girl was to be called *philelftheri*—freedom-loving, or a free spirit. One can only imagine what undue pressure, control, restrictions, and responsibilities were imposed on the daughter in addition to her role in preserving the family's honor.

I frequently visit a village on an island in Greece and have long talks with the women concerning those issues. It is interesting to note that women 50 years of age and older, who were raised with such values, have been on Valium or Prozac for many years. Most of them complain of suffering from *anchos* (anxiety) and *melancholia*, as they call depression.

The contemporary Greek American family

Greeks in the United States have a reputation of being "close families," meaning that they care for, protect, and stand by their family members. Greek mothers in America are known to be "pushy" for encouraging their children to succeed. They have understood that education is a prerequisite to success not only for their sons but also for their daughters. One can very often meet not very well educated mothers who encourage their daughters to study and become professionals, wanting them to achieve what they themselves couldn't. This sounds commendable, and it happens in a majority of Greek families. In cases where the parents feel insecure concerning separation, however, or have problems with encouraging independence, any attempt by the daughter to make her own decision results in a family upheaval. In these cases the mother struggles to maintain control over her daughter by imposing—or trying to—what profession to chose, in which geographical area to live, and whom to marry. Daring daughters who decide their own course in life are rejected and as a consequence may not speak to their mothers for many years at a time. This may partially explain the numerous "cut-offs" in Greek families.

One can say that this inability to accept the daughter as an individual who has her own mind, goals, and search for individuation may have its roots in a multigenerational pathology through learning, which, in fact, is very difficult to eradicate. One can be more understanding of mothers who are not educated and who just repeat the pattern because they have not been exposed to different environments. But it is more difficult to comprehend how first-generation mothers who have themselves had more education and more exposure to other cultures, who are well read, have travelled, and have moved about in the society, can repeat the same patterns. This rigidity, inability to change, and lack of openness can probably be attributed to their own difficulties with separation issues and fear of abandonment than to multigenerational repetition of cultural principles, since they themselves had the opportunity to be exposed and learn differently.

Tasks of the first separation-individuation stage

It is well known and well described in both scientific and popular literature that by the age of two (the so-called terrible twos) the child strives to become autonomous (Erickson 1979). She stands solid on her feet, is able to discern the meaning of the "I" and "you," "me" and "mine," tries new activities, and wants to do things on her own. If the external controls are too rigid—that is, too many "nos," restrictions on exploring the physical environment, insistence on complying with all parental demands—the child may regress, her freedom of self-expression may be suppressed, and eventually there will be loss of self-esteem. The second year of life is the period for setting the framework for which choices are permissible and desirable and which are not. Example: A six-year-old girl was raised by the grandmother almost since birth. The parents were working in a neighboring town and saw their daughter on occasional weekends. The girl had developed elective mutism. The grandmother, being physically unable to run after a young child, restricted the child's exploration, e.g., opening the cabinets, playing with the utensils, and running in the house. The grandmother did not like noise in the house, and therefore forbade singing, crying, and too much talking. In fact she wanted a "doll-like" child who would sit quietly on the couch and not move or talk. As a consequence, the girl decided to behave as such, a speechless doll. After several sessions, when she felt comfortable with her therapist, she began to talk.

It is also about age two that the child tries to separate from the dyadic (mother-daughter) relation. Mahler (1961) called it the separation-individuation stage, where the child prepares for the triadic-oedipal stage. While the mother remains the center of attention, the child tries to increase the distance between them. The toddler explores the environment and is preoccupied with independence, expression, and the performance of pleasurable activities. This is definitely a painful period for all mothers. The child, who was completely symbiotic with and dependent on the mother, exercises and practices autonomy and separation, becomes interested in others, is able to walk away and to say no, and forms bonds with others in the family.

There is a difference between how Greek mothers deal with autonomy, separation, and individuation in boys and in girls. Independence is encouraged in boys and is rewarded. Attempts at independence in girls are discouraged, as mothers become more controlling and somewhat sadistic in response. This may be instinctual in that mothers subconsciously know and are reassured that their sons can't go very far, that the coming oedipal stage is dedicated to them, while the daughters are preparing for other pastures, that is, interest in the father. Some of my observations of how Greek mothers handle the separation-individuation stage among sexes are as follows: The boy moves away from the mother. The mother laughs with pride and may say, "Ah, you are becoming a big boy now," or "You are going to meet your girlfriend, but do not forget I am your mother," or "You are going to work like your father," and other encouraging remarks. When the daughter does the same, the mother may say: "Ah! You are leaving me, so now I will also go away," and sometimes she walks away or leaves the room until the child cries in distress. Or "You are leaving me; I will cry," and pretends to cry. Or, when the daughter goes toward the father: "Oh! You do not love me anymore, you love your father so I will go away," or sometimes, "I will leave you both," or "I do not love you anymore." Therefore separation is punished and individuation forbidden.

The case of Mary. Mary is a 32-year-old professional who finished her studies in Greece and came to the United States with a fellowship. Her family is affluent and educated. She came to see me because she was suffering from anxiety attacks and feelings of sadness. She had just finished her fellowship and been offered a job. She liked the idea because she found her work interesting, was able to publish extensively, and was in a relationship with a colleague with the intent to marry. All these successes, she said, made her very anxious, because she knew that her parents would be displeased if she followed a career and married in the United States. Her parents wanted her to return to Greece, since she was the only daughter among four children. They insisted that her future husband should also move to Greece, although he had an established career in the United States. Mary, without realizing it, had been raised to be the caretaker of the parents. Her mother insisted that she was the only person in the family with whom she could talk. When Mary was living in Greece and her mother was sick, she did not go to the doctor by herself unless her daughter took her. A subtle manipulation consisted in making Mary believe that her presence was indispensable to the welfare of her parents. The messages consisted of how her mother counted on Mary for everything, and indicated that she was dependent on the daughter, and with the latter away her life was empty and had no meaning. In return, Mary tried most of her life to please her parents and did not contradict them from fear of loss of love. When she lived in Greece she followed their advice without questioning their intent. She tried to fulfill their dreams by being an outstanding student throughout her academic career, thus serving as their showcase for outstanding parenting. The ideal scenario from the mother's point of view would have been that Mary return to Greece, have a house next to the parents', have daily contact with them, and take care of her parents' medical and emotional needs.

This case is a typical example of lack of individuation. Mary had interpreted this dependency as "love." She used to call her parents in Greece every few days to report how her days went and ask for advice for every small problem that she encountered. This was an effort to show her mother that she was not very happy away from her and that she still needed her guidance. She was afraid to tell her parents of her professional and interpersonal successes for fear of retaliation. The unspoken threat was that "if you dare to be your own person I can't love you anymore." Mary has also mentioned that she did not want to hurt her father's feelings. During a telephone conversation her mother told her that if she did not come back, she and her father would not talk to her anymore—finally an open threat. It became evident that any attempt of the daughter to emotionally separate and individuate, decide where she wants to live, and make her own professional decisions would be punished by withdrawal of support, and as a consequence withdrawal of love, followed by terminal separation and rejection.

When this very important developmental stage of separation-individuation, at about age two, is not facilitated, the individual fails to become independent later in life, fails to develop a "self," and is unable to solve life problems alone and make the correct life decisions. The early onset of depression, anxiety, and their spectrum disorders, such as school phobia, separation anxiety, dysphoric mood, at early ages may be attributed to the inappropriate resolution of this stage. In most pathological cases, of course, this is the period when borderline personality disorder may develop.

The second separation-individuation stage

Human development is a continual elaboration of past and present tasks that facilitate future emotional growth, and it continues throughout life. For this specific developmental stage of separation-individuation the second chance to reorganize is about age 12, or the peripubertal period. This stage offers another opportunity for both children and parents, if needed, to catch up and correct what was mishandled the first time around. According to Mahler, at this stage the youth's urge to separate from the parental influence is much stronger. In the most optimal circumstances the girl enters into a best-girl-friend relationship, and uses this relationship as a bridge to achieve separation from her mother and to help her individuate. Ironically, the chosen best friend usually has some of the personality characteristics of the mother.

This is a very difficult period for the peripubertal girl, who has to negotiate physical and emotional changes, narcissistic tendencies with a fragile self-esteem, and ambivalence consisting of wanting to remain a little child in the presence of the propelling forces of maturation. At this point the Greek mother who has difficulty letting go may become reprehensible. She may find fault and criticize the best friend because she takes her little girl away, and she feels very competitive. Home country morality or pathology, or both, reappear, and restrictions are put in place under the pretense that friends may encourage the daughter to deviate from the family's values and principles. Mothers at this stage become more "protective" (strict), and follow very closely the activities of their daughters. One may say that nowadays in the United States, this protective disposition is a good attribute because we know what happens to unsupervised youth. These prohibitions are not, however, limited to only physical restrictions and supervision. Mothers seem to subtly blackmail the daughters emotionally in order to encourage dependency. The message is that everyone, except your mother, is out to get you. In addition, the fear is created in the daughter that if she does not follow the mother's wishes something bad will happen. Of course, the worst that can happen in the mind of the young girl is withdrawal of love, disapproval, and rejection.

There are several ways the girl may react to this conflict. Since she is older now, this struggle may evolve into a serious revolt. On the one hand, the daughter may act out and sometimes may get involved in antisocial activities, abuse drugs and alcohol, cut classes, and get into fights. Sometimes she may sneak out of the house at night when everyone is asleep to meet her friends, have sex, and steal money from her parents or from others. The more the daughter acts out, the more severe the restrictions become. Example: I saw an adolescent patient who besides doing badly at school, which is a humiliation to the Greek parents, stole money from the parents' business, and ran away with a friend. She returned home when someone else stole the money from her at gunpoint. The parents put her in a military-style boarding school for girls, where she continued to smoke marijuana daily and use cocaine until she was thrown out of the school.

On the other hand, the girl may become submissive, afraid to experiment with her own ideas and thinking. She may follow parental guidance and try to appease the parents by being obedient and dependent on them. She may become a good daughter to the parents, but she can't be good to herself. The possibility is that when she becomes adult, she will find a controlling husband on whom she will depend for problem solving and decision making. Or she will run back to her mother for advice, since she has not learned how to stand on her own feet.

When this second stage of separation-individuation is not worked through satisfactorily, the outcome may be the development of internalized disorders. If both the first and the second stage were handled unsuccessfully, we may witness the expression of the first episode in any of the internalized disorders. Another risk is the suppression of cognitive abilities. I have seen many Greek adolescents who did badly at school and seemed dull, but when I gave them a test that measures intellectual abilities, the results indicated that they were of superior intelligence. It is possible that whatever the reaction to the parental handling of this stage, the child's cognitive functioning may be affected. Some children may be too busy revolting (externalization), using their cognitive abilities to find ways to deceive others instead of using them to learn new skills. Others, if they remain submissive (internalization), may lack the motivation to learn and reach their potential.

For mothers who have difficulty separating, the last attempt to influence their daughters is during the period of transition from high school to college. Although, as I mentioned previously, the majority of Greek mothers want their daughters to be educated and become professionals, mothers that cannot encourage independence have ambivalent feelings. They fear that college will lead to autonomy, and that the influence of others such as the teachers and friends may result in emotional and sometimes physical distancing from the mother. I have seen many mothers whose daughters were accepted to prestigious universities persuade their daughters to attend a state or other college in the area and live at home. They fear that their daughters may never return to them. This is not the case, however, with boys, who are encouraged to get the best education possible, even if they must move far away to do so.

Families with many daughters

What happens when families have more that one daughter? Do mothers respond to the each daughter in the same way at the separation-individuation stages? In fact they do, mainly using rivalry as a tool: "If you leave me I will love your sister more." In this case, however, the most vulnerable daughter, the one who is more sensitive to rejection, is chosen to be very close to the mother and is groomed to be her caretaker. The other daughters are just encouraged to be dependent on the mother. In many cases this rivalry may give the other daughters the opportunity to become close to the father and become more independent. The family then may be split into the father's daughters and the mother's daughters. The following case is a characteristic example.

The case of the P. family. This family consists of six daughters ranging from 22 to 31 years of age. The father came from a small village in Greece to study in the United States and obtained a professional degree. The mother received a high school education in Greece. They met in the United States, married, and became financially successful. The mother remained a housewife and was the main caretaker of the children. As soon as each daughter reached 12–13 years of age, she revolted. This included violent fights with the mother, cutting school, using alcohol and drugs, and being promiscuous. One daughter became a pathological liar and a thief. Another was expelled from various schools because of conduct problems. One daughter was sent to an out-of-state boarding school for disturbed adolescents because she was unmanageable. Only one daughter remained very close and dependent on the mother—"the good, obedient girl," according to the mother's reports.

The mother always felt inferior because of her lack of education. Her dream was to see her daughters educated so that they would not have to suffer the same "inferiority complex." In fact, all but one of the daughters managed to obtain bachelor's degrees, and a couple of them obtained graduate degrees. They all went away to college, but after college they all returned to live in the house of the parents. The original family was reconstructed after several years of one or the other's being away. The mother again assumed control over the daughters and expected that her opinions and instructions would be followed. The daughters, to the contrary, felt that they were older now and did not need to follow Mother's orders. Subsequently, the fights became more intense, and the triangulations flourished. The mother encouraged rivalry among the girls, rejected the ones that "liked" or continued a relationship with the father, and talked to one against the other. In addition, Mother, who was eager for her daughters to get married, kept criticizing all the young men they met, indicating that none was good enough for them. The daughters, according to the mother, had to marry Greek doctors from good families—meaning rich families. Even if a daughter dated one, however, the mother would find something wrong, intervene, and ruin the relationship. The excuse usually was that the young man was not from an aristocratic family, or that his parents were divorced, or that the mother did not like the influence he had over her daughter. Mother also considered her daughters' friends "bad girls, and unethical." She insisted that the daughters had to listen to the mother and not to the friends. "Only I know what is best," she used to say. In order to impose her will, the mother dragged her daughters from one therapist to another for many years. Counseling lasted for only a short period with each therapist. If she detected any attachment to the therapist, or if the latter did not follow her instructions, she would move her daughters to another one. When she came to me she said, "You are Greek and you know our mentality." She made the appointments for her daughters, although they were legally adults. Before every session with each one she would call me and tell me what to tell them. The message was "Tell her to find a good boy [a prince] to marry; to listen to her mother; tell her to stop seeing this young man; tell her that her friends are no good; I only know what is best for them," and like. Several times when I was in session with one or the other of the daughters, she would barge into the session unannounced "to help me." What the mother expected from the therapist was an ally who would help her daughters to stay dependent on her. As for the father, he was nonexistent. He submerged himself in his work in an effort to avoid the home situation.

The outcome: All of the daughters had problems maintaining jobs. They had difficulties relating to colleagues, revolted against bosses, were fired from or quit jobs very often, and couldn't maintain an intimate relationship. When the father died, all the daughters moved to other states. The mother blamed father, friends, and therapists, because her daughters did not turn out the way she had planned. "This is not the Greek way," she said; daughters should stay close to the mother. That is, they should live with her in the same house like a good Greek family and take care of her. She believed that because she dedicated her life to her daughters, they owed their own lives in return to her. She believed that others, including therapists, influenced her daughters to become heartless. After a few years, however, one of the daughters, the most vulnerable, returned to live in the same house with the mother.

This example of a severely psychopathological case was given insofar as it concerns the topic of this chapter, separation-individuation. In other cases, separation-individuation may be expressed in various forms ranging from normal to those in which there is severe disturbance. In some cases, normal parental feelings of pain at separating from one's child exist, but the parents try not to influence their children's life choices. In some cases parents intervene slightly in the form of "I hope you follow my advice." In other cases, they resort to more threatening expressions such as "I will never talk to you if you move to another city." Finally, in a more severely unhealthy form, are cases like the one described above.

Treatment

Patients do not go to treatment because they feel that their separation-individuation stages were handled inappropriately by their mother. No female would seek help because she feels dependent on her mother. When individuals or families seek help it is because they have reached an impasse in their personal lives or because of overt psychopathology. Only as therapy progresses can one see the extent of the mishandling of the separation-individuation stages. Therefore, clinicians need to be attuned to those issues when working with Greek families. For the treatment of adolescents it is important to involve the parents (or the mother only) almost as intensively as the daughter. In that way the mother will not feel threatened or fear that the therapist will subvert or wrongly influence the daughter. Psychoeducational training is one of the techniques that can help the mother understand that independence does not mean the collapse of a relationship but the genesis of an adult, friendly, caring relationship. At the same time, it is important to help the daughter to develop insight into and awareness of her feelings, relieve her guilt for wanting to be independent, and help her to become an autonomous person while understanding the mother's feelings and dealing with them.

To conclude, I hope I have conveyed the importance of the separation-individuation stages and the role of their appropriate resolution in the development of a healthy, independent personality. Some of the Greek mothers seen in the clinical settings have more difficulty in letting go of their daughters: some because they follow the old country's traditions; others because of identification with the aggressor; some because of their own fear of abandonment; and some because of serious psychopathology. Psychotherapy may be beneficial in helping the parties involved to acquire insights concerning human development and the ensuing resolution of conflicts.

References

Erikson, E. R. 1979. *Identity and the life cycle.* New York: W.W. Norton & Company.
Mahler, M. 1961. On sadness and grief in infancy and childhood. *Psychoanalytic study of the child* 16: 332–51.
Tsemberis, S., and S. D. Orfanos. 1996. Greek families. In *Ethnicity and family therapy,* ed. M. McGoldrick, J. Giordano, and J. Pearce. New York: Guilford Publications.

List of contributors

Dr. PETER D. CHIMBOS is professor of sociology at Brescia College of the University of Western Ontario. Professor Chimbos has published widely in sociological journals and is the author or two major works: *The Canadian Odyssey: The Greek experience in Canada* and *Marital violence: A study of spousal homicides.* He has also served as councillor and advisor in various Canadian ethnocultural organizations.

DEMETRIOS J. CONSTANTELOS is a retired protopresbyter of the Ecumenical Patriarchate and Charles Looper Townsend Sr. Professor Emeritus of History and Religion at the Richard Stockton College of New Jersey. He holds degrees from Holy Cross Greek Orthodox Theological School (B.A.Th., honorary D.D.), Princeton Theological Seminary (Th.M.), and Rutgers—The State University (M.A., Ph.D.). His several books include *Byzantine philanthropy and social welfare,* 2d ed. (New Rochelle, N.Y.: Caratzas, 1991); *Understanding the Greek Orthodox Church: Faith, history, and practice,* 3d ed. ([will check place]: Hellenic College Press, 1998); *Poverty, society, and philanthropy in the late medieval Greek world* (New Rochelle, N.Y.: Caratzas, 1992); and *Christian Hellenism: Continuity and discontinuities* (forthcoming).

DAN GEORGAKAS is an associate adjunct professor of social science at New York University. He is the author of 10 books on various cultural topics, an editor of *Cineaste,* a contributing editor to *The Greek American,* and the initiator of the Greek American Studies Committee of the Modern Greek Studies Association. His most recent work includes a revised second edition of *Detroit: I do mind dying* (Cambridge, Mass.: South End Press, 1998) and an essay, "Angelopoulos, Greek history, and the *Traveling players,*" in *The last modernist: The films of Theo Angelopoulos,* ed. Andrew Horton (Flicks Books, 1997).

Dr. PERRY N. HALKITIS, M.S., Ph.D., is a clinical assistant professor in the Department of Applied Psychology, New York University, and the associate director of the Center for HIV/AIDS Educational Studies and Training. Dr. Halkitis is a researcher funded by the Centers for Disease Control and Prevention. His work has focused primarily on prevention of HIV disease among gay men.

Dr. EUTHYMIA D. HIBBS was born in Greece and studied in both western Europe and the United States. She has been working for twenty years at the National Institute of Mental Health as a clinical researcher, and for the past nine years has been chief of psychosocial treatment research for child and adolescent disorders. She has published numerous peer-reviewed articles, chapters, and books in the area of child and family psychopathology and treatment. She also maintains a private practice.

ANNA KARPATHAKIS received her Ph.D. in 1993 from Columbia University. Her dissertation was on the Greek immigrants of Astoria, Queens, in New York City. Her current areas of research interest include Greek immigrants; immigrant incorporation into American mainstream institutions; and religion. Her theoretical interests include race, class, and gender. She is currently with the Department of Behavioral Sciences and Human Services of Kingsborough Community College of the City University of New York, where she teaches sociology.

ALEXANDER P. KAZHDAN, Ph.D., was an authority on Byzantium who edited a three-volume dictionary on that subject and was for 18 years a research associate of the Center for Byzantine Studies at Dumbarton Oaks in Washington, D.C. Kazhdan was born in Moscow, where he received his doctorate at the Institute of History of the Academy of Sciences. Anti-Semitic discrimination in the former Soviet Union prevented him from holding more than provincial teaching posts for many years, but after Stalinist repression eased, he returned to Moscow and did research at the Institute for Universal History of the Academy of Sciences from 1956 to 1978. Kazhdan came to the United States in 1979. Besides his work at Dumbarton Oaks, he wrote numerous works, including, with Giles Constable, *People and power in Byzantium* (Washington: Dumbarton Oaks, 1982), and was chief editor of the 2,232-page *Oxford Dictionary of Byzantium* (Oxford: Oxford University Press, 1991), declared "a major breakthrough" in Byzantine studies by the British historian of

Byzantium John Julius Norwich. In an interview given at the time of its publication, Kazhdan observed that the study of the Byzantine Empire gives insight into "how the totalitarian organism works." Dr. Kazhdan died in Washington, D.C., on May 29, 1997, appropriately enough on the anniversary of the fall of Constantinople to the Turks in 1453.

HARRY J. PSOMIADES is a professor of political science at Queens College and the graduate school of the City University of New York. He founded and is director of the Queens College Center for Byzantine and Modern Greek Studies and is co-founder and co-editor of the *Journal of Modern Hellenism*. His numerous publications include *The Greek American community in transition*, ed. with A. Scourby (New York: Pella, 1982), *The teaching of modern Greek in the English-speaking world* (co-editor, 1985), *Education and Greek Americans: Process and prospects*, ed. with Spyros D. Orfanos and John Spiridakis (New York: Pella, 1987), and Ethnic politics in America: Greek Americans, *The Mediterranean Quarterly*, Winter 1994.

PAUL SANT CASSIA lectures in social and cultural anthropology at the University of Durham, England, and is visiting professor at the University of Paris (Nanterre). He was previously lecturer in social anthropology and museum curator at Cambridge University (1985–91) and a research fellow at Christ's College, Cambridge (1981–85). He has also been visiting professor at the University of Turin, Italy (1985), and at the University of Malta (1988–92, 1992–94). He has conducted fieldwork in Cyprus (since 1978), Tunisia (1982), Malta (1993–94), and Australia (1982), where he conducted research on migrant and youth unemployment for the Australian federal government. He is the author, with Constantina Bada, of the University of Ioannina, of *The making of the modern Greek family* (Cambridge: Cambridge University Press, 1991) and has published articles on politics, kinship, property transmissions, banditry and violence, museums, political oratory, traditional music, and historical political economy; the articles have appeared in *Man, JRAI, Comparative Studies in Society and History, Byzantine and Modern Greek Studies, The European Journal of Sociology, Modern Greek Studies, Ethnomusicology, Museums Journal, Archaeological Review from Cambridge, Cambridge Anthropology*, and other journals, as well as in numerous edited books published in France, Italy, and Greece. He is also the founding editor of the *Journal of Mediterranean Studies*.

He is a fellow of the Royal Anthropological Institute and a member of the Association of Social Anthropologists of the United Kingdom and the Commonwealth. He is currently working on a book dealing with memory, power, and ethnicity, based on field research in Cyprus and Malta.

SUSAN BUCK SUTTON is an anthropologist who has investigated changing patterns of settlement, migration, household, and gender relations in several areas of Greece. She has edited or written three books: *A contingent countryside: Settlement, economy, and land use in the southern Argolid since 1700* (Stanford University Press, forthcoming), *Constructed meanings: Form and process in Greek architecture* (Modern Greek Studies Yearbook, 1995), and *The landscape and people of the Franchthi region*, with Tjeerd van Andel (Indiana University Press, 1987).

ALICE-MARY TALBOT is director of Byzantine studies at Dumbarton Oaks and formerly served as executive editor of the *Oxford dictionary of Byzantium*. She has published two books on the patriarch of Constantinople Athanasios I and edited two volumes of translations of saints' lives. Her scholarly interests lie primarily in the areas of monasticism and hagiography.

SAM J. TSEMBERIS, Ph.D., is a clinical assistant professor in the department of psychiatry at New York University Medical Center and an adjunct professor in the department of psychology at New York University. He is also co-director of the Greek American Research Project at the Center for Byzantine and Modern Greek Studies, Queens College of the City University of New York. Dr. Tsemberis is a clinical psychologist and researcher whose interests include Greek American families, homelessness, and mental illness, topics on which he has published various works. He worked as a family therapist in Astoria, Queens, from 1980 to 1990, and is founder and executive director of Pathways to Housing, a nonprofit agency providing housing and support services to those who are homeless and suffer from severe mental illness.